Delhi Dialogue V

India-ASEAN:

Vision for Partnership and Prosperity

Delhi Dialogue V

India-ASEAN:
Vision for Partnership and Prosperity

Edited by

RAJIV K. BHATIA

VIJAY SAKHUJA

ASIF SHUJA

ICWA

SHIPRA

First Published 2014

India-ASEAN: Vision for Partnership and Prosperity

Some of the contents of this volume have been transcribed from the audio recordings. Some chapters have also been drawn from power point presentations made at the Delhi Dialogue V. The text has therefore been edited and suitably modified for the readers.

The views expressed in this volume are of individual contributors and do not represent the viewpoint of the editors or the Council.

Rs. 1800 US $ 90

ISBN: 978-81-7541-729-8

Published by:

SHIPRA PUBLICATIONS
H.O.: LG 18-19, Pankaj Central Market, I.P. Ext.,
Patparganj, Delhi 110092, Ph. 22235152, 22236152
Br. Off.: 4617/18, Ansari Road, Daryaganj,
New Delhi 110002; Ph. 9650028065, 9810522367
Email: info@shiprapublications.com
Website: www.shiprapublications.com

Contents

Part II

Non-Traditional Security Challenges: Food Security, Water Management and Pandemics

Part III

Future of Global Energy Market: Role of New and Renewable Energy in Sustainable Development

Part IV

Cooperation between CLMV Countries and North-East India: Opportunities and Challenges

Part V
Expanding Networks through Connectivity: Land, Sea and Air

Abbreviations

ADMM+	ASEAN Defence Ministers' Meeting Plus
AEGCD	ASEAN Expert Group on Communicable Diseases
AFFC	Agriculture and Forestry towards Food Security
AHA	ASEAN Humanitarian Assistance
AHMM	ASEAN Health Ministers Meeting
AHN	Asian Highway Network
AI	Avian Influenza
AIFS	ASEAN Integrated Food Security
ALTID	Asian Land Transport Infrastructure Development
AMAF	ASEAN Ministerial Meeting on Agriculture and Forestry
AMF	ASEAN Maritime Forum
AMM	ASEAN Foreign Ministers Meeting
AMME	ASEAN Ministerial Meeting on the Environment
AMM-TC	ASEAN Ministerial Meeting on Transnational Crime
APAEC	ASEAN Plan of Action for Energy Co-operation
APTERR	ASEAN Plus Three Emergency Rice Reserve
ARF	ASEAN Regional Forum
ASAM	ASEAN Single Aviation Market
ATFOA	ASEAN Task Force on AIDS
ATWGPPR	ASEAN Technical Working Group on Pandemic Preparedness and Response
AVLRC	ASEAN Virtual Learning Resource Centres
bcm	billion cubic metres
BIMSTEC	Bangladesh, India, Myanmar, Sri Lanka and Thailand Economic Cooperation
BLO	Border Liaison Offices
BPO	Business Process Outsourcing
CADP	Comprehensive Asia Development Plan
CAEXPO	China-ASEAN Expo
CBRN	Chemical, Biological, Radiological and Nuclear Weapons
C-DAC	Centre for Development of Advanced Computing

CDM	Clean Development Mechanism
CECA	Comprehensive Economic Cooperation Agreement
CII	Confederation of Indian Industries
COC	Code of Conduct
CSI	Container Security Initiative
DGICM	Directors-General of Immigration Departments and Heads of Consular Affairs Division of the Ministries of Foreign Affairs
EAS	East Asian Summit
EID	Emerging Infectious Diseases
ERIA	Economic Research Institute for ASEAN and East Asia
GBM	Ganga-Brahmaputra-Meghna
GDA	Ganges Dependent Area
GQ	Golden Quadrilateral
HVDC	High-Voltage Direct Current
IABF	India-ASEAN Business Fair
IEA	International Energy Agency
IGNOU	Indira Gandhi National Open University
INDG	India Development Gateway
IONS	Indian Ocean Naval Symposium
IOR-ARC	Indian Ocean Rim Association for Regional Cooperation
ISEAS	Institute of Southeast Asian Studies
ITI	Industrial Training Institutes
JRC	Joint River Commission
LEP	Look East Policy
MAAS	Multilateral Agreement on Air Services
MAFLAFS	Multilateral Agreement on the Full Liberalisation of Air Freight Services
MAFLPAS	Multilateral Agreement on the Full Liberalisation of Passenger Air Services
MARKET	Maximising Agricultural Revenue through Knowledge, Enterprise Development, and Trade
MCDV	Myanmar Comprehensive Development Vision
MGC	Mekong-Ganga Cooperation
MIEC	Mekong-India Economic Corridor
MoU	Memorandum of Understanding
MPAC	Master Plan on ASEAN Connectivity
NAM	Non-Alignment Movement

NER	Northeast Region
NHAI	National Highways Authority of India
NHDP	National Highways Development Programme
NSEW	North-South and East-West Highways
NTS	Non-Traditional Security
NUS	National University of Singapore
ONGC	Oil and Natural Gas Cooperation
PIPVTR	Philippine Institute for Peace, Violence and Terrorism Research
PPP	Public Private Partnership
PPR	Pandemic Preparedness and Response
PSI	Port Security Initiative
RE	Renewable Energy
RIS	Research and Information System
RMSI	Regional Maritime Security Initiative
SARS	Severe Acute Respiratory Syndrome
SEANFZ	Southeast Asian Nuclear Weapons Free Zone
SKRL	Singapore Kunming Rail Link
SLOC	Sea Lines of Communications
SOM-AMAF	Senior Officials Meeting on Agriculture and Forestry
SOM-HD	Senior Officials on Health Development
SOMs	Senior Officials Meetings
SOM-TC	Senior Officials Meeting on Transnational Crime
SPA-FS	Strategic Plan of Action on Food Security in the ASEAN Region
SPV	Solar Photo-Voltaic
TAC	Treaty of Amity and Cooperation
TTR	Trade Transport Routes
UNESCAP	United Nations Economic and Social Council for Asia Pacific
VLRC	Virtual Learning Resource Centres
WEC	World Energy Council
WFP	World Food Programme

About Delhi Dialogue

The India-ASEAN Delhi Dialogue is an annual international conference of political and economic leaders, officials, academics and opinion-makers of ASEAN countries with their Indian counterparts to discuss how to intensify and broaden political, strategic, economic and civil society interaction between the two regions. Focusing on India-ASEAN regional cooperation, five editions of Delhi Dialogue have been held since 2009.

Delhi Dialogue I, 21-22 January, 2009

The Delhi Dialogue I was inaugurated by H.E. Shri Pranab Mukherjee, the then Minister for External Affairs and H.E. Dr. Surin Pitsuwan, ASEAN Secretary-General. The two-day conference was attended by about 250 participants and dealt incisively with three key topics, i.e. Energy Security: The Way Forward for ASEAN and India; Global Financial Turmoil: Economic Security Concerns for India and ASEAN and India-ASEAN Connectivity, Logistics & Security Concerns. Prominent international speakers, who attended the dialogue, included Ambassador Pou Sothirak (Cambodia), Dr. Suthad Setboonsarang (Thailand), Mr. O.K. Daraiddh (Cambodia), Mr. Kazuhiko Higuchi (Philippines), Dr. Theo Sambuaga (Indonesia), Mr. Zulkifli bin Baharudin (Singapore) and Dr. Pavin Chachavalpongpun (Singapore).

Delhi Dialogue II, 21-22 January, 2010

Continuing along the same lines, the Delhi Dialogue II, held on 21-22 January, 2010, focused on regional security and cooperation with the theme of examining 'India and Southeast Asia in the Changing Regional Economic Dynamics of Asia: Shared Interests and Concerns.' The Hon'ble External Affairs Minister of India, H.E. Shri S.M. Krishna and the Deputy ASEAN Secretary General H.E. Mr. Pushpanathan Sundram graced the Delhi Dialogue II. Prominent international participants in the dialogue included Dr. Nam Viyaketh (Laos), Mr. Hidetoshi Nishimura (Indonesia),

Mr. Rodolfo C. Severino (Singapore), Ambassador K. Kesavapany (Singapore), Ambassador See Chak Mun (Singapore), Mr. Johnny N. Chotrani (Philippines), Mr. Deepak Mittal (Thailand) and Mr. Fukunari Kimura (Indonesia), to name a few.

Delhi Dialogue III, 3-4 March, 2011

The third in the series, the Delhi Dialogue III was hosted by India's Ministry of External Affairs (MEA) in partnership with the Indian Council of World Affairs (ICWA) and the Federation of Indian Chambers of Commerce and Industry (FICCI). It was supported by the Institute of Southeast Asia Studies (ISEAS), Singapore, SAEA Group Research, Singapore and the Economic Research Institute of ASEAN and East Asia (ERIA), Jakarta. The theme of the Delhi Dialogue III was 'Beyond the First Twenty Years of India-ASEAN Engagement.' The Dialogue provided an additional avenue for policymakers, think tanks, academics and business leaders to engage in fresh policy thinking and innovative solutions to challenges facing the region. It emerged during the discussion that both India and ASEAN should proactively engage each other in the political, social and economic spheres. A number of ASEAN ministers including Mr. Kasit Piromya (Thailand), Dr. Mari Elka Pangestu (Indonesia) and Pehin Dato Lim Jock Seng (Brunei) as well as ASEAN Secretary General Surin Pitsuwan graced the occasion. Other eminent speakers including Mr. Pham Quang Vinh (Vietnam), Mr. Kao Kim Hourn (Cambodia), Ambassador K. Kesavapany (Singapore), Dato Dr. Mahani Zainal Abidin (Malaysia), Mr. Rodolfo C. Severino (Philippines), Mr. Kavi Chongkittavorn (Thailand), Datuk Seri Samy Vellu (Malaysia), Mr. R. Ravindran (Singapore), Mr. Hidetoshi Nishimura (Indonesia), Mr. U. Nyunt Maung Shein (Myanmar), Prof. Tan Tai Yong (Singapore), Ambassador Mushahid Ali (Singapore), Prof. Aileen San Pablo-Baviera (Philippines), Mr. Aye Lwin (Myanmar), Mr. Samuel B. Bagasin (Philippines), Prof. K.S. Nathan (Malaysia), Mr. Sabam P. Siagian (Indonesia) and Ms. Connie Rahakundini Bakrie (Indonesia) enriched the discussions.

Delhi Dialogue IV, 13-14 February, 2012

Delhi Dialogue IV on the theme 'India and ASEAN: Partners for Peace, Progress and Stability' was held on 13-14 February, 2012 in New Delhi, India. The event was jointly hosted by the Ministry of External Affairs (MEA), Government of India, in partnership with the Indian Council of World Affairs

(ICWA) and the Federation of Indian Chambers of Commerce and Industry (FICCI). The event was supported by the Institute of Southeast Asian Studies (ISEAS), Singapore, SAEA Group Research, Singapore and the Economic Research Institute of ASEAN and East Asia (ERIA), Jakarta. Delhi Dialogue IV was inaugurated by H.E. Shri. S. M. Krishna, Hon'ble External Affairs Minister of India. The other notable dignitaries included Hon'ble Deputy Prime Minister and Foreign Minister of Cambodia H.E. Mr. Hor Namhong; Hon'ble Minister of Foreign Affairs of Thailand H.E. Dr. Surapong Tovichakchaikul; Minister of State for Foreign Affairs of Singapore H.E. Mr. Masagos Zulkifli bin Masagos Mohamad; Hon'ble Deputy Minister of Foreign Affairs of Malaysia H.E. Senator A. Kohilan Pillay; Hon'ble Deputy Minister for Foreign Affairs of Myanmar H.E. Dr. Myo Myint and Hon'ble Deputy Minister of Foreign Affairs of Vietnam H.E. Ms. Nguyen Phuong Nga. ASEAN Secretary-General was represented by H.E. Mr. Bagas Hapsoro, the Deputy Secretary-General for Community and Corporate Affairs of ASEAN. Delhi Dialogue IV covered four thematic issues in its four sessions: (a) Towards Economic Integration: Prospects and Challenges; (b) Non-Traditional Security (NTS) Challenges and Response Strategies; (c) The Evolving Security Architecture in the Asia-Pacific and (d) Building Networks of Knowledge and Science. The 'Valedictory Address' was delivered by Dr. A.P.J. Abdul Kalam, the former President of India.

Introduction

The Delhi Dialogue V, titled 'India-ASEAN: Vision for Partnership and Prosperity' was held on 19-20 February, 2013 in New Delhi, India. The Dialogue was organized by the Ministry of External Affairs, Government of India, in partnership with the Indian Council of World Affairs (ICWA) and the Federation of Indian Chambers of Commerce and Industry (FICCI), and it was supported by the SAEA Group Research, Singapore, and Economic Research Institute of ASEAN and East Asia (ERIA), Jakarta.

The Delhi Dialogue V was inaugurated by H.E. Shri Salman Khurshid, Hon'ble External Affairs Minister of India. The other notable dignitaries, who were present on the occasion, included H.E. Mr. Le Luong Minh, Hon'ble Secretary-General, ASEAN; H.E. Dr. Soeung Rathchavy, Secretary of State, Ministry of Foreign Affairs, Cambodia; H.E. Mr. I. Gusti Agung Wesaka Puja, Director General of ASEAN Cooperation, Ministry of Foreign Affairs, Indonesia; H.E. Y.B. Senator A. Kohillan Pillay, Deputy Minister of Foreign Affairs, Malaysia; H.E. Mr. U. Zin Yaw, Deputy Minister of Foreign Affairs, Myanmar; H.E. Ms. Erlinda F. Basilio, Undersecretary for Policy and SOM Leader, Philippines; H.E. Mr. Simon Wong Wie Kuen, Deputy Secretary of Foreign Affairs, Singapore; H.E. Mr. Nopadol Gunavibool, Deputy Permanent Secretary, Ministry of Foreign Affairs, Thailand and H.E. Mr. Pham Quang Vinh, Deputy Minister of Foreign Affairs, Vietnam; H.E. Mr. Dato Paduka Haji Sidek Ali, High Commissioner of Brunei Darussalam; H.E. Mr. Thongphanh Syackhaphom, Ambassador of the Lao People's Democratic Republic.

This volume emerges from the proceedings of the Delhi Dialogue V and covers five thematic issues representing five sessions of the dialogue: (a) India-ASEAN Security Cooperation: Towards Peace and Stability; (b) Non-Traditional Security Challenges: Food Security, Water Management and Pandemics; (c) Future of Global Energy Market: Role of New and Renewable Energy in Sustainable Development; (d) Cooperation between CLMV Countries and North-East India: Opportunities and Challenges; and (e) Expanding Networks through Connectivity: Land, Sea and Air.

The first plenary session titled 'India-ASEAN Security Cooperation: Towards Peace and Stability' underscored the need for strengthening the relationship between India and ASEAN and making it a truly Strategic Partnership, one that should demonstrate a clear commitment to work together to effectively promote common goals, shared interests and the vision of making the Southeast Asian region a zone of peace, progress and prosperity, while emphasising India's indispensable role in any regional security and strategic architecture.

The plenary session was followed by two concurrent sessions on (a) Non-Traditional Security Challenges: Food Security, Water Management and Pandemics and (b) Future of Global Energy Market: Role of New and Renewable Energy in Sustainable Development. These two sessions discussed in detail different sets of non-traditional vulnerabilities facing the common people of India and ASEAN and their growing needs for energy as they grow together. Likewise, issues of food security, water management and pandemics have gained salience during the first decade of 21st century warranting innovative thinking and comprehensive strategies from both India and ASEAN in addressing these 'Non-Traditional Security Challenges'.

The third plenary session titled 'Cooperation between CLMV Countries and North-East India: Opportunities and Challenges' highlighted the need of connectivity between India's Northeast and CLMV countries because Southeast Asia actually begins with India's Northeast and Myanmar connects India with Southeast Asia. Intensive deliberations were made pertaining to developing the tourist potential in India's Northeast, harnessing energy resources of Myanmar, facilitating greater academic exchanges from the CLMV countries, connecting the local markets across the border and developing roads and rail connectivity between India's Northeast and the CLMV countries.

The fourth plenary session on 'Expanding Networks through Connectivity: Land, Sea and Air' highlighted three components of connectivity between India and ASEAN – physical, institutional and people-to-people. Various ongoing connectivity projects between India and ASEAN, such as India-Myanmar-Thailand Trilateral Highway, Delhi-Hanoi railway line and Dawei port as the key maritime linkage were highlighted.

The valedictory address was delivered by Mr. Sanjay Singh, Secretary (East), Ministry of External Affairs, Government of India. In his address, he acknowledged the emergence of Delhi Dialogue as a premier ASEAN-centric forum. He stated that India and ASEAN were natural partners which were working closely to deal with contemporary challenges that confront them in a globalized world.

This volume provides new ideas and insights towards forging a stronger partnership between India and ASEAN. It is hoped that it will make a valuable contribution to the scholarship on the expanding relationship between the two regions.

Rajiv K. Bhatia
Director General
Indian Council of World Affairs

Delhi Dialogue V: Recommendations

India's relations with the ASEAN countries have traditionally seen a constant flow of ideas, culture, knowledge and practices. With the passage of time, this relationship has advanced to diverse areas for mutual benefit of the peoples of the two regions. Since the launch of India's 'Look East' policy in early 1990s, the multifaceted partnership has come a long way and India-ASEAN relationship remains a key component of this policy. In the recent times, as the global dynamics witness unprecedented changes and trends, Asia is assuming new responsibilities commensurate with its capacities. The shifting of the US pivot towards the Asia-Pacific region is a major geo-political and geo-strategic development that is shaping the regional security environment. The Chinese military modernisation, especially its naval power projection capabilities, has set off varied reactions among its neighbours in East and Southeast Asia.

Non-traditional security issues such as food security, water management and pandemics are of critical importance for both India and ASEAN. Ensuring food security for its populace remains one of the primary concerns of every nation of this region. Similarly, water is a critical resource and its management is a subject of debate and discussion; and pandemics and disease are no longer limited to national boundaries and have assumed a transnational dimension.

Similarly, India's economic growth is highly dependent on sustained supply of energy resources and ASEAN countries, particularly Myanmar, Vietnam and Malaysia can potentially contribute to India's energy security. India and several ASEAN countries are net importers of hydrocarbon and it is important to reduce reliance on fossil fuels. The need to develop alternative energy sources in the region has been gathering momentum.

Since ancient times, India and Southeast Asia have enjoyed the benefits of connectivity and the traditional trade relations need to be augmented further to meet the demands of a globalized world. India and ASEAN need to focus on cooperation in enhancing connectivity through land, sea and air. This can be synergised through joint development of infrastructure such as transport networks, ports, shipping and air connectivity for greater regional economic integration.

The natural resource potential of Northeast India and CLMV countries offers opportunities for developing an export-oriented economy. It also serves as a tool for encouraging investment and industrial development in the region. At another level, the political transformation of Myanmar, enormous economic, commercial and trade opportunities have opened up, which can give a new impetus to the India-ASEAN relationship.

In this context, Delhi Dialogue V provided a number of recommendations to consolidate and further enhance India-ASEAN partnership for peace and prosperity in the region. Significantly, the Delhi Dialogue has been mentioned in the Vision Statement issued at India-ASEAN Commemorative Summit in December 2012, in that context these recommendations assume particular importance.

Defence and Security

a) The relationship between India and ASEAN should be strengthened and it should be made a truly Strategic Partnership. This partnership should demonstrate a clear commitment to work together to effectively promote common goals, shared interests and the vision of making the Southeast Asian region a zone of peace, progress and prosperity. India's role is indispensable in any regional security and strategic architecture.

b) India should eschew bilateralism, promote multilateralism and play a greater role in promoting multilateral institutions and rules-based regional and security architecture. The India-ASEAN partnership ought to take credit for its achievement while ASEAN must value India in its own right and not as being poised against China.

c) Even though there are regional anxieties about China's growing military capability, positive aspects associated with the economic rise of China should be appreciated in the region.

d) While the US is receptive to the concept of the 'Indo-Pacific', ASEAN does not seem ready and is obviously wary of being caught in the midst of what it apprehends as a likely US-India-led containment of China.

Non-Traditional Security

a) There is a consensus that bilateral and trilateral arrangements between the countries of the region is critical to deal with transnational issues such as food security, water management and pandemics.

b) The time is appropriate to discuss India-ASEAN river management issues, particularly the issue of water sharing.

c) The rise in the urban populations in both India and ASEAN regions is likely to exacerbate socio-economic problems and therefore a new paradigm for food supply and demand and policy formulations is needed.

d) The multi-national maritime exercise 'Milan' initiated to support India's Look East policy of closer relations with the nations of Southeast Asian navies is a fine example of regional cooperation.

Energy Security

a) The role of renewable energy in the future development of India and the ASEAN region cannot be underestimated and therefore cooperation in this field is significant.

b) There is a great need to expand cooperation in the renewable energy sector by enlarging business opportunities and making it people centric.

c) The shale gas discoveries in the US are likely to have their influence on Western energy policies, resulting in a possible geopolitical realignment in West Asia.

d) In the current global primary energy demand, hydrocarbons continue to remain dominant as the coal usage is increasing. Nuclear energy may slow down while renewable energy might have a major role in the changed scenario.

e) India and ASEAN should collaborate in R&D in power generation from solar, wind and tidal sources and also from biomass.

f) India should share experience and expertise with ASEAN in the field of hydro- power generation.

g) Solar is a viable form of alternative energy and should be encouraged and incentive should be provided for its usage. The optimum mix of technology and people friendly banking initiatives, especially informal banking can provide tailor-made finance for making people bankable as well as provide finance for decentralised solar energy.

h) India's new energy initiatives and policy moves must be both centralised and non-centralised, with emphasis on technology breakthroughs, efficient handling of supply fluctuations and long-term risk mitigation.

CLMV Countries and Northeast India

a) Trans-border crimes, smuggling of narcotic drugs and light weapons and insurgency are the main challenges that are impeding the development of the Northeast region. The answer to these problems is economic development of the region.

b) There is a need for the Northeast Vision 2020 to be enlivened and engagement by the private sector should be encouraged. Northeast India has the potential to be developed and promoted as a tourist destination.

c) There is an increasing need to avoid delaying of projects that have been or are currently being undertaken in the Northeast region.

d) The countries of the ASEAN need to be more closely involved in jointly executing projects, like the US and European Union have done.

e) Governments have a major role in the development and integration of India with the CLMV countries.

f) Connectivity through land, sea and air would help in bringing together people as well as markets of Northeast India and CLMV countries.

India-ASEAN Connectivity

a) Enhancing physical connectivity alone would not enable closer ties; this would have to be done along with creating institutional, digital and agri-connectivity.

b) There is a growing awareness that the bulk of efforts in greater India-ASEAN connectivity would have to come from the private sector in both the regions.

c) It is important to expedite projects involving building of transport infrastructure in Myanmar for strengthening connectivity with ASEAN. Dawei Port in Myanmar has the potential to transport Indian exports to ASEAN much quicker.

People-to-People Contacts

a) Language, culture and shared values play a seminal role in increasing connectivity between India and ASEAN, along with their common interests and potential for enhancing the partnership.

b) Media connectivity remains a missing link and needs to be critically examined. There should be promotion of more cinema and film festival exchanges on a mutual basis.

List of Contributors

H.E. Mr. Salman Khurshid, Hon'ble External Affairs Minister, Government of India.

H.E. Mr. Sanjay Singh, Secretary (East), Ministry of External Affairs, Government of India.

H.E. Mr. Le Luong Minh, Hon'ble Secretary-General, ASEAN.

H.E. Dr. Soeung Rathchavy, Secretary of State, Ministry of Foreign Affairs, Cambodia.

H.E. Mr. I. Gusti Agung Wesaka Puja, Director General of ASEAN Cooperation, Ministry of Foreign Affairs, Indonesia.

H.E. Y.B. Senator A. Kohillan Pillay, Deputy Minister of Foreign Affairs, Malaysia.

H.E. Mr. U. Zin Yaw, Deputy Foreign Minister of Myanmar.

H.E. Ms. Erlinda F. Basilio, Under Secretary for Policy and SOM Leader, Philippines.

H.E. Mr. Simon Wong Wie Kuen, Deputy Secretary of Foreign Affairs, Singapore.

H.E. Mr. Nopadol Gunavibool, Deputy Permanent Secretary, Ministry of Foreign Affairs, Thailand.

H.E. Mr. Pham Quang Vinh, Deputy Minister of Foreign Affairs, Vietnam.

Chief Organisers

Ambassador Rajiv Kumar Bhatia, Director General, Indian Council of World Affairs, New Delhi.

Ms. Naina Lal Kidwai, President, FICCI, Country Head - India & Director - Asia Pacific, HSBC Ltd., New Delhi, India.

Mr. R. Ravindran, Chairman, SAEA Group Research, Singapore.

Ms. Jyotsna Suri, Senior Vice President, FICCI & Chairperson & Managing Director, Bharat Hotels Ltd., India.

Dr. A. Didar Singh, Secretary General, FICCI, New Delhi.

Plenary Session 1: India-ASEAN Security Cooperation: Towards Peace and Stability

Professor Kanti Prasad Bajpai, Professor and Vice Dean Research, Lee Kuan Yew School of Public Policy, National University of Singapore.

Professor Rommel C. Banlaoi, Chairman and Executive Director, Philippine Institute for Peace, Violence and Terrorism Research (PIPVTR), Manila.

Dr. K.S. Balakrishnan, Head, Department of International and Strategic Studies, Faculty of Arts and Social Sciences, University of Malaya, Kuala Lumpur, Malaysia.

Dr. Evi Fitriani, Head, International Relations Department, University of Indonesia, Jakarta.

Concurrent Session 2A: Non-Traditional Security Challenges: Food Security, Water Management and Pandemics

Professor Nayan Sharma, Head of Department, Department of Water Resource Development and Management, Indian Institute of Technology (IIT), Roorkee.

Dr. Termsak Chalermpalanupap, ASEAN Studies Centre, Institute of Southeast Asian Studies, Singapore.

Dr. Dinna Wisnu, Director, Paramadina Graduate School of Diplomacy, Paramadina University, Jakarta, Indonesia.

Concurrent Session 2B: Future of Global Energy Market: Role of New and Renewable Energy in Sustainable Development

Mr. Harish Hande, Managing Director, SELCO Solar Light Private Limited, India.

Mr. Gautam Vivek, World Energy Council, New Delhi, India.

Mr. R. Ravindran, Chairman, SAEA Group Research, Singapore.

Plenary Session 3: Cooperation between CLMV Countries and North-East India: Opportunities and Challenges

Professor Gautam Barua, Director, Indian Institute of Technology (IIT), Guwahati.

Ambassador U. Nyunt Maung Shein, Head, Myanmar Institute of Strategic and International Studies, Yangon, Myanmar.

Professor Tan Tai Yong, Director, Institute of South Asian Studies (ISAS), National University of Singapore (NUS), Singapore.

Mr. Sunand Sharma, Country President, Alstom India and South Asia, India.

Plenary Session 4: Expanding Networks through Connectivity: Land, Sea and Air

Mr. Brijeshwar Singh, Former Chairman, National Highways Authority of India, India.

Mr. K.L. Thapar, Chairman, Asian Institute of Transport Development, New Delhi.

Mr. Hidetoshi Nishimura, Executive Director, Economic Research Institute of ASEAN and East Asia (ERIA), Jakarta, Indonesia.

Dr. S. Narayan, Head of Research, Institute of South Asian Studies (ISAS), National University of Singapore (NUS), Singapore.

Ambassador Pradap Pibulsonggram, Member, ASEAN Connectivity Coordination Committee, Thailand.

Welcome Remarks

Ambassador Rajiv K. Bhatia

Ambassador Rajiv K. Bhatia

Director General,
Indian Council of World Affairs (ICWA), New Delhi

I extend a warm welcome to the Minister of External Affairs, other special guests seated with him as well as all our distinguished guests who are present here today. I am particularly delighted to welcome all those guests who have come from the ASEAN region to participate in Delhi Dialogue V, a special and unique conference.

Let me begin by thanking the Ministry of External Affairs for their valuable support and the Federation of Indian Chambers of Commerce and Industry, our principal partner in organising this event. We are, of course, grateful to all other supporting institutions, i.e. the SAEA Group Research, Singapore, Economic Research Institute of ASEAN and East Asia, Jakarta and Institute of Defence Studies and Analyses, New Delhi.

As one of the two principal hosts, the Indian Council of World Affairs – offers Delhi Dialogue V as a most befitting platform of Track 1.5 dialogue on India-ASEAN relations. As the country's oldest foreign policy think tank, ICWA has contributed immensely to deepening India's relations with Asia for the past seven decades.

The theme of this year's conference, as you are aware, is 'India-ASEAN: Vision for Partnership and Prosperity'. Previous four conferences, held since 2009, have secured tangible gains towards deepening our mutual understanding and strengthening our cooperation. It is, therefore, a matter of shared pride that Delhi Dialogue, as an institution, found an apt mention in the Vision Statement issued at India-ASEAN Commemorative Summit in December 2012.

Since the launch of India's Look East policy in early 1990s, our multifaceted partnership has come a long way. As Prime Minister Manmohan Singh observed at the historic summit in December 2012, "The breadth and intensity of India's engagement with Southeast Asia is, unmatched by any of our other regional relationships." At present, there are approximately 25 mechanisms coordinating the ASEAN-India partnership in the areas of political-security cooperation, economic ties and socio-cultural cooperation. A relationship based on strong historical foundations and rooted in mutual interest, it has now been elevated to a Strategic Partnership and is poised to scale new heights in future. Now that this partnership has entered the third decade, it is a task of utmost importance that we earnestly begin to enlarge our convergence of views and strengthen our strategy for cooperative action.

In addressing this challenge, the political leaders, senior officials, captains of business and industry and members of strategic, academic and media community should exchange views regularly and candidly on the changing environment. Keeping this in view, we have, through mutual consultations, crafted an innovative agenda for this year. It will place a special focus on security cooperation, non-traditional security challenges (including food security, water management, pandemics and energy cooperation), likely expansion of cooperation between CLMV (Cambodia, Laos, Myanmar and Vietnam) countries and Northeast India, and the trends towards expanding networks through connectivity between India and ASEAN.

I am happy to announce that between today and tomorrow, we would have the opportunity to listen to 39 speakers out of which 21 have come from the ASEAN region. I gratefully acknowledge their presence among us as the testimony of their commitment to the cause of a stronger relationship in future.

Finally, it is sincerely hoped that this conference would further assist us in raising public awareness about the stakes and issues involved in the India-ASEAN partnership, undertaking its objective appraisal and generating new ideas and recommendations for the benefit of policy makers and other stakeholders.

Keynote Addresses

H.E. Mr. Salman Khurshid

H.E. Mr. Le Luong Minh

H.E. Dr. Soeung Rathchavy

H.E. Mr. I. Gusti Agung Wesaka Puja

H.E. Y.B. Senator A. Kohillan Pillay

H.E. Mr. U. Zin Yaw

H.E. Ms. Erlinda F. Basilio

H.E. Mr. Simon Wong Wie Kuen

H.E. Mr. Nopadol Gunavibool

H.E. Mr. Pham Quang Vinh

H.E. Mr. Salman Khurshid

Hon'ble External Affairs Minister, India

I am delighted to welcome you all to the inauguration of Delhi Dialogue V. Delhi Dialogue V has emerged as a successful Track 1.5 venue for discussions between government representatives, Track II experts and business representatives on political, economic and security issues of interest to both India and ASEAN.

Today, Delhi Dialogue V assumes far greater significance since it is the first event after the ASEAN-India Commemorative Summit in December last year, where we enhanced the level of our relationship to a Strategic Partnership. The Vision Statement adopted at the Summit presents vast opportunities for stronger cooperation between ASEAN and India.

The theme for this year's Delhi Dialogue, 'India-ASEAN: Vision for Partnership and Prosperity' sums up our common aspiration in furthering our Strategic Partnership for collective peace, progress and prosperity.

India's relations with the ASEAN member countries have seen a constant flow of ideas, culture, knowledge and practices. It has been a two-way civilizational connect and a history of trade, commerce and educational exchanges. In modern times, we are not only able to rediscover it but also advance it to diverse areas for mutual benefit of peoples of India and the ASEAN region.

In the recent times, as the global dynamics witness unprecedented changes and trends today, Asia is assuming new responsibilities commensurate with its capacities. Political, economic and security structures are evolving globally, and, in a more pronounced manner, in East Asia. ASEAN and India are, and will remain, natural partners in defining their perspectives and addressing their common requirements of economic growth and prosperity.

India and ASEAN member countries share a vision of a peaceful, prosperous and resurgent Asia, which contributes to global peace and security. We share a dynamic economic space, which houses a quarter of humanity and has a combined GDP of US$ 3.8 trillion. We have put in place the Free Trade Agreement on Trade in Goods in 2009 and have now concluded negotiations on the FTA on Services and Investment, which will help create greater synergy between our people, our industry and capacities.

ASEAN-India trade has been growing at over 22 per cent during the last few years, and as much as 37 per cent in 2011-12, which helped cross the target mark of US$ 70 billion last year, ahead of time. We are now striving for the target of US$ 100 billion by 2015 for ASEAN-India trade. As we look to the future, we must empower our youth across the spectrum of higher education, practical skills and vocational training, oriented to trade and technological advancement.

We have simultaneously resolved to meet non-traditional challenges and safeguard our collective politico-security environment, important for smooth flow of raw materials, merchandise and energy supplies. ASEAN-India engagement is proceeding well in the East Asia Summit, ASEAN Regional Forum, ADMM+ (ASEAN Defence Ministers Meeting Plus) and the Expanded ASEAN Maritime Forum (EAMF), which are important initiatives for evolving an open and inclusive regional architecture. We continue to support ASEAN's central role in this regional architecture.

International terrorism, transnational organised crime, money laundering, drug-trafficking, information and cyber security issues are today demanding greater collaboration of effort by the international community. With repercussions for global and regional security, these issues require new, innovative solutions that can remain ahead of the growing complexity in these issues.

Brainstorming and finding synergy of interest and effort in these areas is all the more important when we consider the global economic situation. The economic crisis of 2008-09 continues to persist. Our hitherto resilient economies are getting compounded by the Eurozone crisis. Our rates of growth have depressed but are still healthy and respectable. ASEAN member countries and India continue to be growth centres in Asia, widely expected to lead the global economy out of the ongoing economic crisis.

Connectivity with ASEAN – geographical, institutional or people-to-people – is a strategic priority for India. Relevant mechanisms established under the ASEAN-India framework to further connectivity, including some at Ministerial level, have been held during the Commemorative year.

India-Myanmar-Thailand Trilateral Highway project is progressing well. Route alignments for extending this Highway to Cambodia, Lao PDR (Lao People's Democratic Republic) and Vietnam need to be pursued further. The Mekong-India Economic Corridor, which will connect the industrial and freight corridors in India with the production networks in the Mekong region through the Chennai-Dawei sea link and the land connectivity to our Northeast, will have a beneficial effect on all our economies. These connectivity projects are capital intensive and we need to think of innovative means of financing them. Public-Private Partnership is one such method, but there are several other as well, which I am sure would be discussed at tomorrow's session on connectivity.

In this digital age, we also need to think of virtual networks as a way forward for connecting the region. We have welcomed the ASEAN Information and Communications Technology (ICT) Master Plan 2015 and also the efforts to strengthen ASEAN-India Connectivity in ICT. As a beginning, we are exploring capacity building programmes and sharing best practices in technological development and policy regulations related to e-connectivity.

We support the Initiative for ASEAN Integration (IAI) so as to contribute to the ASEAN vision of an ASEAN Community by 2015. As integration within ASEAN proceeds, it is also important that integration between ASEAN and India progress apace. We have already seen some traction on this as the 6th East Asia Summit called for a 'Connectivity Master Plan Plus' which would expand Connectivity beyond ASEAN.

We can bring about progress and shared prosperity only when the people of ASEAN and India are able to co-author Asia's economic growth and resurgence. I would like to hear recommendations tomorrow for making geographic borders open to trade and investment and the movement of professionals and experts. We will be continuing our capacity building emphasis in the ASEAN-India Strategic Partnership.

Development of effective energy systems, ensuring energy access utilising all forms of energy to all the sections of population, promotion of energy efficiency technologies and use of renewable energy should see urgent prioritisation on our cooperative calendar. The meetings held for the first time by my colleagues last year with their ASEAN counterparts in environment and renewable energy took cognisance of this. To my mind, the current predicament on these issues call for a sharing of expertise and knowledge, capacities and technology, a conviction that India has subscribed to for the last 65 years.

I am confident your deliberations will come up with recommendations on transforming the vision of our Leaders into reality, thus furthering the ASEAN-India Strategic Partnership to the next high level.

I would also like to compliment the Organisers of Delhi Dialogue V, the Indian Council of World Affairs (ICWA), the Federation of Indian Chambers of Commerce and Industry (FICCI), the SAEA Group Research of Singapore, Institute for Defence Studies and Analyses (IDSA) as well as the Economic Research Institute (ERIA) in Jakarta. I wish you success in your deliberations and look forward to receive your recommendations.

H.E. Mr. Le Luong Minh

Hon'ble Secretary-General, ASEAN

Allow me to express my sincere appreciation to the Ministry of External Affairs of India, the Indian Council of World Affairs (ICWA) and the Federation of Indian Chambers of Commerce and Industry (FICCI) for hosting and inviting me and the ASEAN Secretariat to participate in this important Delhi Dialogue on the ASEAN-India vision for partnership and prosperity.

The Look East policy that India has been implementing since 1991, which includes efforts to strengthen its relations with ASEAN, has been well reciprocated by ASEAN as an outward-looking organisation.

Over the past two decades, ASEAN has engaged India in a relationship which had grown rapidly to a full dialogue partnership in 1995, further strengthened with the convening of annual summits since 2002 and most recently, last year, elevated to Strategic Partnership. From a relationship which mainly emphasised economic cooperation, the ASEAN-India partnership has developed into one of ASEAN's most comprehensive, dynamic and fast-growing partnerships spanning across a whole spectrum of political-security, economic, socio-cultural and development collaboration. The consistent sequence of elevating the ASEAN-India partnership not only reflects the two sides' interest and desire to intensify their engagement, but also constitutes a solid foundation for further effective joint actions for peace, progress and shared prosperity.

As ASEAN is in the process of building the ASEAN Community, we appreciate India's support for ASEAN community building and its implementation of the Master Plan on ASEAN connectivity, the Initiative for ASEAN Integration and ASEAN centrality.

The leaders of ASEAN and India at their Commemorative Summit last December adopted a Vision Statement, which will serve as guidance to the pursuit of our Strategic Partnership for the years to come.

In this Vision Statement, our leaders called for greater effective implementation of the Plan of Action to implement the ASEAN-India Partnership for Peace, Progress and Shared Prosperity (2010-2015). The Plan of Action encompasses activities under the various existing ASEAN sectoral work plans, declarations concluded between ASEAN and India, as well as priority activities under the roadmap for an ASEAN Community that could be implemented with India.

In this regard, we would like to suggest that both ASEAN and Indian officials undertake a mid-term review of the implementation of this Plan of Action and map out the course of actions and possible joint activities from now until 2015, which would better correspond to the Vision set out by our Leaders, and study the important recommendations in the Report of the ASEAN-India Eminent Persons Group presented to our Leaders at the 10th ASEAN-India Summit in November 2012.

In the economic field, ASEAN and India have set the aim of achieving a free trade area. With a combined market of over 1.8 billion people and a GDP of US$ 3.8 trillion and relative geographical proximity, there is huge potential awaiting to be tapped. The signing and entry into force of the ASEAN-India Trade in Goods Agreement (TIG) and the conclusion of the negotiation on the Agreement on trade in services and investment paved the way for the creation of one of the world's largest free trade areas. In this endeavour, we need to devise measures to ensure that this Free Trade Agreement (FTA) benefits the business community on both sides.

Also at the 10th ASEAN-India Summit in December 2012, our leaders set the target of US$ 100 billion by 2015 for ASEAN-India trade. In achieving this target as well as in the long run, inter-connectivity would play a key role. ASEAN is embarking on an ambitious and long-term strategy to improve the region's physical, institutional and people-to-people connectivity. Enhanced ASEAN connectivity would promote ASEAN centrality in the regional architecture, facilitate the building of an ASEAN Community and serve as a foundation for a more enhanced connectivity beyond the region. ASEAN and India are located within an economically vibrant Asian region. Effective implementation of the Master Plan of ASEAN connectivity would be of great significance.

Expanding and improving road, rail, maritime and air linkages will be critical to further increase ASEAN-India trade and investment. The development of the Mekong-India Economic Corridor, the early construction of the new Indian-Myanmar-Lao PDR-Viet Nam-Cambodia Highway and the extension of the India-Myanmar-Thailand Trilateral Highway to Lao PDR and Cambodia would promote transport infrastructure linkages between ASEAN and India.

At the same time, we can strengthen ASEAN-India air connectivity by working towards greater liberalisation of air services, both cargo and passengers. Early conclusion of the ASEAN-India Air Services Agreement not only promotes trade, investment and tourism but also people-to-people connectivity, which are all mutually reinforcing.

Another key area of connectivity is Information and Communications Technologies (ICT), which can be enhanced through sharing of best practices in policy, regulations, technological development and capacity building programmes.

To explore concrete ways and means to support the Master Plan on ASEAN Connectivity in areas where India has strong expertise and interest, regular exchanges between the ASEAN Connectivity Coordinating Committee (ACCC) and India's Inter-Ministerial Group on Connectivity would be essential.

Over the years, ASEAN-India socio-cultural cooperation has been expanded to include human resource development, Science and Technology (S&T), people-to-people contacts, health and pharmaceuticals, transport and infrastructure, small and medium enterprises (SMEs), tourism, Information and Communication Technology, agriculture and energy.

India has also been actively contributing to narrowing the gaps of development through a number of projects and programmes. India's support for the Initiative for ASEAN Integration (IAI), particularly the programmes for Cambodia, Laos, Myanmar and Viet Nam in training and capacity building in entrepreneurship development, English language training and ICT has been well-recognised and appreciated by ASEAN.

The present regional and global dynamics are rendering to discussions on a regional architecture in East Asia even more urgent than ever. The dynamics bring along uncertainties, challenges and opportunities that the region has to manage.

As the new realities dawn on the region's horizon, ASEAN as the fulcrum of relations in the East Asia region is very well aware that it faces more challenges in preserving its relevance and centrality.

In expanding ASEAN's external relations with a view to constructively engaging its friends and partners to shape the evolving regional architecture, and at the same time to ensure that ASEAN will have a united voice and will be at the centre or form the core of the evolving regional architecture, ASEAN will strive to continue to exercise leadership and remain proactive in managing the cob-web of processes and cooperation in the region.

ASEAN welcomes and appreciates India's participation, continued commitment and support for the development of ASEAN-led regional processes which are open, transparent and inclusive, and based on principles of international law such as the East Asia Summit, ASEAN Defence Ministers Meeting Plus (ADMM-Plus) and the ASEAN Regional Forum.

Twenty years of cooperation has yielded great mutual benefits for both ASEAN and India. Looking ahead, the work we have to accomplish to ensure peace, promote progress and shared prosperity for our 1.8 billion people is much more comprehensive than what I only briefly mentioned and as reflected in the Agenda for this Fifth Dialogue. I wish success to the deliberation.

H.E. Dr. Soeung Rathchavy

Secretary of State, Ministry of Foreign Affairs, Cambodia

It is my great pleasure and honour to represent His Excellency Hor Namhong, Deputy Prime Minister and Minister of Foreign Affairs and International Cooperation of the Kingdom of Cambodia to participate in this very important inaugural session of the Delhi Dialogue V which we consider as an important international conference for political and economic leaders, diplomats, academia, think-tanks and opinion makers from the ASEAN countries and India to exchange views on political, strategic, economic and security cooperation.

Over the past years we have made significant achievements under the ASEAN-India partnership across all areas of cooperation, including political, security, economic, social and cultural cooperation. The year 2012 was another milestone for ASEAN-India cooperation as the two regions marked their twin celebration of the 10th Anniversary of ASEAN-India Summit and the 20 years of ASEAN-India dialogue relations. As for the political and security cooperation both sides have made remarkable progress in promoting mutual understanding and friendship through exchange of high level contacts and consultations at different levels on various regional and international issues of common interest and concern.

On the economic front, ASEAN and India have also made a giant leap forward with the successful conclusion of the negotiation on ASEAN-India

Trade in Services and Investment Agreement, the last piece of jigsaw for the establishment of ASEAN-India free trade area. Given the enormous economic and trade potentials, we should ensure the signing of this agreement soon so as to maximize benefit from our regional economic integration. At the 21st ASEAN Summit in Phnom Penh last year the negotiation on regional comprehensive economic partnership was launched. Thus, it is imperative for ASEAN and India to work closely to ensure the successful conclusion of the negotiations. As for the socio-cultural cooperation, ASEAN and India have promoted people-to-people interaction through expanding of the exchange of visit of students, media personnel, academia, think-tanks, parliamentarians, etc. in order to make ASEAN-India relations more fruitful for the years to come.

During the ASEAN-India Commemorative Summit held last December in New Delhi, the leaders of ASEAN and India adopted the Vision Statement which declared that the ASEAN-India partnership stands elevated to a Strategic Partnership. Therefore, ASEAN and India should focus on this and this should also be the way forward for ASEAN-India partnership in the coming decades. We need to deepen and enhance our cooperation across all areas of cooperation with a view to elevate this partnership to a real Strategic Partnership. To realise this important vision, it is also imperative for ASEAN and India to actively engage all important stakeholders such as the private sectors, academia, think-tanks and civil society in our joint effort. It is important to stress the need to enhance collaboration between and among the private sectors as well as to promote public-private partnership to strengthen regional integration, particularly in the fields of agriculture, connectivity, tourism and SME (Small and Medium Enterprises) development. In this regard, I also would like to highlight and share some points for future cooperation between ASEAN and India which are as follows:

To enhance regional integration and to support the realisation of ASEAN community by 2015 we should encourage India to continue supporting various programme of activities under the Initiative for ASEAN Integration Work Plan II and also the Phnom Pen agenda for the ASEAN community building which was adopted by the ASEAN leaders in April, 2012 in Phnom Pen. Also there is a need to further promote trade, investment, tourism and people-to-people connectivity between the two regions and to this end ASEAN and India should speed up the establishment of the ASEAN-India Centre as soon as possible. To enhance regional connectivity there is also a need for ASEAN and India to further strengthening the effort to implement the Master Plan on ASEAN connectivity comprising the physical, institutional and people-to-people connectivity and we also need to start considering the Master Plan on Connectivity Plus.

On agriculture, ASEAN and India should implement the Medium Term Plan of Action for ASEAN-India cooperation on agriculture and forestry for the period 2012-15 which was endorsed by the 1st ASEAN-India Agriculture Ministers Meeting in Jakarta, 2011, in particular, through the exchange of best practices and expertise. On tourism, ASEAN and India should also speed up the process of concluding an ASEAN-India air transport agreement as soon as possible and fully implement the MoU between ASEAN and India on strengthening tourism cooperation and more importantly both sides should also consider having direct flights from the major cities of India to the capitals and other important tourist destinations of all the ASEAN countries and vice versa.

We also need to streamline the cooperation under the Mekong-Ganga Cooperation under this particular sub-regional framework. ASEAN and India should further strengthen cooperation, in particular the activities with the focus on human resource development and also the e-initiative. I am also of the view that the challenge lying before us now is to gear up our full effort by utilising the existing mechanism to ensure the effective and timely implementation of all the key decisions of our leaders as enshrined in the Vision Statement and other ASEAN-India documents as well as the practical recommendation by the ASEAN-India Eminent Persons Groups.

Last but not the least, ASEAN and India should do more homework in terms of promoting public awareness on ASEAN-India cooperation since our cooperation is quite dynamic. However, the people of both sides still have little access to the information and also they need to know more about our cooperation. I would like to stress that ASEAN highly values the continued support by India to our ASEAN Community building as well as to the ASEAN centrality in the evolving regional architecture. I think ASEAN and India should ensure that the evolving regional security and economic architecture would maintain peace, security, stability and also bring prosperity to our region.

H.E. Mr. I. Gusti Agung Wesaka Puja

Director General of ASEAN Cooperation, Ministry of Foreign Affairs, Indonesia

First of all, let me convey my Minister for Foreign Affairs' warm regards to His Excellency Mr. Salman Khursid, and all participants of the Delhi Dialogue V. My profound appreciation to all parties involved and colleagues for the excellent arrangements made for the Delhi Dialogue.

I am delighted to be able to attend the Delhi Dialogue V, a Track 1.5 forum which gathers prominent persons from many fields of cooperation between ASEAN and India. With its theme of 'India-ASEAN: Vision for Partnership and Prosperity', I am confident that today's Delhi Dialogue V will be fruitful and would contribute positively to the significant growing ties and relations between ASEAN and India. Let me take this opportunity to highlight certain ways which we may enhance the ASEAN-India partnership, from the perspective of Indonesia.

In reviewing our past activities last year, ASEAN and India has undertaken a series of successful and memorable events. At the highest level, we held the 10th ASEAN-India Summit in November 2012 in Phnom Penh, Cambodia and the 20th Anniversary of ASEAN-India Commemorative Summit in December 2012 in New Delhi.

Indonesia is highly pleased with the convening of two major events in the light of the 20th Anniversary of ASEAN-India Dialogue Relations, namely:

First is the Indian Navy Sailing Ship Expedition of I.N.S. Sudarshini to ASEAN Member States. The ship visited three major sea-ports of Indonesia in Padang (West Sumatra), Bali and Manado (North Sulawesi).

Second is the ASEAN-India Car Rally (AICR), whereas the Indonesian Leg was represented by the initial flag off in Yogyakarta to Solo. During this leg, participants had the opportunity to visit the Borobudur Temple. During their stay at the Borobudur Temple, the participants planted trees and witnessed the inauguration of the bust of Rabindranath Tagore, to commemorate the visit of Tagore to the Temple while expressing his admiration through his poem that he wrote in 1927.

Along this line, I would like to emphasise the need to follow up and ensure the benefits of these events, especially with regard to the ASEAN-India Vision Statement as the landmark outcome of the Commemorative Summit. We need to further organise our joint and concerted efforts in implementing it so as to further ASEAN-India Strategic Partnership in the future.

ASEAN-India Dialogue Partnership was established 20 years ago, and the ASEAN-India Summit began 10 years back. India has also recently introduced its Look East policy. Nevertheless, it is believed that India and the nations of Southeast Asia, particularly Indonesia, have been engaging in trade and cultural links for the last many years. India has been ASEAN's active partners for 20 years, and for Indonesia bilaterally, our friendship began well before formal diplomatic relations were established. Indonesia as well as ASEAN, sees India as one of the emerging strategic powers in Asia. Enhancing relationship and cooperation with India should be the core interest of ASEAN, and vice versa.

Under ASEAN-India dialogue relations, we can certainly state that we have made significant and encouraging progress. It should, however, be emphasised that our cooperation shall be even more determined to accelerate the undertakings towards the ASEAN Community in 2015 and to achieve a common platform for ASEAN in the global community of nations beyond 2015. India's continued support as our dialogue partner would indeed remain valuable.

Our world recently is confronted by global economic crisis. We witnessed recessions caused by slowing growth, coupled with slowing global trade. Simultaneously, the crisis can be further deepened by the volatility of global food and energy prices and supply.

As part of the wider community of nations, ASEAN is confronted with the dynamics of the 21st century, where issues have become more complex, multifaceted, trans-national, interlinked and interdependent. Moreover, ASEAN is relatively resilient from the current crisis.

With this challenging background, countries must work together to overcome the threats and crisis. We have to address the roots of the problems, while also appreciate their complexity. The role of dialogue partners, including India, international financial institutions as well as regional and multilateral organizations becomes ever more critical. Cooperation and collaboration must continue and strengthened sustainably.

Geographically, ASEAN and India are next-door neighbours and share maritime boundaries. ASEAN and India share a huge interest in maritime cooperation with the emerging challenges of sea piracy, vessel accidents, oil spills, terrorism and natural disasters. ASEAN-India maritime cooperation is an emerging important field that need to be further enhanced, through various activities, cooperation and sharing of best practices.

In the economic field, India will remain one of ASEAN's most important trading partners. The growing trade volume between ASEAN and India has surpassed the 2012 target. Considering this fast growth, we should be very confident that the US$ 100 billion trade target for 2015, as outlined in the ASEAN-India Vision Statement, is achievable.

On the bilateral front, Indonesia is pleased with the progress achieved on the bilateral trade of US$ 17 billion. Currently, our two countries attempt to reach the new bilateral trade target of US$ 25 billion in 2015.

ASEAN-India trade can still be further accelerated on both sides by enhancing connectivity. It should therefore be encouraged that ASEAN and India develop more projects on connectivity, especially to share India's expertise in digital connectivity, within the Master Plan on ASEAN Connectivity (MPAC).

On the question of food and energy security, Indonesia continues its call for a closer concrete collaboration between ASEAN and India. As the global demand for food and energy continue to rise, our region as one of the largest population in the world will have to address these imminent challenges with immediate action. We deem it necessary for ASEAN and India to identify and implement tangible projects and cooperation on food and energy security as mentioned in our ASEAN-India Plan of Action (POA 2010-2015).

On a final note, I would like to emphasise that in our pursuit for common security, common stability and common prosperity, ASEAN-India have a collective responsibility to contribute positively to both our people, our region and to the world at large. Indonesia truly hopes that after more than 20 years, ASEAN-India relations will continue to be meaningful and mutually beneficial.

H.E. Y.B. Senator A. Kohillan Pillay

Deputy Minister of Foreign Affairs, Malaysia

I have been told by my Minister of Foreign Affairs Dato' Sri Anifah Hj Aman to represent him at this Dialogue. At the onset, allow me to congratulate and thank the Government of India for organizing the Delhi Dialogue V. The Delhi Dialogue has now been an annual event as stipulated in the ASEAN-India Vision Statement adopted by our leaders during ASEAN-India Commemorative Summit in December 2012 in New Delhi. Over the years Delhi Dialogue has become an important instrument for our thinkers to deepen the relations between ASEAN and India and to achieve the Strategic Partnership as aspired by our leaders in their Vision Statement.

It is with this realization that the Prime Minister of Malaysia Dato' Sri Najin Tun Razak during his intervention at the Commemorative Summit emphasised the importance of expanding ASEAN-India relations through intensified political, economic and people-to-people cooperation. Strategic Partnership could only be achieved completely through the fulfilment of initiatives in these three areas of collaboration. While we should be proud of remarkable progress that we have made in the past, our focus should now be on the implementation of the brilliant ideas and plans discussed last year, especially through the ASEAN-India Vision Statement and the report of the ASEAN-India Eminent Persons Group.

As adopted by our leaders during the ASEAN-India Commemorative Summit last year, India will assist and cooperate closely with ASEAN to realise the ASEAN Community in 2015, the year that Malaysia will take the chairmanship of ASEAN. The success of ASEAN Community in fact needs continued support from all ASEAN dialogue partners. Given that 2015 is just 2 years away, it is important for us to ensure the successful realisations of the community through speedy implementation of some important initiatives. As the strategic partner of ASEAN, India could play a major role in the run-up towards 2015. There are indeed numerous fields in which India and ASEAN could work together.

For the purpose of this dialogue allow me to share with you five priority areas that would enable India to contribute significantly to the ASEAN Community in 2015. First, from the perspective of dialogue relations, ASEAN and India need to enhance efforts in executing the Plan of Action to implement the ASEAN-India partnership for peace, progress and shared prosperity, 2010-2015. The full implementation of this Plan of Action would considerably enhance ASEAN-India dialogue relations as well as to assist ASEAN to realise the ASEAN Community blueprints. As the Plan of Action is fast approaching its termination, a successor document should be thought of from now to ensure the continuation of important programmes and to intensify our future collaboration.

Second area concerns the role of India in the regional architecture of East Asia. India is already an integral part of the East Asia regional architecture. Therefore, it is important for India to continue to engage in ASEAN led regional mechanism such as ASEAN Defence Ministers Meetings Plus and the ASEAN Regional Forum to foster constructive dialogue and consultation on political and security areas. India could also come out with initiatives and measures to further deepen these processes.

Third area pertains to the commitment in realising and implementing the ASEAN-India Free Trade Area (FTA). The success in concluding the negotiations of the ASEAN-India trade in services and investment agreements in December 2012 should pave the way for our private sectors to further enhance linkages in promoting trade in services and expanding cross border investment. The implementation of these agreements together with the continuation of the earlier agreed free trade in goods will double, or even triple, our economic targets in the shortest time possible, before 2015. A successful implementation of complete ASEAN-India FTA would also greatly facilitate future negotiations of the regional comprehensive economic partnership which was agreed at the last ASEAN summit and related summit in Phnom Penh, Cambodia.

Fourth area, India's involvement in ASEAN's connectivity process should be strengthened while ASEAN endeavours to intensify the connectivity among the member States in inter-relations with the dialogue partners. India has come up with several initiatives to enhance its connectivity with ASEAN and promotion of connectivity with ASEAN should continue. At the same time efforts should also be made to ensure that this process is not only limited physically but also encompasses institutions, mechanisms and processes as well as people empowerment.

Fifth area relates to the promotion of people-to-people exchanges between ASEAN and India. I firmly believe that understanding each other better would create productivity and lasting friendship. In this regard, both sides should intensify people-to-people programmes and activities. An early establishment of cultural centres in respective countries such as an ASEAN Centre in New Delhi would contribute towards more people-centred activities especially among the younger generations. Youth interaction can also be set up through sporting events and students exchange programmes.

With focus given to these five priority areas and implementing the initiatives under the ASEAN-India Vision Statement, I believe that India's role in supporting ASEAN Community in 2015 would be strongly felt and greatly appreciated. They also will contribute significantly to the realisation of the true Strategic Partnership between ASEAN and India. In conclusion, let me say that our Strategic Partnership would serve not only our common interests but also peace, stability and prosperity of our region.

H.E. Mr. U. Zin Yaw

Deputy Minister of Foreign Affairs, Myanmar

I am honoured to participate in Delhi Dialogue V, with the distinguished policy makers, academics and members of think tanks from ASEAN and India. The bilateral relations between Myanmar and India have been progressing through exchange of visits of different levels in the past two years. President of Myanmar Thein Sein paid a state visit to India in October 2011 and the Prime Minister of India Dr. Manmohan Singh visited Myanmar in May 2012. The visits of the two leaders have opened a new chapter in our relations. We are very encouraged with the remarks made by Prime Minister Dr. Manmohan Singh in which he expressed that India was very appreciative of the efforts being made by the President of Myanmar for national reconciliation and democratisation for the good of the people of Myanmar. Myanmar highly appreciates the goodwill of India and its kind offer to enhance cooperation in various sectors.

During the visit of Prime Minister of India, a total of 12 agreements and MoUs were signed, including the US$ 500 million line of credit to Myanmar. Furthermore, the two leaders have agreed to cooperate extensively in the security and counterterrorism, connectivity, information technology, agriculture, trade and investment, culture, science and technology, infrastructure, health, education and human resources development. In the regional and multilateral cooperation, the Prime Minister of India extended his good wishes to Myanmar for its successful term as the Chair of Bay of

Bengal Initiative for Multi Sectoral and Economic Cooperation (BIMSTEC). Myanmar will host the 3rd BIMSTEC Summit in 2013. Furthermore, Myanmar will take the chairmanship and host the ASEAN Summit in 2014.

Myanmar is pleased to witness the development of ASEAN-India partnership which has now been elevated to a Strategic Partnership. This accomplishment was announced in New Delhi at the ASEAN-India commemorative summit that marked the 20th anniversary of dialogue relations in December 2012. In this respect the theme of the dialogue 'India-ASEAN: Vision for Partnership and Prosperity' is the most relevant to all of us. We are striving to achieve prosperity while strengthening partnership between us. The discussions at the Delhi Dialogue V based on the recommendations of Dialogue IV will be a leverage to add momentum to the development of ASEAN-India relationship in the years to come. I sincerely hope that through these sessions critical ways and means to implement the Vision Statement of the ASEAN-India Commemorative Summit 2012 will emerge.

We are also thankful to the ASEAN-India Eminent Persons Group for their efforts to take stock of the 20 years of cooperation and chart future direction of ASEAN-India dialogue relations. We have witnessed remarkable progress in the implementation of the Plan of Action of ASEAN-India Partnership for Peace, Progress and Shared Prosperity 2010-2015. We also worked on the conclusion of the negotiations on FTA in service and investment. We hope to see early signing of agreements by both sides. The momentum of progress should be maintained and the future plans beyond 2015 should be studied henceforth. We look forward to the establishment of ASEAN India Centre to further strengthening our cooperation.

The Delhi Dialogue is a premier ASEAN centric Track 1.5 platform to discuss regional and international issues of mutual importance. We support this dialogue that covers wide range of important issues of security cooperation, non-traditional security challenges, energy and connectivity. Myanmar attaches great importance to the principle of the Treaty of Amity and Cooperation in South Asia and commitment of ASEAN member states to find a peaceful resolution to issues that affect peace and stability in the region. Myanmar is ready to actively participate in addressing food and energy security, management of water resources and connectivity of land, sea and air. In addition to the geographic position of Myanmar, the favourable political climate and series of economic and social reforms of the government have further consolidated Myanmar's goodwill and desire to engage with India bilaterally as well as within the framework of ASEAN.

Myanmar also serves as a land bridge between India and Southeast Asia. Hence, the location of Myanmar offers great opportunities for the Indian business to make Foreign Direct Investment (FDI) and do business in the country. The Economic Research Institute for ASEAN and East Asia conceptualised a corridor named Mega India Economic Corridor. The corridor will further expand ASEAN-India connectivity in addition to the existing connectivity network.

In conclusion, may I take this opportunity to raise at this forum that there exists great opportunities ahead for us to expand the ASEAN-India Strategic Partnership at a time when our region and the rest of the world continues to face complex political, economic and social issues. Let us continue to maintain and develop our common appreciation to expand our Strategic Partnership that will bring prosperity to our people and yield success to our partnership.

H.E. Ms. Erlinda F. Basilio

Undersecretary for Policy and SOM Leader, Philippines

It is an honour to be back in New Delhi to represent Philippine's Foreign Secretary Albert F. del Rosario, who conveys his deepest regret for being unable to attend this Delhi Dialogue V, but conveying at the same time his good wishes for the success of the Dialogue, which is an important Track 1.5 venue for discussing important regional and global issues.

The Philippines welcomes the Delhi Dialogue for the opportunity it gives to delve deeper into the ASEAN-India partnership and identify how it can be further strengthened and made more effective. Strategic Partnership with India is significant to ASEAN, economically and politically.

The direction of ASEAN-India cooperation has been mapped by the current 2010-2015 Plan of Action to implement the 'ASEAN-India Partnership for Peace, Progress and Shared Prosperity'. The Plan of Action proposes 18 areas of cooperation, which when pursued with the same rigor as intended by the Vision Statement of the ASEAN-India Commemorative Summit, could very well address many crucial areas of common concern that may be raised during this Dialogue.

Foremost among them is security cooperation. Security is a *sine qua non* or prerequisite for sustained growth, development and prosperity. ASEAN and India's trade with the rest of the world are shipped through our contiguous waters. Hence, security cooperation – particularly maritime cooperation to maintain the freedom of navigation and safety of the sea lanes – is a decisive prerequisite for our two regions' sustained growth, peace and stability.

Crucial also in this Dialogue's discourse are the non-traditional security and energy issues. Our respective countries must be able to provide for the food, water and health needs of our growing populations and increasing appetite for energy of our growing economies, not just satisfying minimum levels but providing in surplus. The adverse effects of climate change should also be addressed. Otherwise, economic growth and development could plateau or come to a standstill.

The Philippines is pleased to note India's increasing contribution to ASEAN's development and integration, notably in the areas of connectivity, agriculture, energy, pharmaceutical products, human resource development and, most recently, biodiversity conservation. However, in considering the requirements for sustaining our regional growth, cooperation in food and energy security should be prioritised. The challenges posed by these two areas may be daunting at first glance, but the prospects of cooperation between our regions are positive as well, because our individual countries have relevant competencies, experts, programs and success stories to share among us. By having our national agriculture and alternative energy experts collaborate on specific challenges, solutions could very well be made. We can complement our national programs to address the pressing needs of our growing populations and economies.

As Prime Minister Manmohan Singh had said during the ASEAN-India Commemorative Summit last December, the destinies of ASEAN and India are intertwined. Indeed, our two regions' needs and prospects are linked. Therefore, ASEAN and India have to closely cooperate on the promotion of common interests and mutual concerns in the years and decades to come.

In summary, the Philippines urges us all to capitalise on the strong ASEAN-India relations and our geographic proximity in addressing our common aspirations, especially in maintaining peaceful co-existence with our neighbours through active maritime cooperation, observance of rules-based regime in resolving disputes and closer collaboration in non-traditional security areas, such as food production, renewable energy and climate change. I hope this Delhi Dialogue V will provide us with fresh insights on how we can attain our noble aspirations for the benefit of our peoples.

H.E. Mr. Simon Wong Wie Kuen

Deputy Secretary of Foreign Affairs, Singapore

Two months ago, I was here in Delhi for the ASEAN-India Commemorative Summit to mark the 20 years of ASEAN-India dialogue relations. The Summit left deep impression on me for two reasons. The first was the ever growing bond between our two regions as manifested in the wonderful performance staged by the cultural troops from India and the 10 countries of ASEAN at the majestic hall of the Presidential residence on the 20th December, 2012. Many in the audience that evening, me included, were simply blown away by the dynamic and seamless performances. The various songs and dance traditions fused in perfect harmony in a rich cultural milieu is a brilliant metaphor of the rich synergies between India and ASEAN. The second reason that I was so impressed was that ASEAN and India reaffirmed the desire to strengthen their Strategic Partnership as encapsulated in the Vision Statement during the Summit.

When our leaders met here in New Delhi in December 2012, they not only came together to celebrate a long standing partnership, but also renewed the firm commitment to build stronger and lasting linkages between the two regions. ASEAN is today a key pillar of India's Look East policy. India in turn as an emerging power has become an indispensable partner for ASEAN. Indeed, India's engagement with ASEAN is helping to create a more open, dynamic, peaceful and prosperous region. I hope as the discussion at the Delhi Dialogue gets underway we will explore new ways in which

ASEAN and India can work together. I wish to highlight just two areas for participant's consideration.

The first is the Regional Comprehensive Economic Partnership or RCEP. Our vision for the RCEP is to be a modern, comprehensive and high quality Free Trade Area (FTA) that will broaden and deepen the current economic engagement that has been achieved through existing ASEAN+1 FTAs. The RCEP will lead to significant improvements over existing ASEAN+1 FTA. Beyond trade in goods, services and investments, the RCEP will also cover economic cooperation, intellectual property, competition, dispute settlement and other issues to be discussed. ASEAN therefore welcomes India's decision as announced by Prime Minister Manmohan Singh in December 2012 to participate in this forum.

RCEP will enhance market access to the region but more than that RCEP is about deepening engagement with the region and supporting the regional architecture that is open, inclusive and outward looking. We think it is important for India to join RCEP right from the onset.

In our globalized world, our futures and fortunes are closely tied and interdependent than ever before. It is heartening to note that India's leaders are committed to achieve growth. In a recent speech by India's Finance Minister Mr. Chidambaram, he made an impassioned case that India needs to focus on growth without which there would be neither development nor inclusiveness. In ASEAN we also recognise the robust investment, economic integration and connectivity are the superhighways that we need to get on, to achieve strong, sustainable and balanced growth. This brings me to the concept of connectivity, the second area, which I believe India can and will contribute meaningfully to ASEAN's community building efforts. Prime Minister Manmohan Singh himself highlighted that ASEAN connectivity is a strategic objective for India at the ASEAN-India summit in 2011. I am glad that India has been an active supporter of the Master Plan on ASEAN connectivity and I had the privilege to open the ASEAN-India seminar with my Indian counterpart in Singapore last November.

I am also happy to be present at the ASEAN-India car rally ceremony in Singapore on the 28th November and a flag down ceremony here in India on the 20th December, 2012 after the drivers of all ASEAN and India completed the gruelling 8000 km journey from Indonesia and ASEAN to Assam in their Mahindra SUVs. As the only two countries with a land border with ASEAN, India stands to gain from a well connected and integrated ASEAN, which will allow India to benefit from better production and distribution networks in the region and to leverage on the comparative strengths of the various ASEAN member States.

However, there is still another way to enhance connectivity between ASEAN and India; it is through the aviation sector. The ASEAN-India Aviation Cooperation Framework (ACF) was adopted in November 2008 following Prime Minister Singh's announcement at the 12th ASEAN Summit in 2007. We feel that this is a bold initiative which Singapore supports strongly. Enhanced air connectivity will bring tremendous benefit to both ASEAN and India that would further facilitate regional integration and the flow of people and goods. ASEAN and India should double their efforts to negotiate on an ASEAN-India air transport agreement.

The past two decades have witnessed enormous progress in ASEAN-India relations in many ways. In December 2012 we started a new chapter by elevating our relationship through a Strategic Partnership. ASEAN and India are natural partners. We are bound by history and culture and we share a common desire to deepen the links between our people, promote commerce, enhance cooperation and improve connectivity. It is my sincere hope that the Delhi Dialogue V will reinforce our commitment to build and intensify those links

H.E. Mr. Nopadol Gunavibool

Deputy Permanent Secretary, Ministry of Foreign Affairs, Thailand

First of all let me say that I am honoured to be here on behalf of my Foreign Minister who has asked me to convey his best wishes for great success of Delhi Dialogue V. I was also privileged to be here last year with him for the Delhi Dialogue IV. I think many of my colleagues have talked about the importance of ASEAN-India relations and cooperation. I think all our colleagues underscored the importance of the 20th anniversary of ASEAN-India dialogue relations in 2012 which concluded here in New Delhi with a Commemorative Summit which elevated our partnership to a strategic one. So, I think at the Delhi Dialogue V, we look forward to hear how we could advance the ASEAN-India Strategic Partnership for the benefit of the region in the next decade.

I want to remind everyone here that the ASEAN-India relations date back more than 20 years. I think Indian culture is indeed a major component of Southeast Asia's culture and we find a trace and deep heritage of Indian culture everywhere in Southeast Asia. So, that is why it is not difficult for ASEAN and India to work together. While we now talk about ASEAN-India connectivity, I believe that we need to connect each other not only through physical linkages, trade and investment, but also through our peoples. In what way are we looking at people-to-people connectivity that contributes to the ASEAN-India Strategic Partnership?

I would like to say that now India has become a vibrant modern nation in the eyes of ASEAN. India is now a source of innovation, technology, knowhow, taking the lead in the world's software business. Modern India's success is admired and sought after everywhere. I believe that India's success lies in her investment in her people, empowering them with modern education, science and technology. This has created a solid foundation for India's innovations and an outburst of creativity and new entrepreneurship that propelled the Indian economy today.

Thailand sees that India's technology-led economy is to a great extent because of its English proficient people who can use new and world class technologies. Moreover a large pool of English speaking professions has attracted the big multinationals and other companies around the world to India for outsourcing contracts in telecommunication, legal and other fields from every corner of the world. By learning from India's experiences in making the knowledge based economy, ASEAN countries can apply it to their own development models.

Similarly, we must not also forget the Indian Diaspora, around 5 million people of Indian origin who live all over the world including Southeast Asia. This Indian Diaspora constitutes professionals such as doctors, engineers, diplomats, scholars, scientists, business executives, artists, journalists and skilled labour to the economy of over 70 nations worldwide. They have had a significant impact on the Indian economy and they have not only brought back wealth and reputation to their homeland but also changed the way the world looks at India. The Indian Diaspora serves as a wider bridge between our two peoples i.e. the people of ASEAN and India and helps in the cooperation between them.

Most of the people-to-people contacts naturally lead to the sharing of common values and ideology constituting ASEAN and India's growing bond. India's commitment to democracy is well known and admired. The growth and the strength of India today has taken place within the framework of democracy, one that is based on secular and inclusive principles. India's experience and best practices in democracy, openness, inclusiveness and tolerance could be shared with ASEAN, especially in a time when we are working towards a rule based ASEAN community.

I also want to say something about our young generation. I think our children and grand children will inherit our shared values that are crucial to our centuries-long relations at a time of great flux and transition. I agree with the Minister of External Affairs that in this day and age I think the world is facing complex issues and with the problems in Europe and America, Asia is looked at as the engine of growth in the next few decades. I think it is incumbent upon ASEAN and India to revitalise and cultivate in our young generation deep understanding and appreciation of our shared values, culture and heritage as they are bridge to link our common future.

India-ASEAN connectivity means connection between our 1.8 billion people. Connectivity based on positive elements such as historical relations, affinities and commonalities will lead to a flow of flourishing economic activities, tourism, travelling and contacts and academic exchanges. Let me commend India for its continuing support for exchange programmes of ASEAN diplomats, students and media as well as parliamentarians. They have contributed to the better understanding of growing bonds among our people.

To sum up, we believe that more people-to-people linkages would continue to be in focus of ASEAN and ASEAN-India relations as a main objective of closer integration and supported by our knowledge base and democratic economy. Such linkages are keys to build a durable foundation for ASEAN-India Strategic Partnership in the next decade.

H.E. Mr. Pham Quang Vinh

Deputy Minister of Foreign Affairs, Vietnam

It is a great pleasure for me to return to Delhi and to attend this 5th edition of Delhi Dialogue under the theme 'India-ASEAN: Vision for Partnership and Prosperity.' We attach great importance to this annual event. Actually over the past years the Delhi Dialogue has become one of the premier Track 1.5 platforms for ASEAN and India to discuss regional and international issues of common concern, including also to further promote ASEAN-India partnership as well as to promote regional peace and prosperity. We believe that this Delhi Dialogue V will be very important since it takes place at a very meaningful juncture, when the region has been encountering both opportunities and challenges.

We also witness that in the region we have peace and stability but at the same time we are facing more and more competing challenges both in non-traditional and traditional security fields. So, I think that ASEAN and India have a lot of things to work together to further promote our common and shared objectives for peace, stability and prosperity.

The successful conclusion of ASEAN-India Commemorative Summit in Delhi in December 2012 has given a new impetus for further strengthening of the ASEAN-India partnership especially in the launch of ASEAN-India Strategic Partnership and we believe that this will give a greater momentum for the further strengthening and fostering of both bilateral relations between ASEAN and India and fostering of peace, security, stability and economic prosperity in the region.

In this regard, we do agree with the proposed theme for this dialogue as designed by the sponsors and also the concept paper. On the security issue we share the analysis that there has been an evolving shift in the regional, geopolitical and geostrategic environment. While ASEAN and India continues to play an important role in promoting peace, stability and prosperity in the region, we also witness changes in the region. Among these we may name a few and I share with the analysis that has been presented to us earlier by the speakers. The issues and challenges that we face today are more transnational, more complicated and more cross-sectoral. We also witness greater engagement of the major powers in the region and their interactions. We also see rare efforts in confidence building and dialogue but at the same time we also see competitive developments regarding peace, stability and security in the region. All these have been for us to discuss and to work for a strategy how to achieve peace, stability and prosperity.

At the same time, based on our achievements and experience so far we need to work harder to ensure the effective resolution of non-traditional security challenges such as disaster, climate change, food, energy and water security as well as trans-national crimes. It is imperative for the region to make greater efforts in this regard and to further enhance dialogue, cooperation and confidence building especially to work together for regional architecture that suits the region and better ensures peace, stability and cooperation in the region in the interest of all countries of this region. We therefore continue to support ASEAN initiative and we appreciate India's continued support for ASEAN centrality in the region.

Among the challenges, I wish to mention the question of maritime security that includes the issue of South China Sea. Here, we continue to witness complicating developments and we believe that it is in the interest of not only ASEAN and India but all countries concerned for the continued efforts in the maintenance of peace, maritime security and freedom of navigation in the South China Sea. Similarly, it is important to ensure the peaceful settlement of disputes as well as the respect for international law and UNCLOS, the full implementation of the Declaration of the Conduct of parties in the South China Sea, the DOC as well as the ASEAN six principles. The countries concerned in the region need to work together for the early conclusion of the Code of Conduct in the region.

It is very important that we here at the Delhi Dialogue V work together to ensure the follow up of the vision that has been worked out by our leaders last December. So I think that today and tomorrow at the Delhi Dialogue we will continue to discuss the ways and means of how to enhance further ASEAN-India Strategic Partnership especially on how to achieve the good and effective implementation of the vision and the plan of action that has been adopted since the Commemorative Summit last year.

Finally, I have great confidence that the Delhi Dialogue will take into account all the challenges that we are witnessing today and will facilitate in working together to build a regional architecture that ensures peace, stability and prosperity, greater regional economic integration, greater connectivity and commercial linkages as well as common benefits for ASEAN countries and India and for all other countries in the region.

Special Remarks

Ms. Naina Lal Kidwai

Ms. Naina Lal Kidwai

President, FICCI, Country Head – India &
Director – Asia Pacific, HSBC Ltd., New Delhi, India

First of all, I would like to express my gratitude to Mr. Salman Khurshid, Hon'ble External Affairs Minister, for his inspiring remarks and setting the tone of the Delhi Dialogue V. This amply demonstrates his personal commitment and the commitment of Government of India in taking the India-ASEAN partnership, to the next level.

Sir, your remarks have highlighted the potential areas for enhanced cooperation between India and ASEAN, some of which are on the agenda for discussion. Such an increased dialogue will have positive impact on trade and investment too. Consider this,

a) India is 7th largest trading partner of ASEAN in the Asian grouping.

b) It is estimated that between April 2000 and July 2012, about US$ 19 billion worth of equity investments came into India from ASEAN, while Indians too pledged US$ 6 billion in ASEAN countries.

c) Further, an early conclusion of the ASEAN-India Services and Investment Agreements would give a boost to trade and investment.

We, as industry, are committed to reaching greater trade volume through India-ASEAN FTA and for realising our trade and investment potential under our Strategic Partnership by expanding economic and diplomatic initiatives.

In this direction, it would be apt for me to share with you some very special lines by our Hon'ble Prime Minister, Dr. Manmohan Singh, during the Commemorative Summit, at New Delhi. He said, "I am optimistic that our trade will exceed 100 billion U.S. dollars by 2015 and we should aim for the milestone of 200 billion U.S. dollars ten years from now."

In the spirit of our Prime Minister's vision it is equally important to recognise the fact that India and ASEAN have not fully exploited the benefits and potential of our partnership. The full potential of trade cannot be reaped till the entire region is open to economic engagement on all parameters.

In this direction the recently concluded 2nd India ASEAN Business Fair and Business Conclave, which was organised by FICCI along with Ministry of Commerce and Industry, took India and ASEAN a step closer towards a landmark FTA covering trade, investment and services.

Over the last decade, our cooperation has spread across an increasingly wide range of sectors and fields, such as automotive, light engineering, chemicals, biotechnology, pharmaceuticals, infrastructure, gems and jewellery, agriculture & food processing, textiles, services sector including IT, ITES, tourism, health care and Ayurveda, etc. amongst others. Besides, our cooperation has also intensified in the areas of culture, education and academic fields, e-linkages, capacity building and security cooperation.

Even during the 3rd ASEAN-India Business Council Meeting for which FICCI is the institutional partner, it was observed that we should focus on some of the sectors like skill development, energy sector, food processing, agriculture, tourism and aspects of connectivity.

Besides sectoral focus, for future growth of trade and investment between India and ASEAN, we also need to 'connect better', not only in form of physical connectivity (land/sea/air), but also with regard to digital connectivity, media connectivity and financial connectivity.

In this direction, India is committed to the completion of the India-Myanmar-Thailand Trilateral Highway and its extension to Lao PDR and Cambodia and the new highway project connecting India-Myanmar-Lao PDR-Viet Nam-Cambodia as well as developing the Mekong-India Economic Corridor (MIEC) connecting Southeast Asia to South Asia on the eastern part of India in order to add greater momentum to the growing trade and investment linkages between ASEAN and India.

This congregation of policy makers, think tanks, business leaders, eminent personalities and civil society is critical for a joint effort to promote our partnership and prosperity.

The various topics to be discussed at the Delhi Dialogue V, across the sessions, intends to provide a fresh policy thinking, suggest innovative solutions to challenges facing the region and give an impetus to our growing partnership.

I am sure that the outcomes of this Dialogue would take our relations with ASEAN countries to a new dimension. This objective is aptly presented in the theme of Delhi Dialogue V 'India-ASEAN: Vision for Partnership and Prosperity.' Hence I urge all of you to actively participate in the interaction tomorrow. I also wish all our guests from ASEAN a very pleasant stay in India.

Vote of Thanks

Mr. R. Ravindran

Mr. R. Ravindran

Chairman, SAEA Group Research, Singapore

It gives me great honour to deliver the Vote of Thanks. I would like to thank the Honourable External Affairs Minister for taking time off from his busy schedule to be here with us and for giving the keynote address. I would also like to thank the Hon'ble Secretary-General of ASEAN for his kind presence and keynote address.

Five years ago, with the support of MEA, FICCI, ISEAS and my organisation, SAEA Group Research, we started the Delhi Dialogue. It was conceptualised as a platform for leaders of government and captains of industry from India and ASEAN countries to engage each other on issues related to regional security, economics and contemporary issues. Since then, it has been held annually and has grown from strength to strength.

This year's Dialogue will highlight India's and ASEAN's increasing engagement with each other and explore the agenda for consolidating their relationship in the coming years. It will also assess and incorporate issues and perspectives which have emerged from the India-ASEAN Commemorative Summit 2012 and help identify areas for greater engagement between India and ASEAN countries. I look forward to very fruitful discussion and generation of new ideas and projects.

ICWA, together with FICCI and MEA and supported by IDSA, ERIA and SAEA Group Research, has put in a lot of effort to organise this year's Delhi

Dialogue. I thank all of them for their hard work, commitment and vision for this annual event.

I must also thank the ASEAN Ambassadors and their staff and the ASEAN Secretariat for all their assistance and useful feedback. I take this opportunity to extend our gratitude to the distinguished panel of speakers, delegates, from India as well as overseas, distinguished participants, and learned guests for participating at this event.

I am heartened to see so many from the government and corporate sectors from ASEAN and India at this inauguration. I thank you for your presence. I look forward to your active participation at the various sessions tomorrow.

I would also convey my thanks to the print and electronic media for the efforts they are taking for coverage of the event. Once again, I would like the Hon'ble External Affairs Minister and all present for your kind presence here and we look forward to his continued strong support. Thank you and I wish all of you a pleasant and enjoyable evening.

Part I
India-ASEAN Security Cooperation: Towards Peace and Stability

Professor Kanti Prasad Bajpai
Professor Rommel C. Banlaoi
Dr. K.S. Balakrishnan
Dr. Evi Fitriani

Chapter 1

India-ASEAN Security Cooperation: Dealing with a Rising China

Kanti Prasad Bajpai

India and ASEAN, historically, were not security partners and did not cooperate. For much of the Cold War, the two stood on nearly opposite side of many international issues. Before the formation of ASEAN, India and the Southeast Asian countries felt that cooperation towards peace and stability in the region and Asia more broadly was a common endeavour. That initial moment unfortunately passed. ASEAN was born in a quite different context and, with its arrival, the two sides drifted apart. Whereas the Southeast Asian countries flirted with the idea of Indian involvement in their regionalism, New Delhi saw matters differently, preferring to hold itself aloof. The end of the Cold War allowed India to 'return' to Southeast Asia and to re-examine its stand on ASEAN. ASEAN too was able to put behind its suspicions of India.

More than two decades after the end of the Cold War, it is fair to say that ASEAN sees India in far more benign terms, perhaps more benignly than it sees any other external power. The agenda for cooperation is a measured one. India and ASEAN will not be allies in a formal sense – neither side wants an alliance, indeed any kind of alliance would only exacerbate the geopolitical tensions in the region. This chapter focuses on India-ASEAN cooperation in relation to the rise of China. There are clearly other areas of security interaction between the two sides – extremism and terrorism and non-traditional security (transnational crime, piracy and natural disasters). However, it is the rise of China that is the greatest common challenge.

The chapter is organised in the following sections. The first section examines India's interests in Southeast Asia in the shadow of rising Chinese powers and asks what India and Southeast Asia can do together. The second section turns to the US 'pivot' and examines how India and the ASEAN countries have reacted to it. Section three focuses on three regional problems that India and Southeast Asia must consider once again in the light of Chinese power and influence: the transition in Myanmar, the problem of North Korea and security in the Indian Ocean. Across the three sections, the chapter concludes that India and ASEAN are convergent in terms of their interests and policy approaches. Neither side wants to polarize the region between China on one side and East/Southeast Asia, the US and India on the other side. India has begun to play a soft balancing role in Southeast Asia but along with ASEAN it is keen to explore ways of cooperating with China and promoting regional stability.

Rising China

The geopolitical challenge that India and ASEAN faces in common is dealing with the rise of China. There has never been anything like China's rise in human history. The size, speed and sustained nature of this juggernaut are unparalleled.[1] Not surprisingly, everyone, including China itself, are confronted with a number of questions: To what ends and purposes will Chinese power to be put? How will China conduct itself in the international system? How should the rest of the world, and Asia in particular, react? Is competition and conflict inevitable between China and the leading powers of Asia, especially, India, Japan and the US; while ASEAN itself is split on the issue of China's rise?

It appears that everyone is looking sideways at China strategically, particularly the smaller states bordering China in Southeast Asia, i.e. Cambodia and Laos – are betting that bandwagoning with China is more or less inevitable for them and for others in Asia. Within ASEAN there are also the centrists, such as Indonesia, Malaysia, Singapore and Thailand, who calculate that the region (and the world for that matter) must accommodate China strategically to a degree and that this could induce stabilising behaviour in Beijing. Those least comfortable with China are those locked in a dispute with it over the South China Sea, principally the Philippines and Vietnam. All of Southeast Asia, though, has two things in common on China: they profit economically

[1] On the economic rise of China, see Arvind Subramanian, *Eclipse: Living in the Shadow of China's Economic Dominance* (New Delhi: Viva Books, 2012). Also see Martin Jacques, *When China Rules the World: The End of the Western World and the Birth of a New Global Order, 2nd edition* (New York: Penguin, 2012).

in the relationship with China; and, they are comfortable with the presence of outside powers such as Australia, India and the US as a balancing factor against Chinese power. Put differently, they are all hedging with respect to China – locked into an economic relationship with it and at the same time looking for 'insurance policy' by cultivating big outside powers.

India is a land neighbour of China, and its main worry relates to Chinese power across the high Himalayas and Chinese influence in South Asia. However, New Delhi must be attentive to developments across the seas in East, especially Southeast Asia, for a number of reasons. First, if Chinese power and actions go unchecked in Southeast Asia, Beijing may become emboldened elsewhere including in relation to India. Second, in as much as Chinese influence in South Asia has deepened, New Delhi must return the favour in other regions, to reduce pressures on India's flanks in its own neighbourhood. Third, India has to consider the possibility that the US will depart Asia at some point or will not be able to project force in the way that it has since 1945, thus leaving China as a possible hegemon in the region. If this is a possibility, and the rise of China accompanied by the stagnation of the US presages such a possibility, then India must begin to fashion a regional security system in a post-US Asia.[2]

Fourth, India has material stakes in Southeast Asia in a way that it did not have during the Cold War. According to Indian Foreign Secretary Ranjan Matthai, in a statement made in December 2012, 'ASEAN-India trade has been growing at over 22 per cent during the last six years and, in fact, trade between India and ASEAN in 2011-2012 has increased by more than 37 per cent and the trade now is US$ 79 billion, which is more than the target of US$ 70 billion set [at the 7th ASEAN-India Summit in Thailand in October 2009]'[3]. At US$ 79 billion, India-ASEAN trade matches the volume of India-China trade which has grown since the late 1990s and has been India's largest trade relationship over the past five years or so. China has an even bigger trade and economic relationship with ASEAN. However, India-ASEAN and China-ASEAN relations are not a zero-sum game; China's trade with ASEAN has no great bearing on India's trade with ASEAN. The point is different – India needs trade with ASEAN for its own development and growth. It cannot afford to be denied that trade and access to

[2] On the US choices in dealing with China, see Aaron Friedberg, *A Contest for Supremacy: China, America, and the Struggle for Mastery in Asia* (New York: W.W. Norton, 2011), David C. Kang, *China Rising: Peace, Power, and Order in East Asia* (New York: Columbia University Press, 2010) and Edward N. Luttwak, *The Rize of China vs. The Logic of Strategy* (The Bellknap Press of Harvard University Press, 2012).

[3] Zachary Keck. "India, ASEAN Celebrate 20th Anniversary with Two FTAs," *The Diplomat*, December 21, 2012. http://thediplomat.com/indian-decade/2012/12/21/india-asean-celebrate-20th-anniversary-with-two-ftas/ (Accessed February 5, 2013).

the larger trading community in the Asia-Pacific if China should choose, in a crisis between the two Asian giants, to bottle India up.

What can India and ASEAN do in an increasingly fractious geopolitical setting in East and Southeast Asia? The rise of China is a challenge for both New Delhi and the various Southeast Asian capitals. The deterioration of relations between China and Japan, China and the Philippines and Vietnam, and the ups and downs between China and the US could draw both India and ASEAN into the fray. The pressure to choose sides will be great, but so far, both have resisted doing so. India is certainly building a strategic relationship with Japan and is involved in a bilateral as well as a trilateral dialogue with Tokyo (Washington is the third partner in the trilateral). It has exercised with the Japanese navy. However, it has refused to take sides on the Senkaku/Diaoyu Islands dispute. Likewise, it is building defence relationships gradually and modestly with various Southeast Asian states including the Philippines and Vietnam. Yet, here too, it has not taken sides on the South China Sea disputes, emphasising only that all sides should respect freedom of the high seas and international maritime law. India continues to explore for energy in what Vietnam considers its waters in the South China Sea even though China has berated India for doing so.[4]

Clearly, India would not want to confront China. Besides, it does not have the capacity to project military power so far from home, and it would be extremely vulnerable in any military conflict. Having said that, India has over the past decade pushed its navy into the South China Sea and has made port calls and engaged local navies, including the Chinese navy. India would like to see a resolution of the disputes or at least progress towards stabilisation of the diplomatic and military situation.[5]

The US Pivot

The US pivot or rebalancing in Asia has reassured some states in the region and worried others. There are those who regard it as a way of warning China that despite its rise it must contend with a balance of power led by the US. Even those who support the pivot recognise that this is more of a political than

[4] On India's stand on the conflict in the region and its own involvement with Vietnam, see "India for Peaceful Resolution of South China Sea Dispute," *The Hindu*, July 6, 2012, http://www.thehindu.com/news/india-for-peaceful-resolution-of-south-china-sea-dispute/article3609324.ece (Accessed March 13, 2013). On India's stand on the China-Japan East China Sea dispute over Senkaku/Diaoyu, see Jagannath Panda, "India Guarded Over Diaoyu Dispute, but Secretly Favors Japan," *Global Times*, February 16, 2013. http://www.globaltimes.cn/content/761733.shtml (Accessed March 16, 2013).

[5] On some of India's moves, see C. Raja Mohan, *Samudra Manthan: Sino-Indian Rivalry in the Indo-Pacific* (Washington, DC: The Carnegie Endowment for International Peace, 2012), pp. 157-187.

a military move since the US had never left the region. US strategic attention was in Iraq and Afghanistan, but Washington's military power in East and Southeast Asia was not in fact retrenched. Those who are reassured by the pivot think that the political return of the US is vital.

The pivot is also a diplomatic move in the sense that Washington's aim is not so much to confront China; it is rather to build diplomatic relations with individual Southeast Asian countries and with the various mini-lateral institutions in the region, particularly ASEAN and the East Asian Summit (EAS) as a way of boosting the confidence of regional states. With the pivot, the US wants to signal that it will not forsake the region. Some in Southeast Asia have welcomed this approach, although even those who support the pivot do not want a cold war, crisis or shooting war with China. Thus, the Philippines and Vietnam are careful to maintain a dialogue with Beijing, not the least because they have deep economic links with China.

Others clearly are not so sanguine about the pivot regarding it either as 'too little too late' or as provocative. The 'too-little too late' view rests on the judgment that Washington's actions are largely verbal, that budgetary constraints plus the ageing of the US naval forces will actually see a reduction in the US boats in the area (though not necessarily firepower), and that the promise to station 2,500 US marines in Darwin, Australia, looks tepid at best. In any case, the rise of the Chinese navy and of onshore missiles that could target the US boats suggests that the US will be more vulnerable in the region than it has ever been. Those who see the US actions as provocative think that the pivot will only cause Beijing to be even more insecure and nationalistic than it was before and that the US move has left China less room for manoeuvre in its disputes.[6]

India has been ambivalent about the US pivot. Since at least November 2010, when President Obama visited India, the US has been urging India to take a more active role in East and Southeast Asia. Secretary of State Hillary Clinton and Secretary of Defence Leon Panetta, on their visits to India, over the past two years, have been even more forthright than the President. The silence that has greeted these calls for greater involvement has been deafening. India clearly does not want to sign up for a US-led containment of China or be seen as being a quasi-ally of the US. Indeed, the high point of India-US entente may have passed. Differences over the nuclear deal, over the US arms transfers, over certain aspects of non-proliferation policy (India has not signed up for the Container or Proliferation Security Initiatives), over Iran policy, over Afghanistan and Pakistan, all these have led to a degree of alienation. In addition, New Delhi

[6] For a rather sceptical view of the pivot and the reassertion of the US power by a very influential Australian voice, see Hugh White, *The China Choice: Why We Should Share Power* (New York: Oxford University Press, 2012).

is worried about hitching its wagon to a declining power and would rather go back to a more non-aligned posture given that rising China is just over the horizon.[7] Finally, India, like many in Southeast Asia, does not want the region to be polarized between China and the US and therefore does not want to be identified too closely with the US plans in the area.[8]

The above analysis suggests that India and ASEAN are convergent in their approach to China; neither party wants to provoke China beyond a point or polarize the region behind the US power. Both sides do want the US presence as a part of a larger balance of power but they do not want Washington to be overly provocative. ASEAN is divided on the issue of the South China Sea, as was evident at the last ASEAN summit, in Cambodia. There is an agreement on the need for a Code of Conduct on the dispute; but there is less agreement on how hard a stand to take against Beijing. India and ASEAN, at the very least, would like the *status quo* in terms of control over the islands and seas to be maintained pending a final resolution. Both would prefer a gradually negotiated settlement, one that is forged through negotiations and discussions with ASEAN playing a role facilitating a settlement. Both India and ASEAN are agreed that India should play a greater diplomatic and security role in the region including in terms of a greater naval presence.

In short, India and ASEAN are agreed on avoiding a polarisation of the region, on a continuing US presence in East and Southeast Asia, on an increased role for India and an ASEAN backed process of negotiation with China over the South China Sea. They are also agreed that trade and other economic linkages with China are both inescapable and useful in forging regional stability. Put somewhat differently, India and ASEAN can be said to agree on the idea of 'soft balancing' against China.[9]

[7] India's ambivalence is astutely analysed by a Heritage Foundation analyst in the US. See Walter Lohman. "The Importance of Reality in US-India East Asia Cooperation," Testimony before the Subcommittee on Asia and the Pacific, Committee on Foreign Affairs, US House of Representatives, March 13, 2013. http://www.heritage.org/research/testimony/2013/03/the-importance-of-reality-in-us-india-east-asia-cooperation?mb=true#form_anchor (Accessed March 16, 2013).

[8] On the need for India to avoid alliances and steer a middle course, see Sunil Khilnani, Rajiv Kumar, Pratap Bhanu Mehta, et al., *Nonalignment 2.0: A Foreign and Strategic Policy for India in the Twenty-First Century,* A report of the Centre for Policy Research, New Delhi, 2012.

[9] The concept of soft balancing is discussed at length in a series of articles in *International Security,* vol. 30, no. 1, Summer 2005. Amongst others see T.V. Paul, "Soft Balancing in the Age of US Primacy," pp. 46-71 in that issue of the journal. Soft balancing is distinct from hard – i.e. military balancing – and refers to various forms of resistance and subversion of another state's power. These include various acts of diplomatic dissent and questioning, postures of neutrality or non-alignment, in relation to a rival power, especially within institutional structures. It is not the same as soft power which is the deployment of a state's suasive resources including its culture, its political values and exemplary or moral conduct to attract others to its point of view. Soft power might be a tool in soft balancing but it is not the same thing as soft balancing. On soft power, see Joseph S. Nye, *Soft Power: The Means to Success in World Politics* (New York: Public Affairs, 2004).

Myanmar, North Korea and the Indian Ocean

There are three other China-related problems on which India and ASEAN can work together. The first is the transition in Myanmar. India and ASEAN worked closely to build a cooperative relationship with Myanmar at a time when the Western states tried to isolate and punish Yangon and as China increasingly expanded its influence with the Myanmar army. ASEAN in particular helped to bring Myanmar into the Southeast Asian fold. Myanmar has finally emerged from its self-imposed and externally imposed isolation. To the extent that it has done so, and, as a result, reduced China's influence, this is in the interest of both India and ASEAN. Myanmar has not of course turned completely away from China, which is neither feasible nor desirable. China's economic role in Myanmar remains vital, and a strong relationship with Myanmar is essential if Beijing is to feel that its strategic underbelly is not under threat and that Western powers as well as India do not altogether 'replace' it in Myanmar's development.[10]

India and ASEAN should work together to help Myanmar persist with the political opening that the President Thein Sein has authored. The role of Aung San Suu Kyi in Myanmar's politics has not yet been defined; nor has she taken a very strong stand on any of the transition issues ahead, preferring to work quietly within the present constitutional order and parliament.[11] The position of the military remains very strong, and clearly there are divisions within the military on the release of Aung San Suu Kyi. Ethnic strife continues to bubble. In sum, a lot could go wrong in the transition and if things do go wrong, the military and President Thein Sein may be tempted to turn to China again if his government falls afoul of the West. India and ASEAN can help him resist that temptation and need to work wherever possible with Thein Sein and Aung San Suu Kyi on a range of issues – economic, political, diplomatic and military – and should coordinate their efforts and at the very least not be working at cross purposes with Myanmar, offering contradictory advice and help. A regular Myanmar dialogue between the two sides would be invaluable.

---

[10] On China's deep relations with Myanmar, see Thant Myint-U, *Where China Meets India: Burma and the New Crossroads of Asia* (London: Faber and Faber, 2011). See also the recent testimony of a US expert on China and India's relative influence. See Lohman, "The Importance of Reality in US-India East Asia Cooperation," Testimony before the Subcommittee on Asia and the Pacific, Committee on Foreign Affairs, US House of Representatives.

[11] Aung San Suu Kyi's increasing political problems within Myanmar, with her own supporters, is evident. See Thomas Fuller, "Burmese Laureate Heckled Over Backing Copper Mine," *New York Times*, March 14, 2013. http://www.nytimes.com/2013/03/15/world/asia/daw-aung-san-suu-kyi-heckled-over-support-of-mine-in-myanmar.html?_r=0 (Accessed March 16, 2013).

A second issue that India and ASEAN could quietly begin to talk about is the future of North Korea. North Korea is the most difficult state in the world – difficult to fathom and difficult to bring into international society. India and ASEAN may have a role here. India has had its ups and downs historically with North Korea, being quite close to it during the early to middle Cold War and then being alienated from it because of Pyongyang's nuclear and missile cooperation with Pakistan as well as New Delhi's growing interest in South Korea There has been some interest, apparently, on the US part to see India more involved in working with North Korea to bring it out of its isolation.[12]

North Korea is a member of ARF, and so ASEAN has engaged Pyongyang as well. ASEAN is divided on the issue of how to deal with North Korea. For instance, it was unable to come to a consensus on a statement on the December 2012 rocket launch of North Korea.[13] On February 12, 2013, North Korea reportedly conducted a third nuclear test, so tensions on the Korean peninsula are likely to increase. India and ASEAN have a record of engaging difficult states – most recently, Myanmar for a number of years. Is it beyond their diplomacy to begin to engage North Korea? How is this to be done given the sanctions regime? Given the stalemate in the Six-party talks, perhaps there is a space for India and ASEAN given their more middling role between China on the one hand and Japan, South Korea and the US on the other hand.

The third China-related issue is the Indian Ocean. China will inevitably enter the Indian Ocean in naval terms. This has to be accepted, and New Delhi has understood it. Just as Indian ships push up into the East and South China Sea and will show the flag in the Pacific, so China will assert itself in the Indian Ocean.[14] The Indian Ocean will therefore feature three big power navies – China, India and the US. India and the US already collaborate on naval matters, with an eye partly on China though China is by no means the only reason for India-US naval ties: there is the piracy, terrorism, non-proliferation, transnational crime, in addition.

The Southeast Asian states have not shown a great deal of interest in the Indian Ocean. But it is not far away, and it laps at the western shores of Indonesia.

[12] See K.P. Nayar, "The Food Bridge India Built with Kim's Korea," *The Telegraph* (Kolkata), December 20, 2011. http://www.telegraphindia.com/1111220/jsp/frontpage/story_14904670.jsp (Accessed March 16, 2013). See also Sandip Roy, "India's Secret-ish Romance with North Korea," *First Post World.* http://www.firstpost.com/world/indias-secret-ish-romance-with-north-korea-160590.html (Accessed March 16, 2013).

[13] "Asean Chair Urges North Korea to Call Off Rocket Launch," *Jakarta Globe,* December 10, 2012. http://www.thejakartaglobe.com/international/asean-chair-urges-north-korea-to-call-off-rocket-launch/560890 (Accessed March 16, 2013) on the inability of ASEAN to come to a consensus statement.

[14] C. Raja Mohan, *Samudra Manthan: Sino-Indian Rivalry in the Indo-Pacific* (Washington DC: Carnegie Endowment for International Peace, 2012).

There is an increasing talk of the Indian Ocean and Pacific Ocean as forming a strategic unity given the presence in both theatres now of the three big navies. China, India and the US should probably begin to engage in a trilateral dialogue on naval matters in the interest of peace and stability.[15] India is a key member of the Indian Ocean Rim Organisation for Regional Cooperation (IOR-ARC), and four ASEAN members are part of the organisation – Indonesia, Malaysia, Singapore and Thailand. The US has recently become a dialogue partner of IOR-ARC and China is already a dialogue partner. The question that faces the grouping is: should China be brought in as a full member to increase peace and stability or should it be kept out?

In addition, there is the issue of naval cooperation between India and ASEAN in the Indian Ocean. It would be in India's interest to see Indonesia, the biggest of the ASEAN member, and Singapore, with perhaps the most modern of the region's naval forces, be more involved and to develop greater inter-operability with the Indian Navy. Indeed, India has an interest in seeing the region's navies also take a greater interest in the Bay of Bengal and Andaman Sea where Chinese ships may also be more active in the years to come. Once again, working with ASEAN on naval matters makes sense so as not to be overly tied to the US in this arena.

Conclusion

India and the ASEAN countries have a common interest in promoting peace and stability in Asia in the light of China's rise and the fears and worries that have ensued. India's return to Asia after the end of the Cold War has been good for it and for the region. New Delhi has so far played a modest role, preferring to watch and wait to gauge the direction of change in the region. In the early years of the Look East policy, its interests were mostly economic. Those interests remain important. However, the economic and then the military rise of China, China's greater assertiveness with India and with Japan, the Philippines and Vietnam in particular, the division created in ASEAN at the last summit in Cambodia, and the relative decline of and political paralysis within the US since 2008 have made India look anew at East and Southeast Asia and its involvement in the region.

[15] On the linking up of the Indian Ocean and Pacific Ocean into an Indo-Pacific strategic space, see Raja Mohan, Samudra Manthan, pp. 1-11. On the possibility of dialogue and cooperation among the three big navies, see C. Raja Mohan, *Samudra Manthan: Sino-Indian Rivalry in the Indo-Pacific* (Washington DC: Carnegie Endowment for International Peace, 2012).

There is little doubt that even as India refuses to be drawn into a containment structure against China and even as New Delhi crafts its own engagement with Beijing, it is deepening its strategic involvements with the US, Australia, Japan, South Korea and ASEAN. There is a convergence of approach with ASEAN that makes it a natural partner. They should expect that the two sides will continue to be drawn to each other in a measured way. As Indian power grows, and the growth will be a reasonable 5 to 7 per cent per annum growth rate, New Delhi will be in a position to contribute to a cooperative security structure in East and Southeast Asia which involves all the major states including China, Japan and the US.

Chapter 2

Challenges in India-ASEAN Security Cooperation

Rommel C. Banlaoi

India and ASEAN are long-standing partners in the promotion of regional security in Asia. For more than 20 years, India and ASEAN have established a fruitful dialogue partnership arrangement that aims to foster regional collaboration and multilateral consultations on regional security issues of common interests. From a mere sectoral partner in 1992, India and ASEAN have come a long way in their full and comprehensive dialogue partnership that started in 1995. Yet, there is still a long journey awaiting India and ASEAN in their collaborative endeavour as they squarely face numerous complex challenges of regional security cooperation in the 21st century. India-ASEAN security cooperation becomes more crucial in the context of rising 'maritime nationalism' in Asia.

Since the formal establishment of their Dialogue Partnership in 1995, India and ASEAN have covered a wide range of security issues that have tremendous bearing on regional security. These include combating transnational organised crimes such as maritime piracy, money laundering and trafficking of arms, drugs and humans, fighting international terrorism, addressing illicit trade of chemical, biological, radiological and nuclear weapons (CBRMs), among others.

India and ASEAN promote 'long-term cooperative partnership' in these areas in order to construct a stable and peaceful region that is currently beset by uncertainties resulting from major power competition, territorial disputes and non-traditional security threats and challenges. At the strategic and policy levels, India and ASEAN have already reached a level of mutual understanding about the need to combat international terrorism, transnational crimes and other non-traditional security threats. However, at the tactical and operational levels, India and ASEAN still need to work more to widen the scope of their security cooperation in the area of intelligence exchange, communication procedure and law enforcement coordination.

Threat groups remain resilient because they share their knowledge, skills and resources with each other to make trouble and to wreak havoc. To confront them, India and ASEAN also have to intensify their information and skills sharing. Otherwise, India-ASEAN security relations will be more of talks rather than actions.

Thus, there is a great need for India and ASEAN to take stock of their specific achievements in regional security cooperation through the years in order to define common future. The India-ASEAN Commemorative Summit held in December 2012 was an important step towards this goal. However, India and ASEAN still have a lot to achieve if they want to accomplish more out of their partnership.

There is no doubt that the regular exchanges between India and ASEAN have contributed immensely to the better understanding of their respective outlooks on various security issues. However, actual collaboration on regional security matters is still wanting.

At the Commemorative Summit, India and ASEAN decided to intensify their cooperation in maritime security. The Vision Statement urges India and ASEAN 'to promote maritime cooperation, including through engagement in the Expanded ASEAN Maritime Forum (EAMF) and its expanded format, to address common challenges on maritime issues, including sea piracy, search and rescue at sea, maritime environment, maritime security, maritime connectivity, freedom of navigation, fisheries and other areas of cooperation'. They also committed to foster "greater security cooperation and information sharing in the form of regular and high-level security dialogues to further address traditional and non-traditional security challenges, including transnational crimes, and strengthening the effective implementation of the ASEAN-India Joint Declaration for Cooperation to Combat International Terrorism".

Implementing their vision statement is a formidable challenge for India and ASEAN considering that both parties still have to address out their existing differences on many security issues such as arms control, nuclear non-proliferation and human rights, specifically when it comes to the issue of North Korea, Myanmar, Kashmir and Taiwan Straits.

On the issue of maritime security, India and ASEAN have a vast maritime domain to cover the Indian Ocean and the South China Sea. These two bodies of waters are strategic waterways that are vital for the survival and prosperity not only of the littoral countries but also of the entire world relying on the freedom of navigation and security of sea-lanes of communication. In between the Indian Ocean and the South China Sea is the highly congested Straits of Malacca whose security is vital not only for India and ASEAN but also for the international community.

Maritime security forces of India and ASEAN interact with each other through various meetings, conferences, workshops, official exchanges and port calls. These activities are essential for confidence building. But India and ASEAN still have to exert their best effort in promoting preventive diplomacy and strategic restraint in their shared maritime domain.

At present, India and ASEAN enjoy the freedom of navigation in the maritime areas of the South China Sea and the Indian Ocean. The freedom of navigation, in fact, also allows transnational security threat organisations to operate, proliferate and even cooperate with each other. Transnational security threats like international terrorism, maritime piracy and trafficking/ smuggling of arms, drugs and humans have established a complex and effective nexus as a result of the freedom of navigation they enjoy.

Addressing these transnational security threats is one of the motivations for military modernisation in Asia. However, because of existing maritime territorial disputes and rising nationalism in Asia, arms procurement and military capability development ironically raise insecurities, uneasiness and anxieties putting all countries in a difficult 'guessing game' situation. The maritime security dilemmas of Asian countries are raising speculations whether the ongoing military preparations are for defensive or offensive purposes.

The South China Sea dispute looms large in Philippines. Recently, India expressed its growing interests to play a more constructive role in the peaceful resolution of conflicts in the South China Sea. The main question is what can India specifically do to contribute to the peaceful resolution of conflicts in the South China Sea? What is the strategic interest of India in the peace and security of the South China Sea that it deploys its ships to sail in this troubled water?

In the context of major power rivalry, India's interest to increase its visibility in the South China Sea is something that China will definitely be wary about. China is suspicious of India's growing interest in the South China. As valuable dialogue partners, ASEAN does not want to be caught in the long-standing dispute between India and China. ASEAN also feels the same way in the context of China-Japan relations.

While ASEAN regards the two major powers as important regional partners for regional security, ASEAN does not want to be caught between two important powers. Promiscuous as it may appear, ASEAN wants to get the best of both worlds. In essence ASEAN does not want its security relations with China to be put at risks while pursuing security relations with India, and vice versa.

There is no doubt that ASEAN benefits from China as its largest trading partner. ASEAN, on the other hand, is China's third largest trading partner. China-ASEAN trade relations have been increasing at an average annual growth of 20 per cent, which is currently the largest in the world. In December 2012, China-ASEAN trade reached US$ 362.8 billion. The annual China-ASEAN Expo (CAEXPO) in Nanning is a powerful project that brings China and ASEAN closer economically. However, when compared with other ASEAN dialogue partners, volume of trade and investment flows between ASEAN and India remained relatively low. India-ASEAN bilateral trade target was only US$ 70 billion in 2012.

The India-ASEAN Car Rally in December 2012 was symbolic as both parties need to 'rally a fast car' to speed up the phase of their bilateral trade if they really want to raise their cooperation to a higher level. The annual India-ASEAN Business Fair (IABF) is a useful mechanism to promote and intensify India-ASEAN economic ties. If IABF achieves its desired outcome, it can put pressure on China to improve further the CAEXPO.

India and ASEAN still have different understandings and approaches on how to deal with China. Besides, both have their own respective dynamics when it comes to their bilateral and multilateral security relations with China. Thus, there is a need for India and ASEAN to exchange views on how to deal with China, particularly in the context of the South China Sea disputes.

Like other major powers, India takes a very cautious position on the South China Sea issue by not taking sides on sovereignty claims. This is the same position that the US takes on the issue as it currently pivots or reengages itself in Asia as a Pacific power. So what difference can India make? Can ASEAN rely on India as a constructive dialogue partner in the peaceful resolution of conflicts in the South China Sea?

Officially, India supports the idea of a Code of Conduct (CoC) in the South China Sea, but ASEAN wants to know how India can specifically support the passage of CoC considering that China does not find it ripe yet to do so. Moreover, the proposed CoC is only between China and ASEAN. How can India help ASEAN in persuading China that the CoC is imperative to avoid military crisis in the South China Sea? It may be difficult for India to find its rightful place in the resolution of maritime sovereignty conflicts in the South China Sea; but India's role is essential in armed conflict prevention, strategic restraint and peace promotion in the South China Sea for the benefits of all mankind.

It is public knowledge that India's state-run Oil and Natural Gas Corporation (ONGC) has joint venture activities with TNK Vietnam and Petro Vietnam to pursue exploratory offshore hydrocarbon projects in the South China Sea. Though India clarifies that its interest is mainly commercial, these projects are getting the 'ire' of China and in some countries in ASEAN, particularly those countries with bilateral border disputes with India.

Border security is another issue that India and ASEAN have to address. Specifically, India has land border problems with Myanmar. In the land border, India urges Myanmar to effectively settle the problem of Assamese, Naga and Manipur rebels who reportedly use Myanmar as a base to mount 'armed' activities against India. On the other hand, Myanmar expects India to also take a more proactive action against Kachin rebels who allegedly use northeast Indian state of Arunachal Pradesh as one of their safe havens.

The Kachin conflict in Myanmar creates refugee problems and other security burdens in India. Thus, India and Myanmar often argue over border insurgent issues. Both countries also have irritants over the Coco Islands near the Andaman Sea. The allegation that China is planning to set-up a maritime base in the Coco Islands also creates security anxieties between the two countries. Nonetheless, both countries are finding ways to solve the border problems by encouraging more cooperation. The Kaladan Multi-Modal Transit Transport Project is good example of cooperation.

India also has maritime problems with Indonesia and Thailand. Though India has existing bilateral agreements with Indonesia and Thailand on how to peacefully approach delimitation issues in their maritime boundary, India's military development in some islands neighbouring Southeast Asia is raising security concerns. Indonesia, for instance, protested in the past about India's military development projects in Andaman and Nicobar islands in the Bengal of Bay.

Indeed, India-ASEAN security cooperation is beset by many challenges, and overcoming these challenges is an arduous task. In the promotion of regional security, ASEAN can count on India being the largest democracy in the world and based on the democratic peace principle, democracies are deeply hesitant to engage in war and are committed to promote peace. Thus, ASEAN has a more 'benign image' of India, something that is important for India-ASEAN security cooperation.

Conclusion

The current state of India-ASEAN security relation is a product of India's Look East policy and ASEAN policy of dialogue partnership with major powers? Shared values, common historical experiences, geographic proximity and convergent security interests solidify India-ASEAN dialogue partnership. But as India looks East, it is time for India to 'act East' in order to advance not only its national interests but to promote its regional interests.

India and ASEAN belong to 'a maritime security complex' of the Indian Ocean and the South China Sea. Being in the same maritime security complex, their security interests converge and are inextricably linked with one another. India and ASEAN share common security predicaments in both traditional and non-traditional sense. Thus, their security cooperation is not only a necessity but also a common destiny.

Chapter 3

The Deepening of India-ASEAN Security Cooperation

K.S. Balakrishnan

The amorphous nature of security at the national, regional and global level of the contemporary world is more visible today than ever before. Armed with a Look East policy (LEP) as an important dimension of foreign and security policy, India has successfully penetrated into the imagination of international relations in Southeast Asia. The terms such as South and East too conjure important meanings for the two sides. During the Cold War, the policy of non-alignment was the vital 'lodestar' of India's foreign policy as a whole.[1] The Non-Alignment Movement (NAM) provided the necessary platform for India to interact with leading ASEAN members like Malaysia and Indonesia. Communist state like Vietnam too admired India's role. The principle of non-alignment and non-interference helped sustain India's image, interest and attraction as a possible partner in the eyes of a number of regional countries. During the Cold War, some viewed Delhi's friendship with the Soviet Union in a rather suspicious manner. India too for some decades felt uncomfortable with the United States for being in military alliance with Pakistan. Its military assistance to Pakistan irked India. But this did not stop India from being active in South-South cooperation via the G15 and G77.[2]

[1] See Sumit Ganguly and Majeet S. Pardesi. "Explaining Sixty Years of India's Foreign Policy," *India Review*, vol. 4, no. 2 (2009), pp. 4-19.

[2] See K.S. Balakrishnan. "Malaysia-India Relations: Foreign Policy Convergence and Bilateral Security Cooperation," *Asian Defence and Diplomacy*, November 2001, pp. 39-43.

Over the years, the security scenario and perception of India has completely changed.[3] A new form of alliance is shaping up with the end of the Cold War and in the aftermath of September 11, 2001. The global war on terror has significantly affected the traditional alliance system and created a new opportunities for India. The old Cold War quagmire is very much diluted, as India-US partnership is currently at the height of the game. This has also resulted in players like ASEAN, Japan, South Korea and Australia looking at India with much vigour. There is now a new expectation for India to become the 'linchpin' to the 'pivot' of the US in the Asia Pacific. The enhancement in India-US relationship too has influenced several ASEAN states to look at India positively not only on the economic front but for the purpose of long-term strategic balancing.

Credit can be also given to the US for its strategic and arduous effort in bringing India into the ambit of the RMSI (Regional Maritime Security Initiative) which was not initially welcome by at least two main ASEAN states. But the efforts and recognition for maritime security cooperation improved over time. Both the US and even India began to be viewed as partners. Will India play to this gallery or can it deliver is another question altogether. It is also important to note that without the dimension of maritime security and the potential threats, India's possible and positive entry into the ASEAN's strategic circle may have been limited. The willingness and enthusiasm of ASEAN members to entice India may not be the way it has progressed thus far.

Three key factors can be attributed to the shifting in alliances and the recognition of India and its role as a possible balancer in the region. At the forefront, it is China's economic and military rise, strategic interest and its related security repercussions that affect all the players in the region. Inevitably, it also affects India's long-term security interest. Secondly, India is also growing economically, becoming powerful day by day. No big and small states in the region would want to miss the boat. India's military too is on the modernising mode whereby the exchanges between defence forces can bring about positive outcomes. There is always a strong desire among the Southeast Asian countries that India could be of assistance in beefing up the national defence via various means. Thirdly, it is without doubt that India too has for almost two decades worked hard in building a stronger and durable relationship with the ASEAN states and others who were reciprocating in goodwill.

[3] See K.S. Balakrishnan. "Malaysia-India Relations: Common Principles For Cooperative Prosperity," *Asian Defence and Diplomacy,* November 1997, pp. 29-35.

Today, India is practically in all vital meetings and regional forum involving both ASEAN and other major powers of East Asia. During the early 1990s, with LEP in mind, it started as a sectoral dialogue partner member with ASEAN and this was followed by a full Dialogue Partner status. With some difficulties, India managed to enter into the ARF (ASEAN Regional Forum) security dialogue. India successfully became a member of the EAS (East Asian Summit) by 2005. It has also signed the Treaty of Amity and Cooperation (TAC) prior to that, indicating its adherence to ASEAN's strategic culture of pacific settlement of dispute and widening cooperation. India's support for the Southeast Asian Nuclear Weapons Free Zone (SEANFZ) too cannot be doubted. With this background, this chapter will explain and explore India-ASEAN security cooperation, challenges and dynamics. It will look at the old lenses, ongoing cooperation and future initiatives for a durable peace in the region.

Changing Strategic Scenario, Security Challenges and the Potential for Cooperation

Security is no longer seen in the same manner, the way it was commonly perceived by researchers and scholars who have dominated the field during and prior to the Cold War. The focus was often heavily dominated by the hard power resources for providing explanations and dealing with national, regional and global security. The economic interdependence dimension was somewhat missing during the Cold War. Very few among the greats were sustaining an overarching perspective of security of the post-independence age. Perspectives on security throughout the world were influenced by the massive development of nuclear weapons and conventional arms and ideas such as the state and nation-building, ideology, sphere of influence, arms race and balance of power.

Can humanity or the nation-states in general move 'out of the box' of such systems, structures, framework and mindset? Or, are we constantly stuck with this age old baggage of balancing and bandwagoning? What can we do together to alter or replace the lenses of our understanding of security? Where the solutions for a durable peace lie? These are important questions. An understanding of genuine security and the way we deal with the regional and state security dilemma in many ways can bring immense opportunity to tap into resources never properly examined before.

In fact, India and ASEAN can be the best entities to expand on this new horizon. Moving away from the baggage of the old lenses and the security realities on the ground is not all that simple and demands courage. States too sometime need enemies to justify their defence policies, security policy and military expenditures. Terrorising its own citizens too is not an alien thing in some authoritarian regimes. The climate is indeed right for exploration as both the regional players like India and ASEAN have demonstrated to a greater degree a strong desire for cooperation, economic growth and maintaining peace and stability. India too has been slowly moving out of its old regional strategic ambit of South Asia. It is also vying for a global role in the United Nations Security Council.

After witnessing a sizeable chunk of the economic prowess in recent decades, what should be the role of India in the community of nations is an important point for consideration. Both India and ASEAN had also demonstrated throughout the Cold War a certain degree of the common historical thread of noble principles. Leaders of both have inspired many in the developing world. Some developed countries also celebrate the ideas of the East. Ideas such as non-alignment and non-interference were practiced by both India and some ASEAN members as the 'lodestar' of their foreign policy for quite some time now. The two entities have also established the habit of reaching out to their difficult neighbours in fostering peace in their respective regions.

India is without doubt a huge nation with a population of 1.2 billion of which some 35 per cent is said to be living in the urban areas. It is also commonly reported that some 250 millions of the Indian population belong to the middle-class. ASEAN is almost half of India in terms of population and sustains a significant portion of the middle class. India-ASEAN Trade was about US$ 12.3 billion in 2002.[4] This has gone fivefold reaching US$ 50 billion and is currently being targeted to attain the amount of US$ 100 billion in five years. It is hoped that with the ASEAN-India FTA and the array of Comprehensive Economic Partnership agreements bilaterally, the goal is a possible target.

Both the entities have huge maritime zone to cover with limited assets. The desire for peace and cooperation is immense as both had experienced and continue to face almost similar security challenges. These challenges can be categorised into both conventional and non-traditional security threats. Territorial disputes with neighbours, border problems, separatism, big power rivalry, poverty, resource scarcity and disputes, energy security, environmental

[4] See Philip Day, "Dancing With Giants," *Far Eastern Economic Review*, April 8, 2004.

challenges and natural disasters, pandemics, terrorism, nuclear threats are affecting the region. Numerous other transnational and organised crimes ranging from drug, human, weapons and goods smuggling have become common in recent decades.

Linkages can be established to explain, terror, separatism and organise crime. Human security is now seen as more dynamic than the old way of assessing national security based on conventional and nuclear capabilities possessed by a nation. High level visits to beef up defence and security cooperation between ASEAN and India are constantly growing. New areas and new possibilities are obvious. But this does not mean that India has no competitors in playing almost a similar game.

The Deepening of India-ASEAN Defence and Security Cooperation

Over the last two decades or so, India was able to use its strategic state-to-state diplomacy effectively with some of the ASEAN members. It was looking towards Southeast Asia in a positive manner given the region's economic prowess. New Delhi's desire to enhance trade and investment with the region cannot be dismissed. It was also in India's interest to move out of the dilemma faced in SAARC. ASEAN and East Asia's economic success stories were visible as India was in the mood for economic liberalisation in a world that was rapidly globalising.

The opportunity for widening the economic and cultural cooperation allowed both ASEAN and India to look at security as a potential platform at the bilateral level. With India's successful entry into ARF, its bilateral defence and security agreements with regional countries continued to grow, albeit in a low profile mode and not in a way it is currently perceived. India as a player is also overly cautious about being misperceived and sending the wrong signals to the key players in the region. The preference of its non-alignment mode in foreign and security policy is conspicuous.

Democracy too can be a hindrance to India's defence and security cooperation with ASEAN. This can be seen in the case of defence and security cooperation with Myanmar and Vietnam. But this challenge too has been slowly averted as India moved into a more pragmatic foreign and security policy posture in facing the China challenge. One could easily argue that, despite India's LEP and the willingness of some ASEAN members to look at Delhi for defence cooperation, the China factor plays a vital role in influencing India-ASEAN defence and security cooperation. A reasonable number of states within Southeast Asia do subscribe to the idea of balance of power and deterrence. Vietnam, Singapore, Indonesia and to some extent Myanmar would want India to play a balancing role against other rising regional powers.

Having said this, one must not rule out the case whereby India too has the potential and possesses the ingredient to offer the seriously needed technical and defence capabilities to assist smaller ASEAN states which look outward for cost effective military assistance. As developing states many ASEAN states are unable to undertake massive spending on defence and especially on procurement. As such, the path for defence cooperation was steadily expanding to the level where it is currently manifested. Defence ties were not visible in the 1990s but became a more apparent component in the wake of US-India expanding defence cooperation after September 11, 2001, which paved the path for a number of states in Asia to court India for military ties in the form a new democratic alliance.

Within the context of India-ASEAN defence cooperation, almost all the littoral states of the Straits of Malacca had maintained positive view of the Indian navy in the Indian Ocean. This has kept defence ties on a solid ground for quite some time during the Cold War at the level of naval exercise and visits. India's entry into the security and defence cooperation sector in the ASEAN region on a bigger scale started when Malaysia planned its Memorandum of Understanding (MoU) on Defence Cooperation in 1993.[5] Malaysia was the first in Southeast Asia to procure and operate successfully the Russian advance fighter jet squadron, MiG-29N Fulcrum in the mid-1990s. India was then seen as an important player who had the right experience and engineering capabilities. Language and communications problems too could be averted.

Unlike China, India has never threatened the Southeast Asian region from a historical and political point of view. One could argue that the success in this bilateral air force collaboration and industrial cooperation has influenced Malaysia to upgrade further with the Sukhoi Su-30MKM version of Russia's advance fighters in recent decades. Malaysia's need for technical and engineering assistance in maintaining these aircraft and cost-efficiency as a factor has boosted the bilateral defence cooperation with India. The Indian Air Force played a significant role in developing Malaysia's training and other needs with the MiG-29 and also the Su30-MKM Flankers.[6]

[5] See K.S. Balakrishnan. "ASEAN-India Strategic Partnership: New Developments in Malaysia's Relations with India," in Nirmala Devi and Adluri S. Raju (eds.), *India and Southeast Asia: Strategic Convergence in the 21st Century* (New Delhi: Manohar Publications, 2012).

[6] See "Indian crew bids farewell after training RMAF pilots," *New Straits Times,* September 13, 2010. See also "Grateful partners in quality training," *New Straits Times,* April 19, 2010.

Malaysia-India defence and security ties have expanded in almost all areas at the inter-governmental level and in track two meetings that host strategic dialogue. Malaysia generally sees India as a peaceful player and contributes towards peace in Southeast Asia. Naval exercises, port-calls and cooperation, military education and training, defence technology, space or satellite capability assistance, cyber security, terrorism, transnational crime and numerous other non-traditional security areas are all open wide for cooperation in recent years. The track record and confidence of security cooperation is ever growing.[7]

Maritime Cooperation as an Important Component of Defence and Security for a Durable Peace

Defence cooperation with India cannot be explained in a comprehensive sense if one were to neglect the maritime component. India's naval diplomacy is a defining element in defence ties not only with Malaysia but with few other ASEAN members. India had responded positively to the US on counter-terror cooperation, especially on monitoring the potential for maritime terrorism in SLOC (sea lines of communications) both in the Indian Ocean and in the Straits of Malacca. The RMSI, Proliferation Security Initiative (PSI) and Container Security Initiative (CSI) were platforms useful for India and ASEAN countries to look at avenues for maritime cooperation. In April 2007, India conducted its first trilateral naval exercise with the US and Japan in Guam.[8]

The event marked for the first time India's movement into a new 'military alliance'. Even though, India had indicated to the rest in the region that it is a non-align player but the event put the Indian Navy into a new mould altogether. It showed clearly that Japan and the US has succeeded in luring India into a new structure. Similar exercises were also conducted in the Bay of Bengal. India also made entry into the Western Pacific Command Naval Symposium. Some ASEAN countries have shown interest in such periodic exercises and in participating in the Indian Ocean naval Symposium (IONS). Opportunity for training and intelligence sharing are seen as important by the ASEAN states. India's influence in the Straits of Malacca and South China Sea is growing. Naval exercises have paved ways for counter-terror and other crime related maritime cooperation.

[7] K.S. Balakrishnan. "ASEAN-India Strategic Partnership: New Developments in Malaysia's Relations with India," in Nirmala Devi and Adluri S. Raju (eds.), *India and Southeast Asia: Strategic Convergence in the 21st Century* (New Delhi: Manohar Publications, 2012).

[8] See C. Raja Mohan, "East Asian Security: India's Rising Profile," *RSIS Commentaries*, July 30, 2007.

Likewise, IONS provides another big and positive image for India's role in regional security by enhancing CSBMs. IONS is viewed as inclusive and capable of promoting peace between navies. The Indian Navy's role during the Tsunami disaster was also highly commendable, working together with Western navies. Not only, the navy was playing a positive role in its own shore but also extended the contribution of relief operation beyond India from Sri Lanka to Indonesia working along the Western and Southeast Asian navies. It was also playing a positive role with the naval forces from the US, Australia and Japan during the Tsunami crisis which affected almost half of Southeast Asia.[9] India has also upgraded its early warning system which it is willing to share with interested ASEAN countries such as Thailand.

In June 2012, four Indian Navy ships (INS Shivalik, INS Rana, INS Shakti and INS Karmuk) visited maritime Southeast Asia. The four day goodwill visit to Malaysia in June 2012 was a part of the 11,000 nautical miles voyage which included Japan, China, Vietnam, the Philippines and Singapore. The arrival of Indian warships to the region was generally regarded as part of the diplomatic exchanges that the navy has been doing in the past.[10] The possibility for joint-submarine training is also in the pipeline between Malaysia and India. The increase in India's naval capabilities is obvious and will be sending positive signals to ASEAN members of what India could do in assisting smaller navies in the region. India's aircraft carrier INS Viraat too had made similar visits to several ports of the ASEAN states in the past.

The Indian Navy has been conducting increasing number of exercises with many naval forces in the Indian Ocean. This helps the littoral states of the Indian Ocean from the ASEAN region to take advantage of anti-piracy, counter-terror, disaster relief and command and control type of naval exercises and training. This is received in a positive manner by the ASEAN states, more so after the 2004 Tsunami. Bigger navies from Japan, Australia and the US are also cooperating with India. The increase in piracy in the Gulf of Aden has also provided more opportunity for naval and maritime cooperation with India. Some ASEAN states have now established a very good track record with the Indian Navy in this type of collaboration.

India on its own is fully aware of the importance of the sea lanes on both sides of the Indian Ocean. It is currently regarded as the New Silk Route for India taking into the fact of energy security and shipping. India is also member of ReCAAP (Regional Cooperation Agreement on Combating Piracy and Armed Robberies against Ships in Asia).[11] In fact, one could argue that

[9] See Saurabh Shukla, "Disaster Diplomacy," *India Today,* January 17, 2005, p. 35.

[10] "Indian Navy ships on a 4-day visit", *New Straits Times,* June 28, 2012.

[11] See Dr. Vijay Sakhuja, "New Silk Route," www.sahara.time.com (Accessed January 28, 2007).

India has expanded its security interest and awareness beyond the Indian Ocean moving into the South and East China Sea. It is in this context, the India-ASEAN defence and security cooperation in the maritime zone is likely to expand further. This will likely to create more dilemmas for China because of her maritime disputes in the South China Sea.

Indonesia and India signed a defence cooperation agreement when Prime Minister Vajpayee visited Jakarta in 2001. Armed with a positive attitude for a common foreign policy principle, democracy and trade liberalisation, both the countries pledged support for expanding ties. Naval exercises and potential for defence procurement were among important matters discussed.[12] India and Indonesia have had good experience in the past as regards to naval cooperation even prior to the Tsunami in 2004. Indonesia like Malaysia views India's defence role positively. This is because even though the Indian Navy possesses a better power projection capability in the Indian Ocean, it has always maintained good relationship with the littoral states. Indonesia too is an important player in the Indian Ocean, even though its naval power projection capabilities may not match India's in term of size and firepower.

President Susilo Bambang perceives India as a Strategic Partner which can play a balancing role in the strategic and geopolitical context of the region. He visited New Delhi twice thus far in 2005 and 2011. Both the countries are member of the G20 and are competing for a permanent seat in the Security Council. Indonesia has shown a genuine desire to court India, given its own weaknesses in certain aspects of defence. The bilateral defence cooperation is viewed from the potential for energy security, defence supplies, procurement, technological cooperation and joint-production. Space, rocket technology for scientific purpose and satellite technology are areas that both the states can explore in term of strengthening security cooperation.[13] After September 11, 2001, both India and Indonesia have experienced serious terrorist attacks and are currently looking at potential for counter-terror and intelligence cooperation. Transnational crime and disaster relief are also other important areas that are being explored. Joint exploration and hydrographical surveys were also conducted in some EEZs of the ASEAN countries.

[12] Shishir Gupta, "Mega-plan of Megawati," *India Today*, April 8, 2002.

[13] "India-Indonesia seek closer ties," *New Straits Times*, November 25, 2005. See also Mahendra Ved, "India and Indonesia try to recapture the old magic," *New Straits Times*, January 24, 2011.

The effort to upgrade India-Vietnam defence ties has been expanding in line with the big commercial companies' entry into Vietnam in 2007. It was also a year where Vietnam entered the WTO. Indian corporate giants were already in Vietnam by then.[14] Prime Minister Nguyen Tan Ding's visit to India and the follow-up joint declaration in July 2007 witnessed the continued desire to expand defence ties.[15] But one could also trace Vietnam's positive desire to have India as a balancer and as a reliable partner way back during the Cold War. Vietnam stood by India when war broke between China and India in 1962.

Hostility with China has been the case for many ASEAN states to favour India on strategic matters. Historically, China has not been in peace with post-independence Southeast Asia. Prime Minister Rao visited Vietnam in 1994. In January 2001, Vajpayee visited Hanoi and strengthened the relationship. India began to even gain in term of oil exploration right.[16] Manmohan Singh's visit in 2010 enhanced further the strategic and geopolitical interest of India in line with its LEP.[17] The role of India increased in many ways including repairing ships in Vietnam. Oil exploration opportunity in Vietnam is not all that simple as this has received protest from China. But it has yet to stop ONGC Videsh and PetroVietnam to sign agreement in 2011.[18] India is also becoming more assertive in enhancing its traditional ties.

The role of balancing China can also be witnessed in Myanmar which shares with India some lengthy land borders. Myanmar-India defence and security cooperation is also growing in the right direction. This has given Myanmar to slowly find its own voice, and becoming less dependent on China for military and other development assistance. The leaders in Myanmar are fully aware of the fact that averting too much dependence on China was one of the factors which caused ASEAN to lure Yangon into the regional organisation in 1997. Myanmar's improved ties with India and the US will likely to alter the almost two decades of junta's strong dependence on China. India's policy of cultivating stronger relationship with states bordering its North Eastern frontiers are important in destabilising China 'string of pearls'.

Defence cooperation with Myanmar has been beefed up in terms of border cooperation, counter-terrorism, assistance in transferring old and cheaper military equipments, etc. Transport, building port facilities, energy security and maritime cooperation have been on the increase. Military training,

[14] Anand Adhiri, "Next Stop Vietnam," *Business Today*, July 1, 2007.

[15] See C. Raja Mohan, "East Asian Security: India's Rising Profile," *RSIS Commentaries*, July 30, 2007.

[16] Sumit Mitra, "Oriental Overture," *India Today*, January 22, 2001.

[17] Mahendra Ved, "India building-up 'Look East' ties," *New Straits Times*, October 23, 2010.

[18] Mahendra Ved, "India moves to strengthen 'Look East Policy'," *New Straits Times*, October 24, 2011.

exercises and intelligence sharing for the purpose of enhancing border security are expanding. General Than Shwe visited India in July 2010 which paved way for more engagement on the part of India.[19] Than Shwe had earlier visited India in 2004. Since then India has been quite pragmatic in handling its relationship with Myanmar. Democracy was not strongly used by the Manmohan administration as important criteria in beefing up defence ties. Monetary assistance and oil contracts in return have become a part of the new relationship. Numerous other economic opportunities are made available for India to grab.[20] The protest by Monks in 2007 and other unrest in Myanmar has yet to stop India from the exploration adventure. India will not reverse its policy on Myanmar in the near future. The US is looking at opportunity for defence and security cooperation.

Maritime cooperation has been a crucial element in enhancing defence and security cooperation with the ASEAN region. States that have fear over maritime threats will likely to increase defence and security cooperation with India. Japan too is looking at India in this context. Singapore, the Philippines and Vietnam have shown strong desire to strengthen further naval and military to military cooperation. Malaysia offers a good example on how to deepen security cooperation with India at the Air Force level. Overall, it is fair to argue that the level of trust that many ASEAN countries have shown is remarkable. While India has increased its role as a balancer via defence cooperation, it has been also a responsible player by ensuring China that it remains open and inclusive in promoting peace and stability.

Conclusion

Since the early 1990s, India has been making inroads into the ASEAN states for defence and security cooperation. While the end of the Cold War can be regarded as a vital turning point, India's non-align foreign policy and the LEP has helped significantly in expanding both the commercial and security ties with the ASEAN grouping. India's role in the regional security architecture has been complementary in the last two decades or so, parallel to its growing economic clout vis-à-vis the region. It has participated both at the inter-governmental and track two levels quite effectively in projecting an image of a peaceful player with a long-term interest. Balancing and bandwagoning have also become part of the approach. India is also careful with the region and not overly ambitious given its own security limitations and inability to

[19] See C. Raja Mohan, "Embracing Myanmar: India's Foreign Policy Realism," *RSIS Commentary*, August 2, 2010.
[20] See Mahendra Ved, "India hopes to join the Myanmar gold rush," *New Straits Times*, June 4, 2010.

stretch its defence resources. ASEAN members are fully aware of the fact that they should not use India or the US card strongly against China in a negative manner. This is crucial given ASEAN's economic dependence on China. Except that in the case of exploration in Vietnam, China has not complained on India's role in Southeast Asia.

In fact, all the players are aware of their long-term economic needs. It is hoped that the growth in defence and security relationship between ASEAN and India will constantly be directed for peaceful purpose and not for destabilising. But this can't stop the misperception on the emerging new military alliance, which is generally perceived as targeting China. This is where both ASEAN and India have a lot more to do to move beyond the bilateral context. Working towards a more multilateral and interdependence nature of regional architecture which eventually involves China can be beneficial for all. The ARF and ADMM Plus have become good models thus far. Credit can also be given to the Indian Navy to be in line with such a positive and inclusive mindset in recent years. Its visualisation of an 'extended neighboured' from a strategic perspective is commendable given the need for durable peace in the maritime zone which is also vital for the long-term economic momentum of the region.

The future potential in areas such as peacekeeping, military education, energy security, cyber, nuclear, space, missile defence, organise crime, counter-terror, environmental and climate security and other form human security agendas can be easily imagined as the needs are also constantly expanding. This will test further the will of the two entities in bringing defence and security cooperation to the next level to fulfil their aspiration. The existing process of regionalism and regional security architecture appear quite sufficient and cohesive enough, when bilateralism is added to it. India is also a nation with a sizeable Muslim population which promotes democracy, multiculturalism and good neighbourliness for others to emulate. This is quite in line with ASEAN's practice of moderation for a peaceful region and the world at large.

Chapter 4

India-ASEAN Security Cooperation: Managing Peace and Stability through the Strategic Partnership

Evi Fitriani

India and Southeast Asian countries have been connected since ancient period and Indian influence was spread in the region almost in all dimensions of life such as culture, technology, ideas and philosophy and daily practices. In modern times, India is ASEAN's Dialogue Partner since 1995 and leaders of the two countries have met during 10 summit meetings since 2002. During this period and through the cooperative mechanism, India and ASEAN countries have developed a reasonably strong cooperation, and India and ASEAN promoted the bilateral relations to Strategic Partnership on December 20, 2012.

This chapter attempts to link India-ASEAN security cooperation and the concept of Strategic Partnership. In particular, the chapter focuses on the questions what it means to be a strategic partner, and how the strategic linkage could enhance cooperation between India and ASEAN countries in order to maintain peace and security in South and Southeast Asia. Before focusing on India-ASEAN security cooperation within the framework of Strategic Partnership, the chapter will highlight security problems that concern ASEAN countries in the recent years.

ASEAN and Indian Security Concerns

There have been many studies and opinions expressed on security issues in the last decade that challenge peace and stability in South and Southeast Asia. In general, India and ASEAN countries deal with two types of challenges: traditional security problems that are primarily state centric and non-traditional security challenges that are generated by states as well as non-state actors.

States in the regions as well as from outside the region may challenge the security of South and Southeast Asian region through military build-up, armed conflict, assertion of territorial claims, provocative movement as well as unfriendly official statements. In fact peace and stability in the region has been disturbed by these phenomena especially in the last decades. The transformation of China to engage as a regional power and its assertiveness to pursue territorial claims in the South China Sea has created concerns for countries in Southeast Asia as far as ASEAN and India. The sea-lanes in South and Southeast Asia are vital for trading not only for the regional countries but also the world. Domination and control by any particular state would jeopardize the freedom of navigation and the security of sea-lanes.

India and ASEAN leaders have realised these challenges and expressed concerns in the Vision Statement declared in the India-ASEAN Commemorative Summit in December 2012. Some of the common concerns are relating to China's military modernisation and navy in the last decade, equipping the country not only with advanced nuclear weapons and satellites but also more submarines and an aircraft-carrier. Thus, the re-emergence of China seems coincident with deepening gap in military capability between the regional power and its neighbouring countries in Asia. In the past, China's armed forces' modernisation was accompanied with attractive soft-power instruments and the narrative tried to mitigate suspicion among the neighbouring countries[1]. Last year, however, China exhibited assertive and provocative activities in South China Sea – as well as in the East China sea — which evoked suspicions and insecurity. How China handles its territorial conflicts with its neighbouring countries in Southeast Asia would be crucial for the stability of the region.

[1] T. Yoshihara. "China's "soft" navel power in the Indian Ocean," *Pacific Focus,* vol. XXV, no. 1 2010, pp. 59-88. Also see J. Nye, Jr. *The Future of Power* (New York: Public Affairs, 2011).

The second type of security challenges that India and ASEAN countries have to overcome relate to terrorism, trans-national crimes, piracy and various types of smuggling – be it arms, drug or people. Like ASEAN countries, India also faces these security problems both at sea and on land. Since Indian Ocean is connected with maritime Southeast Asia and India borders with ASEAN countries, India and ASEAN countries actually share common problems. Much of these problems generate inter-state tension including ethnic conflicts and socio-cultural disputes, imbalance economic growth, poverty as well as problems of weak governance and failed states. Several studies argue how these problems impact state security and regional stability despite its 'low politics'[2]. These problems are essentially trans-national in nature, therefore affected countries need to cooperate to handle them.

In addition, India and China seem to have relations that are different from China-ASEAN relations. Given the circumstance, India has risen as an economic power-house almost concomitantly with China; the two countries are perceived as rising regional powers[3]. In recent years, the Government of the two countries have shown intention for engagement and cooperation, including through Defence Dialogue in January 2013 that concluded with an intention to resume joint military exercises. However, the shadow of 1962 war and unsolved territorial disputes has added to 'competing consequence' between the two Asian powers. India and China cannot escape from 'cooperation as well as competition type' of relationship.

The aforementioned India-China relations are different with ASEAN-China relations because ASEAN countries are not perceived as China's competitors. In fact, the two major Asian countries possess nuclear weapons that place them in different 'playing field' from ASEAN countries. Nevertheless, like India, ASEAN has essentially political and security dilemma in its relation with China because ASEAN member countries have no common position and relations with the regional major power. Due to historical linkages as well as current interests, each of the 10 member countries of ASEAN has different relations with China. Some are China's close allies – if not subordinates — whereas others are more independent of the Chinese influence or are even adversaries due to territorial disputes. These circumstances place ASEAN in an uneasy position vis-à-vis China.

[2] A. Tan and J. Boutin. *Non-traditional Security Issues in Southeast Asia* (Singapore: Institute of Defence and Strategic Studies, 2001). Also see S. Baruah. *Durable Disorder: Understanding the Politics of Northeast India* (New Delhi: Oxford University Press, 2005). Also see D. Puchala. "Of Pirates and Terrorists: What Experience and History Teach," *Contemporary Security Policy,* vol. 26 (2005), pp. 1-24.

[3] M. Klare. *Rising Powers, Shrinking Planet* (New York: Henry Holt and Company, 2008). Also see R. Bahl. *Superpower? The Amazing Race between China's Hare and India's Tortoize* (New York: Penguin, 2010). Also see K. Konstradt and S. Pinto. *India-U.S. Security Relations: Current Engagement,* Congressional Research Service, 2012.

The Concept of Strategic Partnership

Despite enormous security challenges mentioned earlier, India and ASEAN countries could gain confidence as the two parties have agreed to work together and promoted their special engagement to 'Strategic Partnership'. What does it mean to be strategic partners and why states or parties bother to establish the so called 'Strategic Partnership'?

Several countries have used the term 'Strategic Partnership' as an indication of their deeper and stronger relations; some seem to use the term to display a special, privileged status either to show off to other countries that are excluded from the 'partnership' or to appease those included in the partnership. Egmont – the Royal Institute for International Relation of Belgium – tried to study the term in order to undertake a critical review of the Strategic Partnership status that has been used by EU with its 10 partners. Despite the study's criticism on the EU usage of the 'Strategic Partnership' term, one could take advantage of the Egmont's paper to understand the strategic importance of the partnership that has been applied to India-ASEAN since December 2012.

To obtain a deeper understanding on the 'Strategic Partnership', the term's definition can be a starting point. According to Egmont paper, 'A true strategic partner can be defined as a key global player which has a pivotal role in solving global challenges... and which is willing to cooperate ... to solve these challenges, preferably in a multilateral framework – e.g. by coordinating our position with those strategic partners in multilateral forums'[4]. The paper argues that the true strategic partners need to share the ultimate objective, which is to safeguard their common vital interests, and to pursue those shared interests though active strategic and diplomatic efforts[5]. In addition, the paper puts forward what is considered 'strategic' of the partnership. It needs to be comprehensive, built upon reciprocity; it has strong emphatic dimensions in which partners needs to share a common understanding of their mutual values and objectives; it aims for a long term and has to go beyond bilateral issues[6].

India and ASEAN countries could analyse as well as benchmark their 'Strategic Partnership' against the above criteria if the relations are to become true, avoiding the trap of such rhetorical jargon. Before doing so, this chapter

[4] T. Renard. "The Treachery of Strategies: A Call for True EU Strategic Partnership," *Egmont Paper 45* (Gent, Belgium: Academia Press, 2005), p. 5.
[5] T. Renard. "The Treachery of Strategies: A Call for True EU Strategic Partnership," *Egmont Paper 45* (Gent, Belgium: Academia Press, 2005).
[6] Ibid.

would like to check the strategic rationale of India-ASEAN relations which should become the foundation of last December's promotion.

The rationale of India-ASEAN Strategic Partnership may be drawn from several factors. First, the two parties are geographically close; indeed, they share borders both on land and at sea. This natural circumstance has created historical bond and interactions between people and societies in India and almost all ASEAN countries that date back to previous millennium. Their connected land and ocean have created similar geopolitical challenges to both sides. Non-traditional security problems such as piracy, trans-national crimes, smuggling as well as terrorism could go through the Indian Ocean to the Straits of Malacca and further east to Southeast Asia while illegal immigrants from South Asian countries have sailed across the Indian Ocean to Australia. Naturally, the two need to take advantage of their historical bonds and connection to work more closely and strategically to address the challenges effectively.

Secondly, despite the difference of their relations with China, India and ASEAN share common security concerns vis-à-vis China. The growth of China's economy and military has been watched with worry by both parties. Despite the fact that China is the biggest trading partner for India and ASEAN countries, respectively, and is the strongest military power in Asia, India and the majority of ASEAN member countries do not want to fall under China's influence. Thus, the two parties share the common security concerns that are generated by the same country.

Thirdly, India and ASEAN countries need each other for sustainable growth. India is a vital partner for ASEAN countries not only because it is the second highest-growing economy in Asia but also because it is located to East of Southeast Asia that connects ASEAN countries with trading partners in Middle East and Europe. Similarly, ASEAN countries provide a connection between India and its major trading partners in East Asia and the Pacific. According to one of the Indian scholars who observed India-ASEAN relations, "it was a natural choice for developing closer relations"[7].

Fourthly, India and ASEAN seem to have enough institutional mechanism that could support cooperation. India has signed the Treaty of Amity and Cooperation (TAC) with ASEAN countries in 2003, involved in ARF, attended ASEAN Defence Ministers' Meeting (ADMM Plus) and participated in the

[7] A. Bhasin (ed.) *ASEAN-India: Progress & Prosperity* (New Delhi: Geetika Publishers, 2012).

EAS. In the Vision Statement of the India-ASEAN Commemorative Summit December 2012, it is mentioned that India consistently supports ASEAN integration and the building of ASEAN Community.

Finally, in addition to having sufficient institutional frameworks for cooperation, India has been an ASEAN dialogue partner for more than 17 years and the two sides have naturally built sufficient trust and understanding to move on to a higher level of mutually beneficial relationship. The two parties could utilise their current close engagement and intertwined history as a social capital to pursue common objectives in multilateral forums.

Based on the above factors, India and ASEAN countries are likely to have strategic rationale to justify their decision to become strategic partners. It would be interesting to observe how this partnership may be used to enhance security cooperation in order to maintain peace and security in South and Southeast Asia.

Enhancing India-ASEAN Security Cooperation through Strategic Partnership

This part of the paper analyses the meaning of India-ASEAN Strategic Partnership in the context of security cooperation. It consists of a brief observation of current strategic environment that circumvents India-ASEAN Strategic Partnership, an assessment of the partnership based on the criteria mentioned in the Egmont's paper, and a short analysis of challenges to the partnership.

When leaders of India and ASEAN countries announced their Strategic Partnership in December 2012, they acted not in a vacuum of geopolitical circumstance. In fact, the partnership was established amidst a delicate strategic environment in Asia, especially in South, East and Southeast part of Asia. The first important fact is China's military modernisation in the last decade and its growing assertiveness since last year. Directly and indirectly, the Chinese building-up has provoked an arm buying spree by East and Southeast Asian countries. In addition, in the last year, conflicts over territorial claims in South China Sea have worsened, escalating from exchange of verbal threats to deployment of military equipments in the conflicting areas. Four of ten ASEAN countries are involved in territorial disputes not only against each other but also, more dangerously, against China. Moreover, the US has returned to Asia Pacific to pursue what the US Government stated as 'the policy of rebalance'.[8]

The 'pivot' is apparently shown by the deployment of the US troops in the northern part of Australia, more engaged US-PACOM and more active US diplomacy in Southeast Asia. The US has also renewed alliances with its traditional partners in the region, who also have conflicting territorial claims with China. Indeed, the US has established special relations with Vietnam, the enemy it fought until four decades ago. Furthermore, the Indian Ocean has also become a competing area. According to Kaplan[9], China cooperates actively with Pakistan to establish port facility in Gwadar and with Myanmar to build a port and energy pipelines that has led India to build Karwar, a naval port on the Arabian Sea. All these developments have created a delicate – and dangerous – strategic environment in South and Southeast Asia that has to be responded wisely and strategically by India and ASEAN countries though their Strategic Partnership.

The aforementioned Egmont's paper gives a set of criteria that one could use to assess whether India and ASEAN have sufficient condition to embark into a true Strategic Partnership. This assessment, however, depends very much on documents that have been created by Indian and ASEAN leaders such as the 2012 Vision Statement and the Plan of Action. Naturally, the documents show plans and commitments; the real actions may be different when India and ASEAN countries face harsh realities. It will need a longer time-frame to observe the behaviours of India and ASEAN countries to judge whether they are true strategic partners or not. Through document analysis, however, one can identify the intentions that these 11 countries are committed to.

Egmont paper's first criterion of Strategic Partnership is the existence of willingness to, together, solve global issues and to cooperate in multilateral forums. With their current positions in the world, India and ASEAN countries are likely to have an important role in solving global challenges. In addition, in the Vision Statement of India-ASEAN Commemorative Summit 2012, the heads of state/government of ASEAN stated that they are '...committed to work closely together on common regional and international issues of mutual concern and supporting each other's role at the global level

[8] This policy was explained by the Commander of US PACOM Admiral Samuel J. Lockear III in his talk in the Breakfast Open Forum with Indonesian business, academics and military staff on February 8, 2013 during his visit to Jakarta. See also K. Konstradt and S. Pinto. *India-U.S. Security Relations: Current Engagement,* Congressional Research Service, 2012.

[9] R. Kaplan. *The Revenge of Geography* (New York: Random House, 2012).

as well as working together to promote and strengthen inclusive and multi-track regional arrangements...'.

Despite the lack of word 'multilateralism' in their commitment, the leaders appeared to softly bind their states to work together to solve global issues. In addition, the leaders also acknowledged that, historically, their countries had exchanged knowledge, ideas, goods and spiritual tradition that provided a strong foundation for cooperation in a globalized work. Thus, India and ASEAN seem to fulfil the first criteria of strategic partners.

The Egmont's paper second criterion for a Strategic Partnership is likely driven by India and ASEAN's common vital interest to maintain peace and to pursue shared prosperity. The 2012 Vision Statement and the two documents of the Plan of Action (2005-10 and 2010-15) show the intentions of India and ASEAN countries to work together on their common interest through active strategic and diplomatic efforts ranging from dialogue to a joint patrol, from free trade agreement and sub-regional development frameworks to cooperation in order to enhance socio-cultural interaction, from government-to-government relations to people-to-people and business-to-business interactions.

Next, according to Egmont's paper, true Strategic Partners need to have comprehensive relations, built upon reciprocity, and a common understanding of their mutual values and objectives. In the 2012 Vision Statement, India and ASEAN leaders declared their Strategic Partnership constituting almost all aspects of relations, comprising not only political and security but also economic, development and socio-cultural cooperation as well as cooperation in connectivity and regional architecture.

The document also includes statements showcasing common values and objectives such as common understanding to place ASEAN's centrality as the driving force for both regional economic and security structures; the common values to pursue a stable and peaceful region which is essential to achieve sustainable development; and the common objectives to raise the partnership for peace, progress and shared prosperity. The emphatic dimension could be traced from the narratives that show intentions to build a peaceful, harmonious, caring and sharing community, and from the commitment to establish several funding schemes for cooperation.

The last criterion mentioned in Egmont's paper is that a Strategic Partnership should be of a long term and goes beyond bilateral issues. The India-ASEAN Strategic Partnership has gone beyond bilateral issues as it covers regional as well as global issues. In addition, the document shows the intentions to work together on macro issues that require long-term cooperation such as maintaining peace and stability, achieving sustainable development, creating harmonious community, ensuring food and energy security, etc.

Based on the Vision Statement, one may categorise India and ASEAN as true Strategic Partners. A fair judgement of this partnership could only be made after the relations evolve for some time and go through various obstacles. To achieve the realisation of their Strategic Partnership, India and ASEAN countries need to works together consistently and full-heartedly through agreeable and accurate strategies. Indeed, this chapter argues that India and ASEAN can take advantage of their Strategic Partnership in order to work together toward peace and stability as long as they can manage and direct their special relationship. The management and direction of the Strategic Partnership may include several conditions.

First, the special status of Strategic Partnership should be used maximally to build a genuine trust and confidence among India and 10 ASEAN countries. They could enhance empathy towards each other and construct positive understanding through deeper dialogue and interaction among different layers of actors, from government and military officers to students and academia, business, NGOs, social workers, etc. The two parties need to build soft powers towards each other if the Strategic Partnership is to be effective, profound and long-lasting to promote peace and stability in the region.

Secondly, India and ASEAN countries need to carefully manage their partnership in such a way that it could serve to balance China's power and put pressure against its assertive behaviour. But India-ASEAN security cooperation should not create so much pressure on China that it may perceive India and ASEAN countries as joining together to contain it. Like any medicine, India and ASEAN security cooperation needs just a right dose: too much weight would create problems as China could feel contained or betrayed while too little cooperation would have no impact to shape China's behaviours.

Thirdly, India-ASEAN security cooperation needs to avoid being a vehicle or an instrument of interests of the external power, i.e. the US. India and ASEAN countries should not get trapped into the problematic relations between China and the US. There are a number of examples in which the Asian countries became the victims of big countries' strategic or economic interests. The India-ASEAN Strategic Partnership has to be used genuinely to pursue own common interests that may not be in line with the US interests.

Fourthly, concern about China's behaviour is understandable; however, India and ASEAN countries should not become overtly preoccupied by 'China's threat'. The Strategic Partnership should be used to enhance regional security and stability by tackling real security problems such as piracy, trans-national crimes and smuggling to secure trade and sea-lanes, as well as by handling refugee and boat people to help enhance human security. As India and ASEAN countries share non-traditional security problems, they could work together strategically to resolve them. By harnessing their Strategic Partnership to tackle security problems, India and ASEAN countries could gain from their cooperation.

Problem of India-ASEAN Security Cooperation

India and some ASEAN countries have had security cooperation that can be traced back to decades. To upgrade the security cooperation into India-ASEAN framework, however, is a challenge of its own because not all ten ASEAN countries have the same relations, and common interests with India. To some extent, the challenges reflect problems of cooperation within a regional institution. Understanding the challenges is crucial for India-ASEAN in order to utilise their Strategic Partnership to enhance India-ASEAN security cooperation.

The classic problems of India-ASEAN security cooperation are defection by defectors and free raiders. As mentioned previously, the 10 ASEAN countries have different levels of engagement with India due to their histories as well as interests. Some countries that share borders with India naturally have more intense relations, either peacefully or not. It is to say that the level of trust between India and individual ASEAN countries is varying. Those who do not consider India as a priority or do not share security concerns in relatively similar degree may jeopardize the India-ASEAN security cooperation by being defectors. Despite their commitment to the 2012 Vision Statement, there is no guarantee that the ten ASEAN countries are consistently willing to cooperate as strategic partners with India to solve problems in multilateral forums if the problems are not perceived similarly.

One of the solutions to overcome challenges from defectors in India-ASEAN security cooperation is to identify clear payoff to all involved countries. The potential defectors need to be informed that they could gain more from cooperation by consistently fulfilling their commitments. They need to be reminded that together with India, ASEAN countries could form strategic movements that strengthen ASEAN's centrality which in turn would benefit all ASEAN member states.

The second challenge for India-ASEAN security cooperation is the fact that China is also an ASEAN dialogue partner and the biggest trading partner for most – if not all – ASEAN countries. ASEAN needs to be careful in order not to make China feel contained or betrayed. There may be an occasion when ASEAN may seem to be very close to China and in this case, India should not feel left behind as India-ASEAN-China relations are not a zero-sum game. In these triangle relations, ASEAN countries need to be tactical and thoughtful so that it becomes a hub and create positive-sum relations. More frequently, intense and open dialogue through various channels – government to government as well as people to people – could be the strategy to build trust and positive understanding.

The third challenge to India and ASEAN security cooperation is other external players in the region such as the US and perhaps Russia. These external players may be interested in investing their energy and resources for the security and stability in the region. They, however, cannot be depended on since they have their own interests and strategic rationale that are not necessarily in harmony with India-ASEAN common objectives.

Conclusion

India-ASEAN security cooperation can be enhanced through their Strategic Partnership; the results are relative to the ability of the two parties to become true Strategic Partners for each other. India and ASEAN security cooperation should be able to prevent China to take unexpected behaviours but at the same time the cooperation need not make China feel constrained or betrayed. The security cooperation between India and ASEAN countries should be used more to overcome non-traditional security threats and challenges that have become real and immediate problems. It must be acknowledged that the Strategic Partnership between India and ASEAN countries is in a 'state of making'. For the partnership to work strategically, both sides need to have better and deeper understanding towards each other so that they can harmonise each other's interests and develop more genuine common objectives. More dialogue and interactions in various channels is the key.

Part II
Non-Traditional Security Challenges: Food Security, Water Management and Pandemics

Professor Nayan Sharma
Dr. Termsak Chalermpalanupap
Dr. Dinna Wisnu

Chapter 5

Prospects and Imperatives for Water Management in South Asia

Nayan Sharma

A number of major trans-boundary river systems of the world such as the Brahmaputra, the Ganga, the Indus, the Yangtze, the Mekong, the Hwang Ho and the Irrawaddy, etc. have originated from the Tibetan Plateau. In most Asian trans-boundary rivers, including the Ganga-Brahmaputra-Meghna (GBM) in South Asia, agreements have been difficult to negotiate between the co-basin countries due to a number of factors such as historical mistrust and rivalries, asymmetrical power relationships, short-term requirements of the national political parties as opposed to long-term national interests, exclusive negotiations on water issues alone (which often reduce the water allocation process to a zero-sum game), non-formulation of a negotiating framework which considers an overall development spectrum that could result in win-win results for all the concerned parties and emergence of numerous single issues. All these constraints have hampered the development of mutually beneficial projects and activities between co-basin countries[1].

The GBM Basins provide excellent examples of very substantial benefits that can be obtained by the countries when they decide to collaborate with each other[2]. The cooperation between Bhutan and India has brought significant

[1] B.G. Verghese. "From Dispute to Dialogue to Doing," in A.K. Biswas and J.I. Uitto (eds) *Sustainable Development of the Ganges-Brahmaputra-Meghna Basin* (Tokyo: United Nationals University Press, 2001), pp. 163-189.

[2] Z.U. Ahmad, "Water Development Potential within a Basin-wise Approach: Ganges-Brahmaputra-Meghna Issues," in A.K. Biswas, O. Unver and C. Tortajada (eds.) *Water as a Focus for Regional Development* (Oxford University Press, 2004), pp. 83-113.

benefits to the two countries. Equally, lack of collaboration between India and Nepal, and Bangladesh and India, has meant that all the three countries have foregone substantial benefits, which can never be recovered[3].

Water is the single most important natural resource of the basin countries; the three GBM river systems contribute an annual discharge of 1,350 billion cubic metres (bcm), of which the Ganges contributes about 500 bcm, the Brahmaputra 700 bcm and the Meghna 150 bcm[4]. Compared to an annual average water availability of 269,000 m^3/km^2 for the world, the availability in the GBM region is 771,400 m^3/km^2, which is nearly three times the world average. In addition to surface water, the GBM region has an annually replenishable groundwater resource of about 230 bcm. However, the countries sharing the GBM basins are beset by a number of water management problems due to gross inequalities in the temporal and spatial distribution of water, mainly floods, droughts and dry season water scarcity. Management of water resources in the region becomes all the more challenging because of the huge population, the anticipated population growth and the prevailing poverty situation[5].

However, while so much more could have been done, achievements in terms of sharing, development and management of water resources of these rivers as well as sharing and exchange of information and data through mutual cooperation have not been encouraging thus far[6]. It is important to recognize that water resources must be developed and managed in a rational, efficient and equitable way, so that it can act as the engine to promote socio-economic development, shaping the future of millions of people living in this region[7].

The GBM River systems constitute the second largest hydrologic region in the world. The total drainage area of the GBM region is about 1.75 million km^2, stretching across five countries: Bangladesh, Bhutan, China, India (16 states in the

[3] A.K. Biswas. "Management of Ganges-Brahmaputra-Meghna System: Way Forward," in O. Varis, C. Tortajada and A.K. Biswas (eds.) *Management of Trans-boundary Rivers and Lakes* (Berlin: Springer, 2008), pp. 143-164.

[4] Q.K. Ahmad et al. *Ganges-Brahmaputra-Meghna Region: A Framework for Sustainable Development* (Dhaka: The University Press, 2001).

[5] A.K. Biswas. "Management of Ganges-Brahmaputra-Meghna System: Way Forward," in O. Varis, C. Tortajada and A.K. Biswas (eds.) *Management of Trans-boundary Rivers and Lakes* (Berlin: Springer, 2008), pp. 143-164.

[6] A.K. Biswas. "Management of Ganges-Brahmaputra-Meghna System: Way Forward," in O. Varis, C. Tortajada and A.K. Biswas (eds.) *Management of Trans-boundary Rivers and Lakes* (Berlin: Springer, 2008), pp. 143-164. Also see T.A. Khan. "Bangladesh, Trans-boundary Rivers and the Regional Perspective" (Paper presented at the short course on River Basin Management, Directorate of Continuing Education, Bangladesh University of Engineering and Technology, Dhaka, 2005).

[7] A.K. Biswas and J. I. Uitto (eds.) *Sustainable Development of the Ganges-Brahmaputra-Meghna Basins, UNU Series on Water Resources Management and Policy* (New York: United Nation University Press, 2001).

Table 1: Catchment Area of the GBM Basins

Country	Ganges basin		Brahmaputra basin		Meghna basin	
	Basin area (1,000 km^2)	Percentage of total area	Basin area (1,000 km^2)	Percentage of total area	Basin area (1,000 km^2)	Percentage of total area
China	33	3	293	50		
Nepal	140	13				
Bhutan			45	8		
India	861	80	195	34	49	58
Bangladesh	46	4	47	8	36	42
Total	1080	100	580	100	85	100

Source: Rangachari and Verghese (2001)[8]; Pun (2004)[9].

north, east and northeast, in part or fully) and Nepal. While Bangladesh and India share all the three river systems, China shares only the Brahmaputra and the Ganges, Nepal only the Ganges and Bhutan only the Brahmaputra basin (Table 1)[10] . About 10 per cent of the world's population live in this region, representing only 1.2 per cent of the world's land mass. The GBM region is characterized by endemic poverty. It is home to about 40 per cent of the poor people of the developing world.

Despite the poor socio-economic status of the region, it has rich natural endowments of water, land and energy. It is indeed an agonising paradox. The abundance of water in the GBM region as a shared resource could be a principal driver of development for the millions of poor people living in the region. The shared river systems can be optimally developed only through collaborative efforts. It is imperative, therefore, to formulate a framework for the sustainable development of this region in a long-term time frame on a cooperative basis. The objective would be to enhance the quality of life through accelerated human development, environmental conservation and efficient institutions for governance[11].

[8] R. Rangachari and B. G. Verghese. *Making Water Work to Translate Poverty into Prosperity: The Ganga-Brahmaputra-Meghna Region: A Framework for Sustainable Development* (Dhaka: The University Press Limited, 2001), pp. 81-142.
[9] S.B. Pun. "Overview: Conflicts over the Ganges," in B. Subba and K. Pradhan (eds.) *Disputes over the Ganga, Panos Institute South Asia* (Nepal: 2004).
[10] T.A. Khan. "Bangladesh, Trans-boundary Rivers and the Regional Perspective" (Paper presented at the short course on River Basin Management, Directorate of Continuing Education, Bangladesh University of Engineering and Technology, Dhaka, 2005).
[11] A.K. Biswas. "Management of Ganges-Brahmaputra-Meghna System: Way Forward," in O. Varis, C. Tortajada and A.K. Biswas (eds.) *Management of Trans-boundary Rivers and Lakes* (Berlin: Springer, 2008), pp. 143-164.

Water is abundant during the monsoon but scarce during the dry season. Harnessing the GBM rivers will require storing the monsoon flows and redistribute the water available over space and time, when and where required[12].

South Asian Regional Cooperation

Due to trans-boundary nature of the Himalayan river systems, it is incumbent upon the co-basin countries to forge regional cooperation agreements for water management of these river systems. In this regard, there are several instances of bilateral treaties amongst the basin countries.

India and Pakistan Cooperation

The Indus water treaty of 1961 was signed between India and Pakistan due to huge potential advantage for development of the Indus waters. This treaty had shown that it is possible to derive mutual economic benefits from a river system despite unfavourable bilateral relations.

India and Bhutan Cooperation

The collaboration agreement between Bhutan and India presents a classic example on exploitation of trans-boundary river waters as an engine for economic development of an under-developed region with mutual benefits to each country. The 336 MW Chukha hydel project was developed across Wangchu River in western Bhutan to meet domestic power requirement of Bhutan and export surplus to India. The 1,020 MW Tala Hydro-electric project has been completed in recent years under cooperation agreement between Bhutan and India.

The agreement between the two countries is that the electricity generated will be first used to satisfy Bhutan's needs. Before the construction of the Chukha plant, electricity was generated by diesel and mini-hydro plants. Thus, total electricity generated was very limited. Transporting diesel to a landlocked and mountainous country is an expensive and complex process. It is also inefficient. Not surprisingly, in 1980, per capita energy consumption in Bhutan was only 17 kWh, which was less than 10 per cent of that of India, at 173 kWh (see Table 2).

[12] R.B. Shah. "Ganges-Brahmaputra: The Outlook for 21st Century," in A.K. Biswas, Uitto J.I. (eds.) *Sustainable Development of the Ganges-Brahmaputra-Meghna Basin* (Tokyo: United Nations University Press, 2001), pp. 17-45.

Table 2: Per Capita GDP, GDP Growth Rates and Electricity Consumption for South Asian Countries

Countries	GDP (US$) per capita 2004	GDP Growth rate (%) 1975-2004	Electricity consumption per capita (kWh)	
			1980	2003
Bangladesh	406	1.7	30	145
Bhutan	751	4.0	17	218
India	640	3.4	173	594
Nepal	252	2.0	17	91
Pakistan	632	2.9	176	493
Sri Lanka	1,033	3.3	113	407

Source: UNDP, *Human Development Report* (New York: UNDP, 2006), pp. 332, 333, 354, 355.

Bhutan's per capita electricity consumption has steadily increased since the Chukha project became operational. For example, by 2002, compared to 1980, per capita energy consumption had increased by a factor of nearly 14, to 235 kWh.

The win-win approach used by Bhutan and India is a good example of how trans-boundary water bodies can be successfully managed by the co-basin countries for regional economic development, which can directly contribute to the improvements in the quality of life of the people of both the countries through income generation, poverty alleviation and environmental conservation. Viewed from any direction, the collaboration between the two countries has been mutually very beneficial, including enhancement of regional peace and stability.

These water-based developments have meant that Bhutan's per capita GDP has increased from being the lowest of any south Asian countries in 1980, to being the second highest (only Sri Lanka has a higher per capita GDP) in the region at present, within a very brief time span of only a little more than two decades. If the current trends continue, and there does not appear to be any reason as to why this should not, by 2015, Bhutan is likely to have by far the highest per capita GDP in the South Asian region, all primarily because of its farsighted and enlightened approach to develop collaboratively its trans-boundary water bodies with its neighbour, India.[13]

[13]A.K. Biswas. "Management of Ganges-Brahmaputra-Meghna System: Way Forward," in O. Varis, C. Tortajada and A.K. Biswas (eds.) *Management of Trans-boundary Rivers and Lakes* (Berlin: Springer, 2008), pp. 143-164.

India and Nepal Cooperation

A number of agreements between India and Nepal had been forged starting with the Sarda Barrage agreement in 1920 followed by the Koshi river agreement in 1954, and the Gandak river agreement in 1959. The Mahakali Treaty was signed between India and Nepal in 1996.

The Mahakali Treaty can be considered to be a framework agreement, whose centrepiece is the Pancheswar Dam. It establishes the general parameters within which bi-national cooperation could be developed. However, the progress on the implementation of this Treaty has been agonisingly slow. The joint detailed project report is still not ready, some 10 years after the treaty was signed. If and when the dam is constructed, it would have major positive development impacts on the underdeveloped far-west region of Nepal, and Pithoragarh District of Uttar Pradesh in India, which is also a backward area. The concept should be to integrate the hardware of the hydropower development with the software of area development, like education, health services, nutrition, employment generation, transportation, communication and gender empowerment. Combination of this hardware and software has the potential to revolutionize the lifestyles of the people of the region within one generation[14].

The 315 m high rock fill dam at Pancheswar is expected to have a generating capacity of 6,480 MW. India is obliged to purchase any excess electricity that Nepal wishes to sell at a mutually agreed price. While there has been considerable discussion on what could be a fair price that will be acceptable to both parties, there has been no agreement so far[15].

In contrast to the approach of Bhutan and India, which has resulted in significant benefits to the two co-basin countries because of managing trans-boundary water cooperatively in a constructive spirit, the last 20 years have proved to be a missed opportunity for India and Nepal[16].

India and Bangladesh Cooperation

In 1977, a five year Ganga water sharing agreement was signed between India

[14] B.G. Verghese. "From Dispute to Dialogue to Doing," in A.K. Biswas and Uitto J.I. (eds) *Sustainable Development of the Ganges-Brahmaputra-Meghna Basin* (Tokyo: United Nations University Press, 2001), pp.163-189.

[15] A.K. Biswas. "Management of Ganges-Brahmaputra-Meghna System: Way Forward," in O. Varis, C. Tortajada and A.K. Biswas (eds.), *Management of Trans-boundary Rivers and Lakes* (Berlin: Springer, 2008), pp. 143-164.

[16] Ibid.

and Bangladesh on Farakka barrage to divert water for solving the siltation problem at Kolkata port. A Joint River Commission (JRC) was established under the agreement clause, which would be responsible for observing and recording at Farakka, the daily flows below Farakka Barrage and in the feeder canal in India, as well as Hardinge Bridge point in Bangladesh, and for implementing the water sharing arrangements and examining any difficulty arising out of the implementation of the sharing arrangement and of the operation of the Farakka Barrage. A mechanism was provided for the settlement of disputes.

An MoU was signed in 1982 to extend the 1977 agreement which finally expired in 1988 after two similar extensions. Negotiations for a permanent water sharing agreement continued in the subsequent years while both the countries focused more on the national river development initiatives and barrages on the Teesta, Ganges and the Brahmaputra. After a period (1989-96) without any agreement, the Ganges Water Treaty was signed between the two governments in 1996 to share the dry season flow of the Ganges and to seek ways for flow augmentation[17].

This 30-year long Treaty has provided Bangladesh an opportunity for environmental restoration of the Ganges Dependent Area (GDA)[18]. India and Bangladesh share 54 rivers, however, the Ganges Treaty is the only water sharing agreement that exists today between Bangladesh and India. Article IX of the Ganges Treaty stipulated that, guided by the principle of equity, fairness and no harm to either party, both Bangladesh and India would conclude water sharing treaties/agreements with regard to other trans-boundary or common rivers. The Joint Committee formed after the signing of the Treaty to implement this had prioritised seven rivers at the initial stage, viz. the Teesta, Dharla, Dudhkumar, Manu, Khowai, Gumti and Muhuri rivers. Later the JRC recognized that the long-term sharing of waters for the Feni river should also be examined along with the other seven rivers. Recent media reports in both Bangladesh and India suggest that sharing agreements for Teesta and Feni rivers have been drafted, which might be signed by the end of 2011[19].

[17] Mashfiqus Salehin et al. "Opportunities for Trans-boundary Water Sharing in The Ganges, The Brahmaputra, and The Meghna Basins," *India Infrastructure Report - 2011, Water: Policy and Performance for Sustainable Development* (New Delhi: Oxford University Press, 2011), pp. 29-43.

[18] WARPO 2002.

[19] Mashfiqus Salehin et al. "Opportunities for Trans-boundary Water Sharing in The Ganges, The Brahmaputra, and The Meghna Basins," *India Infrastructure Report - 2011, Water: Policy and Performance for Sustainable Development* (New Delhi: Oxford University Press, 2011), pp. 29-43.

Damming or Diversion of the Yarlung Tsangpo in Tibet

Several trans-boundary river basins originating from the Tibetan Plateau including the Brahmaputra, the Ganga, the Satluj, the Koshi are shared by India and China. There have been instances of cooperation in sharing of data pertaining to floods, GLOF, etc. by the two countries especially in the case of the Satluj and the Brahmaputra rivers.

Recently, there have been reports in the media on proposed and under-construction dams on the Yarlung Tsangpo (Brahmaputra) in Tibetan region of China for hydro power. The 116 m high Zangmu dam (510 mw) is in advanced stage of construction and another three more dams (Jiexu, Jiacha and Lengda) downstream of it have recently been approved for construction by the Chinese Government. Furthermore, there are unconfirmed reports about possible future plans for probable diversion of stream flow of the Yarlung Tsangpo to Xinjiang province/Gobi desert and resulting in acute water shortage in northern areas of China for various uses including irrigation, drinking water, etc.

There is a need to scientifically study the impact of any such possible future plans for flow diversion of the Yarlung Tsangpo by constructing storage or diversion dams or by simply making dams at a very high altitude for run-of-the-river hydel project. Such a study should appropriately address the potential environmental, socio-economic and safety concerns in the immediate downstream Assam valley of the Brahmaputra in India from a strict technical standpoint.

Notably, out of average annual flow of 455,000 million cubic metres of the Brahmaputra at Pandu in Assam state of India about 44 per cent of the average flow is contributed by the Dihang or Siang main stream which is known as the Yarlung Tsangpo in Tibet[20]. While during monsoon season, the balance 56 per cent flow comes from the tributaries in Assam, the bulk of non-monsoon dry weather base flow of the Brahmaputra is mainly generated from the source glaciers in the Tibetan high Himalayas. It should thus be apparent that any reduction of stream flow in the Yarlung Tsangpo, because of climate change or artificial flow diversion in coming years, will have very serious impact on the quantum of water resources in downstream areas of the Brahmaputra in India and Bangladesh, besides greatly depleting the non-monsoon flows.

[20] K.L. Rao. *India's Water Wealth: Its Assessment, Uses and Projections* (New Delhi: Orient Longman, 1979), pp. 39-70.

The intricate channel morphology of the Brahmaputra makes it one of the most highly braided rivers of the world having stream width varying from 1.2 km near Guwahati to as wide as 22 km near Gumi with very complex fluvial landform configuration and the consequent channel braiding is progressively increasing due to unabated stream-bank erosion process.

The downstream impact of flow reduction due to any future diversion of the Yarlung Tsangpo to acute water scarce regions in northern part of China will induce the river morphology of the Brahmaputra in Assam to undergo further intensification of braiding process along with harmful rise in average stream bed level and loss of channel conveyance capacity. As a consequence due to above likely channel changes, even for moderate kind of monsoon rains, there will be much more magnified incidence of flood events than that are occurring in the present time, since flood carrying capacity of the aggraded channel section will progressively decrease causing stream-bank overtopping and rampant embankment breaches.

In the event of any river diversion of the Yarlung Tsangpo in future, in addition to aforementioned impacts the water use namely – ecology, inland navigation and drinking water will be very severely hit especially in the non-monsoon low flow period. Due to greatly reduced water depth in the highly braided river reaches compounded by intense sedimentation, the prime aquatic creatures like dolphins, turtles, big fishes and other mega fauna will practically become extinct due to irreversible process of habitat shrinkage. The inland navigation fairways will become inoperable due to loss of required navigation draught. The supply sources catering to rising water demand for municipal, industrial and pollution control from the Brahmaputra such as for Guwahati city, refineries, etc. will run dry during low flow season. Even abstraction of ground water is likely to be much more arduous and expensive due to resultant depression in sub soil water levels.

Around the gorge of the Great Bend of the Yarlung Tsangpo near the highest mountain of Eastern Tibet, Namche Barwa at 7,760 m, China's hydro engineers calculate that two great hydro projects could be built, notably—Metok (Motuo) with 38,000 megawatt generating capacity, more than double of Three Gorges 18,600 MW; and Daduo, which could generate even more, 43,800 MW. Both involve diverting water from the river through a man-made short-cut tunnel that avoids much of the great bend, sending huge volumes of water straight across from intercept points where the river is just below 3,000 m, rushing down to rejoin the river on the far side of the bend, where it is only at 850 m (Metok/Motuo) or 560 m, at Daduo, an even greater drop. This makes maximum use of a drop of more than 2 km to drive enormous turbines and produce electricity on a scale that dwarfs even the world's largest power plant Three Gorges. Not only have Chinese hydro engineers sketched such plans, they have published proposed routes for the ultra high voltage cables that would then step across the deep gorges of nearby rivers in order to reach the core cities of western China, Chongqing and Chengdu. China's Xinhua news agency published a map in 2003 showing power lines heading east to the Sichuan basin.

In the event of major earthquakes, any possible structural failure of above dams on the Yarlung Tsangpo sited at an altitude of about 3 km above Assam plains in Eastern Tibet may pose very serious hazard for the Brahmaputra valley in Northeast India.

It is a universally followed convention that while planning any dam – whether run-of-the-river or storage based, especially on such a highly earthquake prone zone-it is a statutory obligation of the planners to conduct comprehensive dam break analysis so as to predict and assess the possible consequences in the downstream areas resulting from any dam failure (due to design/construction faults or earthquake occurrence) for getting the project cleared from safety consideration. This is extremely essential in the case of a trans-boundary river like the Brahmaputra on such a highly seismic region. Notably, the 162.8 m high Tipaimukh dam (1,500 MW) on Barak River in Manipur has remained stalled due to controversy over water rights between India and Bangladesh besides other issues.

Imperatives for Water Management Treaty for Trans-Boundary Brahmaputra & Ganga Basins

In the present juncture, it has now become imperative for the five co-basin nations – China, India, Bhutan, Nepal and Bangladesh to enter into a comprehensive water management treaty for sustainable, equitable, safe and judicious exploitation of the water resources of the Brahmaputra and the Ganga rivers in a climate of trust, cooperation and harmony. There are many instances of similar water use of trans-boundary rivers amongst big and small countries without generating any sense of deprivation or unfairness in a win-win situation for the co-basin countries.

The preliminary findings of a research project undertaken by a European Commission Sponsored international consortium BRAHMATWINN indicated the likely impact of climate change, in which the temperature is projected to increase in Brahmaputra basin in the coming decades with the higher values in the Himalayan region of the Tibetan Plateau especially the winter temperature. The study brought out preliminary evidence of some snow cover loss with possible glacier melting in the eastern Himalayas.

However, further in-depth scientific analysis is warranted to investigate the ramifications of the above phenomenon which will potentially have profound impact on the availability status of water resources from the Yarlung Tsangpo/ Brahmaputra and probably Ganga rivers in coming decades primarily affecting China, India, Nepal and Bangladesh.

In the current context of climate change and rising population growth, it is anticipated that there will be steep hike in water demand in the coming decades which potentially may give rise to discord amongst the co-basin nations in the absence of appropriate water management mechanism. For economic growth of the South Asian region, water management agreement can be equipped with in-built mechanism for sharing relevant data & research, joint project investigation, joint monitoring & planning of water resources projects, sharing of technical expertise for planning, design and construction.

It can potentially promote inter-country commercial agreements to develop water resources, eco-system services and goods, and also marketing cheap hydropower among basin countries which can be abundantly harnessed from the Yarlung Tsangpo/Brahmaputra as well as from the Ganga. Such agreement will engender a favourable environment for trade and commerce boosted by economic growth pulses emanating from water management of the trans-boundary river systems in South Asia. This will be a win-win situation for the South Asian countries ushering in an era of collective economic growth, peace and stability.

Chapter 6

India-ASEAN Cooperation to Cope with Non-Traditional Security Challenges

Termsak Chalermpalanupap

Non-traditional security challenges confronting ASEAN can be divided into two groups: (a) transnational crimes, and (b) those that are not crimes but are nonetheless serious transnational security challenges. In the former, ASEAN focuses on eight major areas: narcotic drugs, trafficking in persons, sea piracy, arms smuggling, money laundering, terrorism, international economic crimes and cyber crimes. The cooperation is undertaken mainly under the framework of the ASEAN Ministerial Meeting on Transnational Crime (AMM-TC), in which ASEAN Member States are represented by their respective Minister of Interior or Minister of Home Affairs. The AMM-TC meets once every two years; its 8th meeting was held in Bali from October 9-13, 2011. The 9th meeting will be hosted by Laos in Vientiane in November 2013.

The AMM-TC is assisted by the ASEAN Senior Officials Meeting on Transnational Crime (SOM-TC), the ASEAN Senior Officials on Drug Matters, the ASEANAPOL (ASEAN chiefs of police) and the Meeting of Directors-General of Immigration Departments and Heads of Consular Affairs Division of the Ministries of Foreign Affairs (DGICM). The AMM-TC also coordinates closely with the ASEAN Foreign Ministers Meeting (AMM), the ARF and the ADMM on broad transnational security issues such as counter-terrorism, and maritime security.

At the same time, ASEAN also has to address other non-traditional security challenges that are not transnational crimes: natural disasters, illegal migration or irregular movement of people, trans-boundary air pollution or haze from forest fires, global warming/climate change, energy security, food security, scarcity of water resource and water management and pandemics.

ASEAN puts its peoples (600 million in combined population in 2013) at the centre of community-building. ASEAN pursues comprehensive security aimed at ensuring human survival, safety, security, well-being, human rights and human dignity, and human development of every individual in each society as well as in the ASEAN Community. Comprehensive security requires closer regional cooperation, involving participation of all stakeholders, to ensure effective response, which will boost the sense of community and belongingness.

ASEAN is also outward-looking in its pursuit of comprehensive security. ASEAN has initiated several processes for dialogue and cooperation with external partners, such as the ASEAN+1 with 10 Dialogue Partners[1], ASEAN Plus with China, Japan and the RoK, the ARF[2], and the ADMM-Plus, and the EAS.[3] This chapter outlines ASEAN efforts in coping with the non-traditional security challenges such as food security, water management and pandemics.

ASEAN Cooperation on Food Security

The ASEAN region as a whole is a net food-exporter. Cambodia, Myanmar, Thailand and Vietnam are major rice exporters of the world. Thailand is also a highly competitive producer and exporter of canned tuna, frozen shrimp and frozen chicken. Yet ASEAN recognizes food security as an important issue.

The first major step was undertaken by ASEAN Foreign Ministers who signed the ASEAN Agreement on the Food Security Reserve in New York on October 4, 1979. Under the agreement, the five founding ASEAN members (Indonesia, Malaysia, the Philippines, Singapore and Thailand) pledged to earmark a total of 50,000 tons of rice to create the ASEAN Emergency Rice Reserve for emergency requirement. In 1997, the reserve was increased to 67,000 tons with the participation of two additional ASEAN members, Brunei

[1] The 10 Dialogue Partners are: Australia, Canada, China, the E.U., India, Japan, the RoK, New Zealand, Russia and the U.S.

[2] Twenty-seven are participating in the ARF: 10 ASEAN Member States, 10 Dialogue Partners, and Papua New Guinea, Pakistan, Mongolia, the DPRK, Timor-Leste, Bangladesh and Sri Lanka.

[3] The same eight Dialogue Partners are participating in both the ADMM-Plus and the EAS, but these two processes are not related; the eight are: Australia, China, India, Japan, the RoK, New Zealand, Russia and the U.S.

Darussalam and Vietnam, and now 87,000 tons with all 10 ASEAN members (including Laos, Myanmar and Cambodia) participating.

ASEAN is also engaged with China, Japan and the RoK to create the ASEAN Plus Three Emergency Rice Reserve (APTERR) with a total emergency rice reserve of 787,000 tons: 87,000 tons from ASEAN, 300,000 tons from China, 150,000 tons from Japan and 250,000 tons from the RoK. Thailand's Office of Agricultural Economics of the Ministry of Agriculture and Cooperatives operates a secretariat of the APTERR in Bangkok to promote ASEAN Plus Three cooperation on food security, nutrition and information for food trade.[4]

The main ASEAN body handling food security cooperation is the ASEAN Ministerial Meeting on Agriculture and Forestry (AMAF). In the Ministerial Understanding of AMAF signed in October 1993, food security was listed as the first among the seven priorities. AMAF is assisted by the ASEAN Senior Officials Meeting on Agriculture and Forestry (SOM-AMAF) in implementing the ASEAN Integrated Food Security (AIFS) Framework, and the Strategic Plan of Action on Food Security in the ASEAN Region (SPA-FS) (2009-2013).

The six strategic thrusts of the AIFS are: to strengthen food security arrangements; to promote conducive food market and trade; to strengthen integrated food security information systems to effectively forecast, plan and monitor supplies and utilisation for basic food commodities; to promote sustainable food production; to encourage greater investment in food and agro-based industry to enhance food security; and to identify and address emerging issues related to food security.

The six objectives of the SPA-FS are: to increase food production; to reduce post-harvest losses; to promote conducive market and trade for agriculture commodities and inputs; to ensure food stability; to promote availability and accessibility to agriculture inputs; and to operationalise regional food emergency relief arrangements. The overall goal under the strategy and plan of action is to ensure long-term food security and to improve the livelihood of farmers in the ASEAN region. The two documents are on the website of the ASEAN Secretariat: www.asean.org.

In the ASEAN Economic Community Blueprint (2009-15), cooperation on food, agriculture and forestry is aimed at three major goals: (a) enhancing intra-ASEAN and extra-ASEAN trade and long-term competitiveness of ASEAN's food, agriculture and forestry products and commodities;

[4] See details of the APTERR at www.apeterr.org

(b) promotion of joint approaches and transfer of technology; and (c) promotion of agricultural cooperatives as a means to empower and enhance market access of agricultural products for the benefit of farmers in the ASEAN Community.[5]

Enhancing food security and food safety is also included in the ASEAN Socio-Cultural Community Blueprint. Its strategic objective is to ensure adequate access to food at all times for all ASEAN peoples and to ensure food safety in ASEAN Member States.[6] The ASEAN Health Ministers Meeting (AHMM) has an ASEAN Coordinating Committee on Food Safety and an ASEAN Expert Group on Food Safety to undertake cooperation in this area.

At the 14th ASEAN Summit in Cha-am/Hua Hin, Thailand, February 26 – March 1, 2009, ASEAN Leaders discussed food security in the ASEAN region and adopted a statement on this issue, expressing their concerns about the rising international food prices in the wake of the financial crisis of 2008-09, which has brought about adverse impacts on food security in the ASEAN region. They emphasized their determination to enhance ASEAN cooperation to ensure food security "through sustainable food production, post-harvest, marketing and trade in the region, especially by strengthening ASEAN initiative/measures already existed as well as a strategic pursuit of actions to be developed/enhanced based on strong commitments and ownership among all Member States. ..."[7]

At the 15th ASEAN Summit in Cha-am/Hua Hin, Thailand, October 23-25, 2009, food security continued to be an issue of common interest among the ASEAN Leaders. They also discussed the issue with their counterparts from China, Japan and the RoK. The outcome of their discussion on this issue was reflected in the Cha-am Hua Hin Statement on ASEAN Plus Three Cooperation on Food Security and Bio-Energy, October 24, 2009. They stated in part that they shared "common concerns over food security and the need to develop sustainable bio-energy in the light of ongoing volatility in food and energy prices which have affected the livelihood of our peoples and our economic growth; ..."[8] Among other things, the ASEAN Plus Three Leaders pledged to "enhance food production capability for the well-being of our peoples as an integral part of the Millennium Development Goals, ... [and to] explore the possibility of establishing an ASEAN Plus Three Emergency Rice Reserve (APTERR) ...". [9] The APTERR came into force in 2012.

[5] See details of the AEC Blueprint at: www.asean.org.

[6] See details of the ASCC Blueprint at: www.asean.org.

[7] See the March 1, 2009 ASEAN Summit Statement on Food Security in the ASEAN Region at: www.asean.org/images/archive/22341.pdf.

[8] See the October 24, 2009 Statement at : www.asean.org/news/item/cha-am-hua-hin-statement-on-asean-plus-three-cooperation-on-food-security-and-bio-energy-development.

[9] Ibid.

Additional Food Security Projects

In recent years, ASEAN has undertaken the following food security projects:

- ASEAN, SAARC, ADB, FAO and USA: Regional Consultation on Policy and Programme Actions to Address High Food Price in Asia and the Pacific (Bangkok, March 9-11, 2011).
- ASEAN Multi-Sectoral Framework on Climate Change: Agriculture and Forestry towards Food security (AFCC) [3 million euro provided by Germany to promote food security in ASEAN 2011-13].
- ASEAN-USA joint project on Maximising Agricultural Revenue Through Knowledge, Enterprise Development, and Trade (MARKET) [3-year project to promote food trade and food security in ASEAN: involve the private sector and civil society in food security; support harmonisation of agrifood sector regulations; improve the ability of the ASEAN Secretariat to monitor and evaluate food security programmes].

Water Management

ASEAN faces a diversity of water issues: in Singapore, for example, the priority is on conservation and renewable use of water; in Thailand, it is the growing fluctuation of water supply from serious floods in one year (July 2011 – January 2012) and widespread droughts in another (2013); riparian States in the lower Mekong sub-region face adverse consequences of Chinese dams upstream; and rising sea level poses another set of problems to several ASEAN countries, especially Indonesia and the Philippines, the world's two largest archipelagic States.

Water management concerns several ministries: agriculture (water for farming), energy (hydro-electric generation), natural resources (water conservation), industry or mineral resource (groundwater) and environment. In ASEAN, the responsibility of handling water management goes to the ASEAN Ministerial Meeting on the Environment (AMME), which is assisted by the Working Group on Water Resources Management. One of the 10 priorities, based on the World Summit on Sustainable Development Plan of Implementation, is about freshwater resources.

The ASEAN Strategic Plan of Action on Water Resources Management was adopted by the AMME in December 2003. The vision in the Strategic Plan for water in the ASEAN region by 2025 is: "The attainment of sustainability of water resources to ensure sufficient water quantity of acceptable quality to meet the needs of the people of Southeast Asia in terms of health, food security, economy, and environment".[10]

The ASEAN Working Group on Water Resources Management convened its 12th meeting in Quang Ninh, Viet Nam, on July 25, 2012, to review the implementation of the Strategic Plan and to recommend its future direction. The Working Group also discussed ASEAN participation in the Clean Environment Summit in Singapore, July 1-4, 2012, the 2nd Asia-Pacific Water Summit, May 19-20, 2013 in Chiang Mai, and the Singapore International Water Week, June 1-5, 2014.

In the ASCC Blueprint, the strategic objective of ASEAN cooperation on the sustainability of freshwater resources is to ensure equitable accessibility and sufficient water quantity of acceptable quality to meet the needs of the peoples of ASEAN. Water management also concerns the promotion of sustainable use of coastal and marine environment, management of natural resources and biodiversity, cooperation on global environmental issues, such as global warming, and disaster management and emergency response.

Pandemic Preparedness in ASEAN

In the past, ASEAN's cooperation on public health was focused on tackling well-known but normal communicable diseases such as HIV/AIDS, malaria and tuberculosis. The sudden outbreak of severe acute respiratory syndrome (SARS) in 2002 caught ASEAN by surprise and led ASEAN to step up its cooperation on public health to cope with the new pandemic.

ASEAN Leaders met in a special summit in Bangkok on April 29, 2003 to examine the SARS pandemic and adopted the measures as recommended by their ASEAN Health Ministers. The ASEAN Health Ministers met in Kuala Lumpur on April 26, 2003 and agreed to recommend several urgent measures.[11] ASEAN Leaders also met with the newly appointed Chinese Premier Wen Jiabao in a special ASEAN-China Summit in Bangkok on April 29, 2003. At the meeting, the Chinese Premier pledged full cooperation with

[10] See text of the Strategic Plan at : www.cil.nus.edu.sg/rp/pdf/2003.

[11] See the Joint Declaration of the Special ASEAN Leaders Meeting on Severe Acute Respiratory Syndrome (SARS) at www.asean.org/communities/asean-socio-cultural-community/item/joint-declaration-special-asean-leaders-meeting-on-severe-respiratory-syndrome.

ASEAN in coping with SARS. That was his first overseas trip as the Chinese Premier and first meeting with ASEAN Leaders.

ASEAN learned several important lessons from the SARS pandemic. These included the following: the need to ensure close surveillance of situation on the ground; to put in place necessary preventive measures; to enforce strict quarantine regulations; to ensure transparency; to share factual information among ASEAN governments; and to keep the media and general public well-informed.

The onslaught of the highly pathogenic avian influenza in early 2004 further alarmed the peoples and governments in ASEAN. However, ASEAN was then better prepared and had a better common understanding of what needed to be done. Mutual trust among ASEAN governments has increased and good working relations among relevant ASEAN authorities have been developed from their joint efforts in tackling SARS.

ASEAN's AMAF set up an ASEAN Task Force on HPAI in October 2004 to spearhead regional cooperation to tackle the pandemic. The Task Force's plan of action addressed eight priority areas, including disease surveillance, emergency preparedness, public awareness and containment measures.[12]

Also responsible for preparing ASEAN for any pandemics is the AHMM. It is assisted by the ASEAN Senior Officials on Health Development (SOM-HD), the ASEAN Expert Group on Communicable Diseases (AEGCD), the ASEAN Task Force on AIDS (ATFOA) and the ASEAN Technical Working Group on Pandemic Preparedness and Response (ATWGPPR). The AEGCD, ATFOA and ATWGPPR are directly in charge of the ASEAN cooperation in communicable diseases and pandemic preparedness and response (PPR). The PPR is linked to ASEAN Member States' implementation of the ASEAN Agreement on Disaster Management and Emergency Response, under which the ASEAN Humanitarian Assistance Centre (AHA) has been established in Jakarta.

ASEAN, China, Japan and the RoK have a cooperation programme on emerging infectious diseases (EID). It includes an ASEAN Regional Risk Communication Centre; linking partnership laboratories into a regional network; and undertaking regional laboratory-based disease surveillance.[13]

ASEAN and Japan have a joint project on stockpiling of anti-virals and personal protective equipment against potential influenza pandemic. The stockpile of 500,000 courses of Tamiful and personal protective equipment for

[12] See details in Anish Kumar Roy's "Addressing Pandemic Preparedness in ASEAN: The Way Forward" in Dr. Mely Caballero-Anthony (ed.) *Pandemic Preparedness in Asia,* RSIS Monograph No. 16, Singapore, 2009.
[13] See details at www.aseanplus3-eid.info.

350,000 people, worth about US$ 30 million, is based in Singapore. USAID have a project on multi-sectoral pandemic preparedness and response. ASEAN and the ADB also have a project on highly pathogenic avian influenza.

ASEAN has also worked closely with WHO, FAO, World Animal Health Organization (OIE, Office International des Epizooties), the UN System Influenza Coordination and the UN Office for the Coordination of Humanitarian Affairs to organize cooperation efforts to cope with the avian influenza and enhancing ASEAN's preparedness.

ASEAN Leaders took personal interest in coping with the avian influenza (AI). They discussed the pandemic with their counterparts from Australia, China, India, Japan, the RoK and New Zealand at their First East Asia Summit (EAS) in Kuala Lumpur on December 14, 2005. In their EAS Declaration on Avian Influenza Prevention, Control and Response, the EAS Leaders acknowledged that "the avian influenza has spread to a number of countries in the region and that its serious impact is not just confined to the poultry industry but also public health, livestock production, trade, tourism, economic and social development in the region; ..." They pledged to "undertake every effort through existing bilateral, regional and multilateral channels, to enhance national, regional and international capacities to deal with the current avian influenza epidemic, inter-alia, to prevent it from transforming into a human influenza pandemic ... ".[14]

According to Dr. Julie E. Fischer, a global health security expert of the Henry L. Stimson Center, "planning in Southeast Asia is at a far greater level of maturity than corresponding efforts in other regions, stemming in part from the [ASEAN] region's experiences with SARS and AI [avian influenza] and its political leadership's acceptance of non-traditional security (NTS) issues as a matter of international dialogue...."[15]

[14] See the EAS Declaration at www.asean.org/news/item/east-asia-summit-declaration-on-avian-influenza-prevention-control-and response-kuala-lumpur-14-december-2005.

[15] Paper of Dr. Julie E. Fischer on "The Way Forward: Strategies to Strengthen Regional Pandemic Preparedness" in Dr. Mely Caballero-Anthony (ed.) Pandemic Preparedness in Asia, RSIS Monograph No. 16, Singapore, 2009.

Chapter 7

Habits, Policies and Food Security in ASEAN: Rooms for India-ASEAN Strategic Partnership

Dinna Wisnu

There are many reasons why the study on food security has continued for decades. One obvious reason is because there have not been enough satisfactory outputs indicating systematic eradication of hunger across the globe. Specifically for ASEAN, the figures on poverty, and consequently the lack of access to food and nutrition, are quite disturbing.

The ASEAN Secretariat has recently adopted A Framework Action Plan on Rural Development and Poverty Eradication 2011-15, which forms the basis for various Senior Officials Meetings (SOMs) in developing the ASEAN Economic Community. The framework was made based on the data coming from IFAD and World Bank. IFAD in its Rural Poverty Report 2011 reports that 53 per cent of the total population of nearly 600 millions in Southeast Asia lives in poverty with less than US$ 2 a day while around 18 per cent of the total population lives in extreme poverty with less than US$ 1.25 a day. Sixty two per cent of this poverty is located in rural areas. The ASEAN Secretariat is most concerned because the World Bank report lists Southeast Asia as second only to sub-Saharan Africa in the percentage of its people who live in poverty.

The World Food Programme of the United Nations (WFP) released its 2012 Hunger Map. Only three countries among ASEAN members that have very low incidence of undernourishment where less than 5 per cent of the population is undernourished: Singapore, Malaysia and Brunei Darussalam. Indonesia is categorized as moderately low in undernourishment (5-14 per cent are undernourished), while Philippines, Vietnam, Thailand are moderately high in undernourishment (15-24 per cent are undernourished), and Cambodia, Laos are high in the incidence of undernourishment (25-34 per cent are undernourished); there is no data from Myanmar. Looking at the bigger picture, India is categorized as moderately high in undernourishment.

Many reports and studies refer to insufficient supply of food, the high cost of food and its challenge to food security[1]; but the findings from Randy Stringer in Australia (2000) was particularly interesting. It says that actually enough food is produced worldwide to feed the world. The study may be a bit old for data reference today, but it reminds of a classic study on agricultural politics written by Robert Bates[2] where he challenged the notion of food scarcity in causing high cost of food. Bates provided compelling sets of data from several African countries that there are policies and systematic politics to keep farmers in disadvantageous position vis-à-vis the urban consumers. Post-colonial governments typically inherited the same type of institution from the colonial regime: a state marketing board that purchased all cash crops and export them itself, while rural people live at subsistence level with the food crops that farmers increasingly reject to grow in order to gain more from growing cash crops. The government, Bates argued, are using the surplus from exporting cash crops to develop processing industries while at the same time control the prices of supply coming from farmers in order to keep urban consumers happy for affordable food crops. The consequence of this, Bates demonstrated, is the economic pressure experienced by farmers.

In Southeast Asia, there is evidence that food security problem is not necessarily a problem of food supply, but rather a problem of public policies and political approach in solving the problem of hunger. This chapter is a brief version of a still undergoing study on the politics of food security in Southeast Asia. It will present the current dimensions of food security in Southeast Asia, the politics based on the policies in the area of agriculture, and some recommendations for the consideration of the Delhi Dialogue V forum.

[1] Henk Breman and Siegfried Kofi Debrah. "Improving African Food Security", *SAIS Review*, vol. XXIII, no. 1 (Winter-Spring, 2003), pp. 153-170.

[2] Robert Bates. *Markets and States in Tropical Africa: The Political Basis of Agricultural Politics* (Berkeley: University of California Press, 1981).

Dimensions of Food Security

The study is driven by the puzzle that many have acknowledged the urgency of solving food security problem and are troubled by the dire consequences of the absence of food and nutrition, but why are the numbers on hunger and malnutrition still high? Southeast Asia in general is fertile and surrounded by rich maritime wealth. There should not be reason for lack of supply of food. There have been problems of population control, also income inequality between rural and urban residents, gaps in education, knowledge, skills and even productivity. Yet, these variables are not necessarily the causes of food insecurity. At best, they are intervening variables that increases the likelihood for experiencing food insecurity.

It has been argued that food security is not necessarily about self-sufficiency in food production.[3] After all, many communities cannot produce enough food for themselves due to shortage in arable land, water, people and technology. Other suggested that food may not be available to individuals if they do not have control over household resources and income. Simon Maxwell[4] cited the work of Thomas[5] who studied families in urban Brazil where unearned income has 20 times the effect on child survival if it is controlled by mothers. There is also the factor of climate change, soil degradation and ecological damage that have made agricultural activities more costly and complicated than it was a few decades ago. Without careful calculation on how policies lead to actions, there won't be satisfactory output coming out of any food security dialogs and frameworks.

Food security is understood in this chapter as the ability of governments to acquire food for the people, distribute it on time to prevent hunger and malnutrition, with the prices that are suitable for target communities. Food security is about the willingness of governments to manage limited resources and to provide instruments for various stakeholders to acquire food and to work together as a community. The policies may vary from place to place, but the goals and idea to face challenges are mentioned above.

It is useful to introduce the notion that governments are responsible to provide tools and to induce the creation of instruments that would overcome different kinds of challenges stakeholders may face to acquire food. Why

[3] Simon Maxwell. "Food Security a Post-Modern Perspective," *Food Policy*, vol. 21, no. 2, 1996, pp. 155-170. Also see Robert Stringer. "Food Security in the Developing World," *Policy Discussion Paper No. 0011*, (Adelaide: Centre for International Economic Studies, Adelaide, Australia, March 2000).

[4] Simon Maxwell. "Food Security a Post-Modern Perspective," *Food Policy*, vol. 21, no. 2, 1996, pp. 155-170.

[5] D. Thomas. "Gender Differences in Household Resource Allocation, Population and Human Resources Department. Living Standards Measurement Study," Working Paper No. 79, (Washington DC: World Bank, 1991).

governments? The supply of food depends on collective actions but the demand is individual. No individual farmers can create and ensure widespread use of quality seeds that is suitable for the changing climate, or distribute fertilizers at affordable prices, or ensure good price for their harvest, or deliver their crops to consumers across the country. Farmers need to work with other farmers, as well as with businesses and entrepreneurs and government officials at all levels to reach the desired level of supply. Fishermen cannot predict how many tons of fish and the kinds they catch, let alone determine the price. Yet demands for food are driven by lifestyle, personal diet and other personal considerations.

Studies have shown that farmers have limited control of how the supply reaches the consumers[6] or whether the target of supply can be achieved at a certain period.[7] The same thing applies to fishermen. Consumers, on the other hand, while they may determine which products would be bought and at what price, they have no control over the security of food supply for themselves. Consumers have little idea of what food security is and often feel disempowered even in educated developed economies such as the United Kingdom.[8]

Intuitively speaking, demand for food can be elastic or inelastic depending on lifestyle trend, marketing gimmicks, distribution and price. All of these can be influenced by the actions or inactions of the governments. This is where 'governments willingness in managing limited resources' becomes critical. Indeed, the keyword is willingness. Even an inch of willingness that is firm and persistent would make a difference in giving directions to producers and consumers on how to create a system that works for the community in terms of securing food. Like a lighthouse, what the governments do, if done consistently, it will become an anchor for the increasingly uncertain challenges of food security.

Food security has numerous interrelated dimensions. For the context of ASEAN, it is argued that following dimensions are what matter most in ensuring food security: first, the dimension of agricultural and fishing business; second, the dimension of network for ecological survival; and third, the dimension of bureaucracy that observes and is adaptive to agricultural and fishing business.

[6] Robert Bates. *Markets and States in Tropical Africa: The Political Basis of Agricultural Politics* (Berkeley: University of California Press, 1981).

[7] Neil Coles and Philip Hall. *"Water, Energy and Food Security"* (Perth: Centre of Excellence for Ecohydrology, The University of Western Australia, 2012).

[8] Maya Kneafsey et al. "Consumers and Food Security: Uncertain or Empowered?" *Journal of Rural Studies*, vol. 29, 2013, pp. 101-112.

The Dimension of Agricultural and Fishing Business

Over the years it becomes clear that there has been mismatch of approach done by farmers and communities and those by governments. Farmers, fishermen and communities are still operating in the framework of producing crops in 'traditional' way, i.e. boosting yields primarily for the sufficiency of self or limited community; while the agreements made at regional and international level assumes that farmers are no longer producing in that traditional way.

Almost everything that farmers and fishermen and rural communities do, in practice, depends on their own interpretation of government policies. Many government programs do not reach the real need of farmers and fishermen anyway. So they learn to adjust to their habits of traditional life where income is limited and room for manoeuvre are limited. All the while, talks on food security, especially those coming from the developed world, focus on sustainable development standard, on safety-labelling and standards of production, which assumes a level of agricultural practices that are modern and easy to adjust depending on the needs of agricultural business.

The reality between traditional agriculture and agricultural business is totally different. Farmers in most parts in Southeast Asia are still using traditional tools, hiring family members and people based on call-bases, their pest eradication is self-help, and so are their marketing, storage and delivery. Most of them do not plan based on what the nations need but more on what they can (or know how to) plant. Therefore once the nation complaints about not having enough supply, there is no other way but hunting for imports from other countries. In the words of a senior member of Indonesia's Chamber of Commerce: "businesses (in Indonesia) are discouraged because they find difficulties in getting supplies for the production of food products…for instance those doing business in making fruit lunkhead or fruit compote must pay very expensive price to ensure continuous supply of raw materials. If one pays for 10 fruits, they should be able to use 10 fruits for the production, but this is not the case yet in Indonesia…".

The way to go, in the minds of businesses, is simply to ensure continuous supply of raw materials, wherever it comes from, including from imports. However imports create a different problem of food insecurity, e.g. local agricultural products often became wasted or sold at very low price because their quality of storage and harvesting is not as good as those coming from other countries. Farmers experience income loss, which creates food insecurity for farmers.

When the government decides to impose import quota to immediately fix the problem for farmers, consumers and farmers are often at disadvantageous position (again) because import quota involves deals made by bureaucrats and the importing companies, namely to settle on what number of quota would be allowed at certain point in time. Such quota may create price hike if the supply is not enough for domestic consumption and if importers are building cartels. This is high risk; after all, farmers with traditional means of production cannot be truly predicted to meet the national target of supply because many things are beyond their ability to control the output of production. Thus, the likelihood of price hike is more likely than not. Worse, of course, is that bureaucrats and importers may create lucrative collusion that would further pressure farmers and consumers.

The Executive Director of PhilMech (Philippine Center for Postharvest Development and Mechanisation disclosed that to date Philippines has one of the lowest rates of mechanical equipment use in Southeast Asia – at half a horsepower (0.5 hp) per hectare, which is equal to the power of a small electric fan. Reading his comparison, it is actually said that other agricultural countries in the region such as Vietnam and Thailand are not so impressive either, only at 0.7 hp per hectare, compared with the fully industrialised Japan that utilises 7 hp per hectare or South Korea at 4 hp per hectare.

This lack of mechanisation is induced by several factors, including the lack of financial capital to buy machines, lack of knowledge on modern treatment of crops, lack of land size that would fit with the price of buying machineries, and some farmers do not want their family members or friends to lose jobs. One must remember that farmers live in communities where everyone knows everybody else, and they sustain living because of good cooperation within the community.

Statistics across the region show that the sector with the largest employment is agriculture, and if there should be employment efficiency in the sector, one must be careful not to create unemployment simply because farmers cannot find jobs in other sectors. When a government decides that farmers must invest in planting different crops, a mechanism to minimize the risk during the transition period (until the new plants can be harvested) must be provided. Otherwise, the risk would be too high for farmers. All of these impose farmers to do 'business as usual'. Farmers are by nature risk-averse.

However, it would be unfair to underestimate the skills in which farmers are capable. Their habit of living by subsistence could be a tool for them to think of ways of surviving mechanisation in their fields. Of course they must be provided with other tools, which is to upgrade their capacity in growing in more sophisticated ways. They can learn gradually on how to grow plants without land (e.g. aeroponics) or diversify to some level of food processing industry.

However, all of the above is impossible if nothing is changed in terms of skills and capital for farmers. Capital for farmers is indeed very limited, if not scarce. Most commercial banks do not provide credits from farmers. Such limit of capital is debilitating farmers. In Indonesia, for instance, many hectares of palm oil trees, coconut trees and tea are very old. Old trees are low in productivity and quality. But replanting needs capital, including during the transition until the new plants can be harvested. The majority of coconut trees and palm oil, for instance in Indonesia, are produced by small holder farmers.

Of course, talking about food security, one must also remember the sector of fisheries. There are two important maritime countries in ASEAN: Indonesia and Philippines. Unfortunately, the livelihood of fishermen is still mostly poor. They rely on whether to go fishing, and cannot do much if consumers decide not to buy their catch. Most fishing boats are still traditional, without decent refrigerators or sophisticated storage cabin. Foreign investors disclosed in a meeting organised by an embassy and Indonesia's Chamber of Commerce that they regret the high cost of developing logistical systems when they want to operate fishing industry. Not only the systems are not in place, the electricity access to parts of fishing spots is absent.

In short, farmers and fishermen have very limited (or no) instruments to acquire food for themselves and the nation. Even if they work together at the community level, they won't have much impact on the national level because they still do things in traditional way. Their contact or network with one another is also traditional, just by residency or familial ties. Food security today needs modern farming and fishing. This is a must rather than an option for today's economy. Modern farming and fishing needs:

- Modern machineries.
- Technology knowhow to fix and create machineries.
- Marketing knowhow to create attractive and suitable wrapping that induce selling, protect food and prolong storage.
- Sharing information on various methods in production or catch and why they are done in certain ways.
- New-frontier research and development, including creating new variety of crops that can grow in unfriendly soil (e.g. in flooded soil, or very dry soil), to create new kind of processed fish, and to do farming that are friendly to earth.

- Patent right that would induce innovation.
- Risk protection so that farmers and fishermen dare to bear the risk of replanting or innovation, including keeping their jobs.

It can be seen that in most places, agriculture and fishing businesses are still done in traditional way. Many businesses and entrepreneurs in agriculture and fishing are not members of any employers association. They operate as micro and small companies, thus inefficient and hard to mobilise in collective action.

The Dimension of Network for Ecological Survival

Food security requires various stakeholders to work together as a community. Community building is part of the identity of ASEAN country members. Many solutions and initiatives for national management and policies start with and are supported by communities.

Unfortunately, community development is often discouraged when policies on price of food or funding for business fail to give attention to the formation of a community. For instance import as a means to meet domestic demand. If import is done without any work being done to the community of producers and businesses, it would result in deterioration of production in the longer runs. Producers may lose incentive to grow, because obviously growing requires more time and money than buying from abroad, but by buying alone, the local producers would experience food insecurity. Also, when business and entrepreneurs receive funding to grow their business up, what means are in place to ensure that they are working to build the community of reliable producers?

The employers' associations should be more active in monitoring areas of production, and entice all business owners and entrepreneurs to be their members. Membership may be voluntary but efforts must be done more persistently to entice newcomers to join the association. When the employers association is more active in monitoring business activities, it should be more effective than if the government is doing the monitoring. After all, businesses need to know and engage all producers in the sector in order to secure supply for their production.

In addition, the cost of doing business in agriculture and fishing industry can only be controlled if businesses and entrepreneurs, along with farmers and fishermen, are minimising damage to the environment. So, when the government set up a plan to develop certain infrastructure project that would destroy ecological balance or give up a piece of land by the river for property business, the network of business, entrepreneurs, farmers and fishermen, should come forward to pressure the government to do otherwise.

In this dimension, food security is the output of a productive and communicative network among producers. As the people who know what means would work best for the plants and fish, the producers must voice their concerns and demands to the government officials at all levels. Certainly they may need help from media professionals, civil society activists and academics.

The Dimension of Policymakers that Observes and is Adaptive to Agricultural and Fishing Business

The last, and certainly not the least dimension of food security is the policymaker that observes and is adaptive to agricultural and fishing business. Policymakers cannot always keep up with the needs of producers and consumers, but they must know that their main job is to secure livelihood for the people. As quoted by Simon Maxwell[9], Amartya Sen[10] mentioned about the need for objective entitlement when it comes to providing food for the people. This means that they must focus on designing policies that caters to the need of as many people as possible (or creating the least evil for most constituents) and is flexible enough for sudden force-majeure.

Capturing the suggestion from Simon Maxwell (1996), the perspective and approach to food security in modern world should be post-modern, rather than modern, in the sense of the following:

[9] Simon Maxwell. "Food Security a Post-Modern Perspective," *Food Policy*, vol. 21, no. 2, 1996, pp. 155-170.
[10] Amartya Sen. *Poverty and Famines: An Essay on Entitlement and Deprivation* (Oxford: Clarendon Press, 1981).

	Modern	**Post-modern**
Underlying reality	Simple, uniform	Complex, diverse
Objectives	Growth Pre-occupation with macro	Development Pre-occupation with micro
Research Approach	Measure Survey Reductionist Deduction Abstract models Aggregate	Listen Participatory Rural Appraisal Holistic Induction Complex reality Disaggregate
Planning Approach	Plan Model Top-down Centralize	Enable Interact Bottom-up De-centralize
Implementation	Blue-print Role culture Standardisation	Process Task culture Flexibility, innovation

Source: Simon Maxwell (1996, p. 161).[11]

One cannot expect to create a single overarching policy that one can copy paste from one place to another. The challenge in food security is complex and diverse across places, not only because of the objective conditions, but also because of the subjective ones. The farmers, fishermen, the communities where they are embedded, also the businesses and entrepreneurs have different habits to adjust. Research must be done in more participatory way, holistic, and by accommodating the complex reality. The governments must plan policies that are enabling, allowing interaction between stakeholders, where decisions on what policy to apply could be decentralized but the principles on what to protect are firm. Monitoring of implementation is also critical, which has been missing in the past.

[11] Simon Maxwell. "Food Security a Post-Modern Perspective," *Food Policy*, vol. 21, no. 2, 1996, pp. 155-170.

Bridging Collective Actions in India and ASEAN

There is a saying that 'a dream is an answer to a question we haven't yet learned how to ask'. In Asia, be it in ASEAN and within the framework of cooperation of India and ASEAN, the dream is to create a community of peace, equality and prosperity. Countries understand well, at least the leaders who sign the framework of cooperation, the worst risk of working individually in the world where challenges are massive and emerge out of new levels of interactions among countries. Without a shared sense of community, people would fight alone, using any tools at hand, creating chaos and desperation to those without sufficient means to fight back.

It is well known that economic integration among countries is inevitable; it is also known that it is creating much anxiety due to the new level of vulnerabilities that people at individual levels must face. One may be tempted to classify the opposition to greater economic integration in the region in the boxes of 'unskilled labour', 'non-competitive sector', 'the camp of anti-liberal market', or 'the pessimists', but it has been learnt earlier that often times, the reason for scepticism is quite practical, thus needing immediate action from policymakers.

The recommendations for India-ASEAN Strategic Partnership to ensure food security in the countries should consider the following elements of success for the partnership:

a) Good Input to the partnership.

b) Neat Process, easy to understand by people in member countries.

c) Responsible monitoring and evaluation.

The good input would rest primarily on the responsibility of all member countries at the domestic level. The partnership may assist in:

a) Campaigning awareness of the approach chosen by ASEAN and India to achieve food security to stakeholders.

b) Engage civil society and academics to broaden the awareness to stakeholders.

c) Develop joint research and development activities to support the creation of new seeds for crops or varieties that can withstand current climate change challenge, identify varieties of modern growing and catching methods suitable for different contexts.

d) Share with farmers and fishermen, through networking with entrepreneurs, civil society and academics, the technology knowhow and business management of modern agriculture and fishing.

e) Improve access to modern machineries.

f) Share with farmers and fishermen the possibilities to reduce risks while introducing modern practices.

It is a good option to develop a website, managed collectively by agreed partners (e.g. among academics in cooperation with certain ministries), where any progress and new tools for better achievement of food security would be easily found by entrepreneurs, business, farmers, fishermen and civil society activists. A regular series of dialogue should be done across the region to enrich and update the website. The Ministry of Foreign Affairs of India and the ASEAN Secretariat could respond to the updates through SOMs or Track 1.5 diplomacy forums. Civil society, entrepreneurs and employers associations should disseminate the information in the vision of building communities free of food insecurity.

Conclusion

The issue of food security must be approached in different ways, accommodating the habits of farmers, fishermen, businesses and entrepreneurs through policies that are flexible and bridging the existing gaps. The big gap today is how farming and fishing are done, how the governments set targets, and how businesses recommend immediate solutions. Farming and fishing are done in traditional ways, with limited access to skill development and capital, where farmers and fishermen are risk averse but the challenges are getting more complex, beyond what they learnt from their predecessors on how to cope. Meanwhile, businesses simply want fast and sustained supply. Governments care more about catering to business and consumer need (at least that's what they think they are doing), so they do more deals on imports and quotas, which in reality do not solve any problems of food security. Instead, they have proven to create food insecurity problems for farmers and fishermen.

What is critical is governments' willingness to manage the limited resources and to provide instruments to various stakeholders to acquire food and to work together as a community to acquire food. It is nearly impossible that any single government can create an overarching policy for all. The approach should be to 'hands on tools and instruments to stakeholders'. With this, it is imperative that producers (growers, catchers, entrepreneurs and businesses working with them) must change their mindset, from individuals and small-segments of communities to bigger communities with important role in food security chain.

Part III
Future of Global Energy Market: Role of New and Renewable Energy in Sustainable Development

Mr. Harish Hande
Mr. Gautam Vivek
Mr. R. Ravindran

Chapter 8

Energy Security: Sustainable Energy Solutions for the Poor through an Integrated Approach

Harish Hande

Securing a country's energy supply especially for a developing country like India is vital considering the population and the related growth challenges. Rising GDP brings along with it scores of questions regarding social and environment sustainability.

There is a high correlation between economic growth and high-energy consumption. This trend is validated even in India's growth story of 77 per cent, which also coincided with a 60 per cent increase in electricity consumption.[1] Thus it is imperative for India to prioritise sustainable development. India has still long way to go as the recent blackouts[2] which crippled over 600 million residents in North India, have shown, which happened because of pressure placed on conventional power infrastructure and further compounded by politics and mismanagement.

Within the contexts of unstable energy security and unchecked global warming, steps are already being taken by governments including India to diversify supply, increase domestic capacity, tap into local energy sources and reduce demand in an effort to manage an impending energy security crisis. While these high level efforts are appreciated, much of the debate has been focused on centralized solutions, grid interactive technology, large power plants that would

[1] Khandher et al. *Energy Poverty in Rural and Urban India. Are the Energy Poor also Income Poor?* Policy Research Working Paper, 2010.

[2] http://www.nytimes.com/2012/08/02/world/asia/power-restored-after-india-blackout.html?pagewanted=all&_r=0.

supplement ongoing grid extension programmes or erratic power supplies. The poor are often neglected as low-income consumers who are not financially viable (or with attractive returns) to warrant significant investments. These constitute over 400 million who currently have no access to basic energy requirements.

Recent estimates[3] by the Government of India show that fuel and electricity expenditures by the urban and rural poor as the third highest expenditure after food and health. Despite these revelations, many of us still find it difficult to imagine that lack of energy perpetuates the cycle of poverty. The common notion is that renewable energy is expensive and thus to provide the poor with immediate access to energy, nuclear and coal are the only options. This is an extremely naive thought process and these solutions thereby are financially and socially unsustainable.

This chapter highlights the importance of thinking in terms of sustainable energy solutions that link energy security, reliable energy supply and the poor in India and steps that can be taken to speed up the process of implementing these solutions.

India is a country of paradoxes, with a mixture of a highly developed world (second fastest growing economy in the world) and underdeveloped (more than 400 million people living below the poverty line). The poor are not a homogeneous segment and thus many of the standardised methods of providing them with energy services will not be sustainable in the long run. Energy is a critical prerequisite to development but it does not imply that development will follow. For economic benefits to flow, reliable energy solutions need to be integrated into a broader development plan that gives importance to sectors such as water, health, education, livelihoods and so on. The sources of energy used and the manner in which energy services are produced and consumed, are of crucial importance for sustainable development and, in particular, to the poor.

Studies[4] have validated the high cost the poor households spend as a percentage of their incomes on energy, and most of the time it is higher than the rich classes. Estimates range from 5 per cent up to 20 per cent of cash income or expenditure. By being forced to spend a significant portion of their incomes on energy, that too, inadequate rustic forms of energy, households and businesses are deprived of other basic goods and services needed to

[3] Level and Pattern of consumption expenditure, 2009-10, NSSO 66th Round.

[4] "Productive Uses of Energy for Rural Development". *Energy and Environment Review.* Co-author with Anil Caabral and Sachin Agarwal. 2005. Also see Hammond et al. *The Next 4 Billion: Market Size and Business Strategy at the Base of the Pyramid.* 2007.

sustain a decent quality of life. These studies indicate that in the absence of reliable energy supply, people spiral deeper into poverty and in turn the socio-economic ladder. For instance,

a) Education: lack of lighting stymies the ability of children to study at home or in schools and consequently lift themselves out of poverty.

b) Livelihoods: stifles productivity if engaged in household businesses.

c) Health: polluting effects of open fires for cooking leads to impaired health due to respiratory congestions as a result of chronic exposure to these fumes.

d) Water: inability to pump water for irrigation or even daily use.

e) ICT: archaic communication technologies that effect efficiencies in business, schools and daily lives.

f) Skilled seamstresses cannot upgrade their manual sewing machines to electric machines with higher efficiencies.

g) Silk weavers use machines with interrupted power supply leading to lower productivity, consequently higher electricity bills (because of inefficient motors) eat into incomes.

The result is very evident – large numbers have remained poor with no avenues to increase their income and quality of life due to lack of access to reliable energy and the cost of delaying the solutions of reliable energy to poverty alleviation although enormous, is often neglected.

Any plan which continues to perpetuate the centralized model of power distribution will surely run into the similar challenges pervading the conventional grid systems. Renewable energy technologies are well-suited to meet India's need for power in remote areas that lack grid and road infrastructure due to the distributed nature of resources and the scalability of system design. Decentralized energy systems close to the point of final use which reduce grid loads and energy losses in distribution should be encouraged to develop. Building up clusters of renewable micro grids, especially for people living in remote areas, will be a central tool in assuring sustainable energy.

However, what is most often heard are statements like: 'Solar energy and other renewable energy sources are expensive'. This statement is valid in comparison to a highly reliable grid, which in itself is heavily subsidized. The statement ceases to apply when we widen the segment to include households that are still unconnected to the grid.

Today, kerosene fuel for lighting is a reality in most un-electrified households. But Kerosene is by no means economical for the poor. For example, each household in the state of Karnataka, India, uses approximately 5 to 7 litres of kerosene per month on lighting. While the first 2 litres are available at a subsidized price (when purchased through the Public Distribution System), the remaining quantity is bought in the market at nearly $1 per litre. Today, nearly all households in rural India own a mobile phone. The lack of electricity connection forces them to charge their mobile phones at 10 cents per charge at the nearest electrified town. Not considering the cost of travelling to and fro, charging mobile phones costs the household a little more than US$1 per month. Consequently, they are forced to spend between US$ 3 and US$ 4 a month on lighting via kerosene – a significant part of their monthly income.

It is worth comparing this to the cost of availing a solar energy system (with a mobile phone charging unit as an add-on) through a bank loan. A basic single-light solar home lighting system costs approximately US$ 160. A bank loan for a similar amount at market rate of interest (12 per cent) over a 5 year period works out to US$ 3.5 per month. An instalment-based payment is in line with the cash flows of the rural household and overcome the burden of putting down a large one-time cost for the solar system.

Contrary to what is commonly believed, the problem is not with the availability of technology. Rather, the difficulty lies in providing energy access through practical, feasible and affordable mechanisms, which are often the missing gaps in technology dissemination and utilisation. A number of solutions and models of business, for the problems mentioned above, already exist in some of the more advanced developing countries like India. They need to be scaled up and replicated.

A recent report[5] in India by Greenpeace showcases the diversity of renewable energy solution tailored to fit the local needs and conditions. The solutions range from waste products like rice husk, grid interactive photovoltaic technology, stand alone solar systems, pico hydro plants in remote locations in order to satisfy a variety of daily energy needs such as cooking, lighting, livelihoods and all this within a diversity of contexts that vary by geography, governance and economic models.

The lessons from the report underline a fact that the poor are not a monolithic structure. Many of the successful models cannot be replicated in total. However, most processes of these successful models can be replicated with certain

[5] Taking Charge. Case studies of decentralized renewable energy projects in India. Greenpeace, 2010.

variations depending on the culture and financial behaviour, etc. Before we jump into replication of processes or models, the eco-systems need to be in place that promotes an integrated energy approach and development angle for the poor. Following are some pathways to consider when developing such an approach:

a) Financial Inclusion: This is a two-fold process involving consumer financing that enhances affordability and purchasing power in line with cash flows and also building capacities within local financial institutions to develop energy portfolios that encourage the dissemination of these solutions. The latter can be through capacity building initiatives, RBI norms such as priority sector lending, easier transaction processes for small quantum loans, etc.

b) Developing locally available energy sources: Rather than promote one type of technology irrespective of its viability, efforts need to be made to develop locally available energy sources and in turn the infrastructure needed to make it viable.

c) Cross sectoral collaboration: Integrate sustainable energy into various pro-poor development programmes in order to provide holistic solutions like powering up digital education tools, equipment for hospitals, safe and clean drinking water and so on.

d) Consultative Policy Process: Improving renewable energy access for rural and underserved communities is an arduous task requiring supportive Government policies. Unfortunately, a number of policies in this sector in India have failed to appreciate ground-level realities and practitioner perspectives. As a result, they have not benefitted the end users and have instead become barriers in the way of enterprises providing energy solutions. Proactive efforts are required to engage various stakeholders to adequately address shortfalls in policy and provide corrective policy measures early, especially in a nascent renewable energy field.

e) Human Resources: The need for skilled human resources in the sector is large and has not been fully addressed. In general, attention needs to be paid in developing human resources at all organisational levels of renewable energy enterprises - operations, sales and marketing, finance, servicing and community involvement. Renewable energy deployment programmes should capitalise on the existing Industrial Training Institutes (ITIs) in the country to increase the capacity of local people to handle technologies on the ground. The emphasis on long-term functioning and sustainability of energy access should take due note of the appropriate manpower requirements at the local level.

f) Promotion of models that tap into decentralized services: At present there are very few incentives encouraging locally brewed models that are attempting to develop market driven forces to address social barriers.

This is by no means a complete list but it does highlight the non-technical aspects that need to be taken into consideration when applying energy (renewable or otherwise) solutions for the poor. Other factors such as politics, urban area favouritism, cultural and demographics are inhibitors in energy development that widen the 'haves' and 'have-nots'.

Worldwide the current reliance on grid extension or large-scale centralized solutions will leave more than one billion people living without access to modern energy services by 2030 according to the International Energy Agency (IEA). The IEA has found that half of all energy services will have to be provided by off-grid clean energy investments in order to deliver universal energy access by 2030.[6] This does not mean that in one sweep renewable energy will solve the energy crisis; rather we have to be mindful that an organic transition needs to take place which takes an integrated approach with a mix of grid extension, grid interactive and off-grid systems to meet the energy requirements of the poor keeping in mind existing practices and contexts.

It is important to note that providing power to the people is not about technology, finance or markets, or even energy. It is about enabling marginalized groups of people to gain access to what most of us see as our rightful entitlement – to make choices that enable us to improve our lives, and the lives of our families. Until this becomes the true core upon which we build all programmes and policies, providing energy solutions – renewable or not – will remain a formidable challenge, relegated to constant dialogue and nothing much.

[6] World Energy Outlook. IEA 2010.

Chapter 9

The Conceptual Framework for Sustainable Energy and World Energy Council

Gautam Vivek

World Energy Council (WEC) works for sustainable supply and use of energy. To understand the sustainability, WEC has developed a model called a conceptual framework for sustainable energy thinking called Energy Trilemma. The trilemma is represented by a triangle and three aspects of sustainability. One is the energy security which is assuring the fuel supplies with due respect to the environment. The second is the environmental impact mitigation. All of us are very familiar with GHG emissions but there are other aspects of environmental impact mitigations, which will not be elaborated here because that itself is a large issue. Third is the social equity where merely securing the energy security for the country does not necessarily translate into energy security for poor.

When dealing with energy security one needs to look at the diversity of energy basket. In 1973, just after the oil crisis, in the energy basket, 46 per cent of the energy came from oil, about 25 per cent from coal, 16 per cent from gas and the balance were from the conventional biomass and hydro and a small fraction was provided by the renewable at that point of time. The global energy requirement was 6,000 million tons of oil equivalents. By 2010 the demand just doubled but the share of coal remained constant. It gets about 27 per cent of the primary energy requirements. The oil shrunk to 32 per cent which was supplemented by the increased use of natural gases and there was a accent on nuclear and 6 per cent of nuclear energy comes from nuclear generation.

The second aspect is the environmental impact mitigation and GHG emissions. Because of the shrinkage in oil usage, the contribution of CO_2 emission shrunk to about less than 40 per cent. At this point of time coal is contributing almost 43 per cent of the GHG emissions and that's why the label of dirty fuel. About 20 per cent is being provided by gas. The emissions also have almost doubled and because of the efficiency, they are less than double. There is about 30,000 million tons of carbon dioxide emission every year.

The third aspect is the energy access which is of some consequence. In fact it was found that poverty and energy access has a correlation. If they provide energy access to poor, there are 1.3 billion people around the world who do not have access to modern form of energy and about 2.7 billion people are without the clean cooking facilities that bring it to our area where 95 per cent of these people are concentrated in the Sub-Saharan Africa and in the developing Asia. In India these figures are between 400 million to 500 million and 84 per cent of these live in rural areas. The present investment in the energy access is about US$ 9 billion. One of the estimates is that if they really want to have energy access by 2030, they need to step it by about five times. So in this period they will require about a trillion of investment and there are barriers that have to be overcome in terms of investment. The privatisation in this sector being done very well in India but there is still a long way to go before moving towards sustainability in this area.

This is the present scenario, and it also gives a quick peek into the future. Based on the data from the International Energy Agency, the WEC created four scenarios. The timeframe for these scenarios is 2035. One is the current policy scenario which means business as usual scenario. The second one is the new policy scenario where the new policies which are emerging are assumed to be policies that are going to be implemented even though there may not be a clear cut plan for it. Finally, there is a wish list scenario which does not seem very feasible. This is called 450 scenarios, where the global temperatures are excepted to go up to 2 degrees. In the current scheme of things that is considered as a sustainable increase.

However, that does not seem achievable and to show at this point of time what would be the concentration of carbon dioxide in atmosphere will be 450 compared to little less than 400 as of now, and then there is an efficient world scenario. This is just a window that the humanity has if they make all the right investment in efficient use of energy which are viable, a 5-year window, so the steps that need to taken probably gets a breather for 5 years.

The renewables are going to play a very important role, however, how much and in what time frame, is something that is a conjuncture at this stage. The gas continues to provide about 22-24 per cent of the energy. In the current policy scenario the oil shrinks and the usage of coal increases. It is predicted that there will be about 21 per cent increase in coal usage. Because of the Fukushima disaster there is going to be slow down in nuclear energy usage as per the current policy scenario.

The renewables still do not find a major role. However, in the new policy scenario the biofuels and waste are providing about 11 per cent and there is a slowdown in nuclear energy because of the political consequences. However, eventually the nuclear will be stepped up because we do not have much lee-way. Then there is the 450 scenario where apart from the fact that the renewables have gone up to 15 per cent, there is a huge cut on the coal consumption bringing down to 16 per cent. In fact one equation which is very important is that the coal is twice as dirty as natural gases. So the use of natural gas is considered friendly in that context.

If we look at the climate change mitigation in the current scenario, by 2035 the emissions are going to touch a dangerous level of 44 gigatons. In the new policy scenario where the implementation of whatever measures they are taking it will go up to about 37 and this would result in instead of 2 degrees temperature variation, it will be about 3.6 and these are probabilistic models. These cannot be predicted with accuracy but there will be a high probability that the temperatures by 2050 would be about 3.6 degrees higher. Then the ideal scenarios, the 450 scenario where if the strong measures are taken such as retiring the coal stations, it will by 2020 to 31.4 and going down to about 22 gigatons per year. The energy supplies constitute about 25.9 per cent of the total global pollution and therefore it becomes very important to have focus on this.

Transport sector is another challenge. We cannot talk about the global energy market without talking about the recent changes, particularly the shale gas boom in the US. In fact 2000 shale gas provided only 1 per cent of the natural gas production. It's now 20 per cent and the prediction is that by 2020 the US will become self-sufficient. By 2030 they will become exporter and that will have huge consequences on global energy market. By 2035 the total contribution of natural gas would be about 46 per cent. But the important thing to note is that the shale gas has a potential to divert investment from fossil fuels and renewables.

The United Nations intervention in the year 2012, the international year of sustainable energy for all, which talks about by 2030 ensuring universal energy access to modern energy services, doubling the global rate of improvement in energy efficiency and doubling the share of renewables in the global energy mix. Here they have estimated that they have to make investments to achieve at least the third target. They have to make investments about a trillion dollar in this timeframe. Important thing to note is that when the MDGs were framed that time they did not refer to energy and now they are saying that the energy is that golden thread that runs through all this goals. So now it has become a mainstream agenda.

There is good news for renewable in the current scenario, there is a huge capacity additions and solar PV for instance is growing almost at 50 per cent rate. The countries have become very active about 118 countries are now in renewables. India along with USA, Germany, Spain and China are taking lead in this area. They can see how the bio-energy use is changing; the biomass which is the traditional biomass is not necessarily energy friendly. It's going down from 60 per cent to 30 per cent and bio-energy, hydro and wind are going to provide important contribution in this kitty. The rate of growth of solar is enormous, however still in a longer timeframe it is going to take a lead but in this time frame these are the three leading energy sources in renewables.

This is India's current scenario. WEC have about 26,000 megawatts of grid connectivity and they are also planning to add another 30,000 megawatts in 12th Plan going over 50,000 megawatt. The renewable is going to have a role both in centralized and decentralized and in fact when they talk about decentralized India essentially they are talking about where the grid cannot reach. But the decentralized generation is now being referred to as a viable model, as a shift from the centralised power generation to a decentralized model.

There are challenges to Renewable Energy (RE) becoming the mainstream. The RE is going to provide anything between 17 and 23 per cent of this thing even that is slightly challenging. So, WEC need technological breakthroughs, they are expecting some disruptive technologies are cost and efficiency for it to come to a grid parity level where the track will be different, the growth will be different. They need standardisation in biomass such that these systems become more rugged and reliable.

One other issue with RE is the fluctuation because RE is not reliable, one cannot have solar all the time and also can't have wind all the time. So these fluctuations are another important aspect. Financing is another issue that needs to be looked at. So, WEC need to have a multi-pronged approach of high-investment energy efficient renewables and clean coal technologies. Nuclear is a question mark at the moment but in a longer timeframe major contribution will come from nuclear. CCS is the bigger question mark now that the shale gas discoveries have been made and US is meeting today 70 per cent of its Kyoto protocol because of these discoveries.

Chapter 10

India-ASEAN Cooperation on Renewable Energy

R. Ravindran

There are multiple factors, ranging from population growth, the structure of the economy, rising fossil fuel prices, enhancing energy security, growing energy demand, greenhouse gas emissions and climate change, improvements in renewable energy technology and cost reduction, rising electricity prices and so on, which have led to the promotion of the use and generation of renewable energy in India and ASEAN countries.

India

India is home to almost one-sixth (approximately 1,210.2 million people, 17.5 per cent) of the world's population. The annual rate of population is increasing by about 1.4 per cent per annum. India's urban population grew from the 290 million in 2001 to 340 million in 2008 and is expected to soar further to 590 million by 2030. The total population of the ASEAN Member States (600 million) is nearly less than half of India's population. There are more than 1.3 billion people in the world today who lack access to electricity and at least 2.7 billion people do not have clean cooking facilities; 289 million people in India do not have access to electricity. Around 160 million do not have access to electricity and rely on traditional biomass for cooking in ASEAN countries.

India registered an economic growth of over 6 per cent in the 1990s and over the last few years it has reached up to 9 per cent. Although economic growth is slowing down due to policy inertia and delayed economic reforms, India is poised to target high economic growth under the 12th Five-year Plan. It has also witnessed changes in the structure of the economy in the post-economic reform era. The Indian economy has shifted away from agriculture to the services sector (contribution of services sector in GDP has been raising. According to Economic Survey of India 2011-12, services sector grew by 9.4 per cent; its share in GDP goes up to 59 per cent in 2011-12). Strong demand for building infrastructure, housing, retail outlets, media and entertainment, and information and communication technologies has gradually been rising. Despite slow down in European Union and the United States, it is forecasted that economic growth in ASEAN countries is expected to remain robust. Average growth rate of 5.5 per cent is forecast for next five years for ASEAN member states.

India's energy requirements are expected to be more than double in the next two decades; by 2030, the country is expected to overtake Japan and Russia and become the third largest global consumer of energy. Oil and natural gas comprised an increasing proportion of consumption, and is projected to account for almost a third by 2030. However with only 0.3 per cent of the world's proven oil reserves and 0.6 per cent of proven gas reserves, domestic supply will not be able to keep up with demand. India has abundant reserves of coal, but the coal has been mined ineffectively, and by 2030 the country is expected to seek almost a third of its coal requirements abroad.

Furthermore, if production grows at 5 per cent annually, India is projected to run out of the currently extractable coal in 45 years. Imports of natural gas and coal are also expected to increase. The growing oil import bill and increasing dependency on imports for coal, oil and gas are creating pressures to increase domestic production and explore alternative sources of energy. It is indeed difficult to predict how oil prices will evolve, but current assessments indicate that they will remain high.

Due to growing population, high economic growth, enhancing energy access, etc., ASEAN's primary energy requirement is set to grow and is projected to triple by 2030 with an annual growth rate of 4 per cent. Therefore, meeting the region's energy needs, which will usher in unprecedented increases in coal use, oil and gas imports and greenhouse gas emissions, will prove to be a challenge.

Energy policy analysts believe that a favourable environment for the generation and promotion of renewable energy is emerging in India and ASEAN countries (in some countries). Growth opportunities in renewable energy have gradually been shifting to the Southeast and South Asia region in recent times. Global investment in renewable power and fuels has also increased by 17 per cent to a new record of US$ 257 billion in 2011. In particular, India displayed the fastest expansion rate for investment of any large renewables market in the world in 2011, with a 62 per cent increase to US$ 12 billion. Both national and international investors have more confidence in the renewable energy sector in the Indian market. With a wider portfolio of customers, a growing manufacturing base and an effective supply chain, the Indian renewable energy sector is an attractive destination for investment. Ernst & Young's 'Renewable Energy Country Attractiveness Indices' of May 2012 rank India as the third most attractive country to invest in renewable energy.

According to the Global Renewable Energy Status Report 2012, renewable energy has grown to supply 16.7 per cent of the global energy consumption. India stands among the top five countries in the world today in terms of renewable energy installed capacity. With over 26 GW installed capacity, India's renewable energy represents about 12.5 per cent of the total installed power generation capacity. India aims to achieve about 55 GW of renewable power by 2017. India's renewable energy programme is primarily private sector driven and offers significant investment and business opportunities, Dr. Abdullah recently said. The minister recently stated that the investment in renewable energy in India has now exceeded US$ 10 billion per year.

ASEAN

ASEAN's energy master plan which is a part of the ASEAN Economic Community Master Plan, is contained in the ASEAN Plan of Action for Energy Co-operation (APAEC), the third series is currently being operationalised for the period 2010–15. The strategic goal on the use of renewable energy (RE) and its technologies under the latest APAEC Plan No. 5 is:

a) To achieve a collective target of 15 per cent for regional RE in the total installed capacity by 2015.

b) To strengthen regional co-operation on the development of RE and alternative energy including hydropower and bio-fuels.

c) To promote the development of centres of research and development on RE in the region.

d) To promote open trade, facilitation and co-operation in the RE sector and related industries as well as the investment in the requisite infrastructure for RE development.

Arising from this, each ASEAN country is to come up with its own renewable energy policy at the national level expecting to achieve the 15 per cent RE target by 2015.

Policy initiatives taken by ASEAN countries vary from country to country. Among the ASEAN countries Philippines has implemented most of the renewable energy policy instruments in interest. There are many steps taken under non-fossil fuel obligations in Philippines, including social cost pricing, diversify the energy mix supporting renewable energy, and priorities in the national list for energy sources, which covers new and/or renewable energy sources and natural gas, etc.

Brunei and Singapore do not have any substantial specific policy on renewable energy yet. Brunei is a country rich in oil and natural gas reserves. Thus, renewable energy is not yet given substantial importance. On the other hand, Singapore does not have any economically viable renewable energy sources and the requirement in introducing new renewable energy sources are at minimum level since Singapore's installed capacity is much higher than the peak demand.

Renewable energy market is less developed in ASEAN countries in comparison to India and European Union. ASEAN Member States do not figure low in the Ernst & Young's 'Renewable Energy Country Attractiveness Indices'. Inadequate funding, lack of experience and knowledge, high cost and limited policy frameworks are the major barrier in the ASEAN countries. ASEAN countries also need to legislate robust policies and institutional framework for making renewable energy market more attractive.

Opportunities for India-ASEAN Renewable Energy Cooperation

Energy security was an important agenda item of Indian foreign policy in the 1990s. The acceleration of India's economic growth rates after the 1991 economic reforms launched a new debate on energy-related issues in India's national security discourse. Energy security is deemed to be an essential component of national security and it has been mainstreamed into India's foreign policy agenda. India has made investments in hydrocarbon fields around the world on a national priority basis and has been exploring and signing agreements with developed nations with a view to diversifying their energy basket, including by making investments in renewable energy and clean technologies.

The Ministry of External Affairs has established an energy security division, entrusted with maintaining close coordination with relevant ministries and supporting 'their international engagement through appropriate diplomatic interventions.' Increasing reliance on renewable sources and promoting energy is one of the main planks of India's energy security strategy. Access to technology for clean energy and exploiting non-conventional sources of energy and investment have become necessary elements of India's economic diplomacy.

Strengthening energy security is also main plank of ASEAN policy. A secure, highly efficient energy interconnected system is the key for realisation of ASEAN Economic Community. ASEAN region is relatively rich in energy resources; some Member States are genuinely self-sufficient. Brunei has quite large reserves for oil and gas. Oil, gas, coal, hydro, geothermal and biomass are available in Indonesia, Vietnam, Malaysia and Thailand. Other Member States have also reserves of oil, gas and hydro. Singapore has no indigenous energy resources, but the country is very important as a major processing centre for oil and petrochemical, and oil bunkers.

India and the ASEAN can cooperate in the areas of solar, wind and biomass energy, small hydro power, energy from waste, bio fuel and clean coal. According to Census 2011, there are 641,000 villages in India; 40 per cent of the country's population is currently denied energy access. Renewables can be used for lighting, heating, cooling, water pumping, cooking and almost any requirement that is presently met by fossil fuels. Under the Solar Mission, it has been proposed to cover 2,000 MW equivalent off-grid power systems by 2022. India has aggressively pursued a policy of harnessing solar power potential.

It has been promoting both grid and decentralized solar power generation. As the national solar mission prioritizes a major expansion in solar energy, business analysts see a huge market potential for processing raw materials for solar cells, large capacity Solar Photo-Voltaic (SPV) modules, film solar cells, SPV roof tiles, inverters, charge controllers, etc. in India. The Ministry of New and Renewable Energy has planned to enhance off-grid production of solar energy, particularly in rural areas.

Renewable Energy sources are abundantly available in most of the member countries of ASEAN. ASEAN countries have huge potential for solar photovoltaic potentials and utilisation. Being in tropical region, all ASEAN countries receive very high daily solar radiation, averaging more than 4.5 kWh/m. Solar photovoltaic technologies are widely used in Indonesia, Thailand, Philippines and Vietnam compared to other ASEAN countries. India and ASEAN Members can cooperate in enhancing energy access in rural areas. Myanmar, Laos, Cambodia and Vietnam where access to energy in rural areas is limited, can cooperate with India for the promotion of decentralized generation of solar energy.

Wind is another sector where immense business opportunities are available and need to be harnessed properly. According to the Confederation of Indian Industries (CII), the Indian wind energy industry is a great success story and the country is ranked fourth worldwide in terms of installed wind capacity and is set to increase its installed capacity figure substantially. Central and state governments have undertaken various policy initiatives to attract investment in the wind sector.

Their policies offer a combination of feed-in tariffs, portfolio standards, subsidized capital and tax incentives to lure investment. Power sector reforms, capital support to renewables, attractive renewable tariffs, domestic equipment and partners, an improved business environment, the establishment of special economic zones and Clean Development Mechanism (CDM) investment have all contributed. India's wind energy sector attracted investments of US$ 4.6 billion in 2011. It is also observed that wind energy sector has a better track record and lower cost, and is relatively less risky.

Some countries in the ASEAN region have good wind power potential. The mountains of central, southern and coastal areas of Vietnam, central Laos, and central and western Thailand are found to be having good to excellent wind resource areas for large-scale wind generation. North and northeast areas of Philippine are also seen as having a good wind potential. Wind measurement, project studies and development are actively undertaken in the Philippines, Vietnam and Thailand. However, the ASEAN countries are lagging in the wind power.

It is estimated that 540 million tons of crop and plantation residues are produced every year, a large portion of which is either wasted or used inefficiently in India. An increasing quantity of rubbish in urban areas caused by rapid urbanisation and industrialisation presents further opportunities.

The national biofuel policy, aimed at facilitating development of indigenous biomass feedstock for production of biofuels, has been approved. It proposes an indicative target of 20 per cent blending of biofuels, both for biodiesel and bioethanol, by 2017. The government had already made 10 per cent ethanol blending with petrol effective from 2008.

ASEAN countries also have a potential for power generation from biomass. The composition of biomass resources in ASEAN vary from one member country to another due to differences in the production structures of agriculture, forestry, livestock and industry. Biomass resource potential is high in Indonesia, Malaysia and Thailand. The biomass resources in ASEAN are mainly from Rice husk, Biogas and Palm Oil waste. There are opportunities for small hydro power projects given India's numerous rivers and their tributaries. India has considerable experience in this field and can certainly undertake similar projects in some of the ASEAN countries.

Energy efficiency is nearly always cost effective in the long run and helps cut emissions and enhances energy security. Energy efficiency must help reduce the energy intensity of the global economy. Application of more stringent performance standards and codes will be necessary, particularly in the buildings and transport sectors. In this regard, information and energy management are proven and effective ways to encourage energy efficiency measures in industry. Economic incentives will be essential to unlock the energy efficiency potential and scale up private finance, but non-economic barriers must also be overcome.

National Mission for Enhanced Energy Efficiency is also relevant here. It has a mandate to adopt a market-based mechanism to enhance cost effectiveness of improvement in energy efficiency in energy-intensive large industries and facilities, accelerating the shift to energy efficiency appliances to make them more affordable, providing energy efficiency financing platform and developing fiscal instruments to promote energy efficiency. The mission aims to save about 23 million tonnes of oil-equivalent of fossil fuels per year by 2014-15, along with an expected avoided electricity capacity in addition of around 19,000 MW; and encouragement of energy efficient building.

All the ASEAN countries except Brunei have implemented decrees and laws supporting energy efficiency programs. Indonesia, Thailand and Philippine have already implemented most of the energy efficiency policy instruments under consideration. Energy efficient fluorescent lamp programmes, street lights programmes and energy efficient ballast programmes are the most common lighting programs implemented. Thailand and Philippines have also implemented high efficient refrigeration and air condition (AC) programmes.

Research and development is necessary for technological and business innovations. India and ASEAN can enhance cooperation in solar, wind and biogas and other areas of new and renewable energy. Expanding cooperation on energy, particularly renewable energy would make India-ASEAN partnership dynamic, robust and people-centric. Both India and ASEAN need energy to spur their economic growth and social development. Cooperation in the areas of renewable energy would provide investment and business opportunities, technology and knowledge sharing and research and development. Two MoUs have been signed between India and ASEAN countries (the Philippines and Thailand) for enhancing cooperation in the field of renewable energy.

India had recently hosted its first ministerial meeting with ASEAN countries to discuss policy and regulatory framework for promotion of renewable energy. The issues relating to financing, research and development, and technology transfer came up for discussion at the meeting. Many of these ASEAN countries have sought cooperation in solar, wind, biomass and small hydro technologies including capacity building from India. This augurs for future co-operation between India and ASEAN in the field of renewable energy.

Part IV
Cooperation between CLMV Countries and North-East India: Opportunities and Challenges

Professor Gautam Barua
Ambassador U. Nyunt Maung Shein
Professor Tan Tai Yong
Mr. Sunand Sharma

Chapter 11

Ways of Cooperation between CLMV Countries and North-East India

Gautam Barua

The North-East region is in a way cursed by geography or may be by politics and in today's Indian economy it is at one end. The entire North-East is connected to the rest of the country by chicken neck of 23 km width, which is connecting Nepal and Bangladesh. Through this bottleneck all the network cables, telephone lines, railway lines, the roads passes and if there are floods, or an earthquake, the entire North-East can be cut off. One road digging in that area results in the entire internet connectivity going off for the entire North-East because of this physical problem there.

Likewise, Myanmar is in a similar situation due to a kind of a wall between India's northeast and Myanmar. So, the obvious thing is to get that wall off and if that can be done, then the markets of either side will open up and it will also become a transit to reach into Laos, Vietnam and Thailand.

In fact Hanoi is closer to Guwahati by air if there was a flight than Delhi. So, Hanoi and Yangon are all closer than Delhi from Guwahati. Yet, there is no flight from any of these places to Guwahati and therefore there needs to be transportation. One way of opening this is to have twice-weekly flight to Mandalay. The Government of India is talking about subsidising air travel in the Northeast because the same economy of scale issues are coming in and not enough private aircrafts are flying and there is this form of compulsion right now which will translate into a subsidy. It will be very easy to expect that to subsidise a twice-weekly flight to Mandalay will help exchange of people.

Today there is flight from Guwahati to Bangkok, courtesy Bhutan Air, and that has made small but significant change. People from Assam are going to Bangkok for holiday which translates small amount of trade. There are goods from Thailand in Guwahati markets and vice versa. And that's how trade moves forward. Therefore, it is important to extend this to Mandalay and the reason for choosing Mandalay and not Yangon is that it would focus on northern Myanmar which is underdeveloped along with upper Assam and other north eastern States. The Stilwell road goes to Kunming, but there are issues with China, which is claiming most of Arunachal Pradesh. But the Stilwell road can be opened to Mandalay, so from India to Mandalay we will have motorable road and there are talks about railway lines through Moreh and Manipur, trans-Southeast Asia to Indian networks.

The Northeast requires alternate outlets. At one time Assam was surplus in oil, but production is down and crude oil is coming in. If there was a separate pipeline to Sitwe, and a separate internet connection from Sitwe port, the entire North-East will benefit and the curse of geography will reduce to some extent. Therefore, from a North-East perspective, there are lots of advantages in opening up and these would require investment by the Government of India for infrastructure. The private industry is not likely to show up in the North-East, which is not a betrayal, but, it is simple economics.

There are also not enough buyers, the market isn't big enough in the Northeast for multinationals and companies to set up factories and there is no way of going out because of the dead end. But Sibsagar, its market can help Northeast India, Myanmar, Laos and Vietnam. Similarly the countries of Southeast region can also export their goods to the Northeast. Today, nearly 80 to 90 per cent of all requirements come in from hinterland India into the Northeast. Part of it can easily be replenished from Myanmar, Laos and Vietnam.

Let us now talk about cooperation in education. We are very keen on having collaborations with institutions in the Southeast Asian region. Already we have some collaboration with universities in Singapore. We are talking with the University of Malaya, Malaysia and IIT Guwahati is also a partner in what's called SAPTRU, South East Asia, South Asia and Taiwan University confederation and through that we have talked to institutions in Indonesia and Vietnam; we have about four or five students from Myanmar currently doing Ph.D. in IIT.

So small beginnings have been made, but there is enormous scope in extending this interaction, in exchange of students among these universities in these countries and it will benefit all. An international student community in any institution is a benefit whether it is located in Guwahati, Vientiane or Hanoi. And we are particularly keen to increase the number of exchange of students. It is going to be easier for students to come and there are a lot of cultural similarities which students would see when they would come.

Chapter 12

Myanmar's Role in Connecting North-East India with ASEAN

Nyunt Maung Shein

Among the CLMV countries, Myanmar is unique in the sense that it is the only country that shares a 1,600 km long border with India. The Northeastern states of Arunachal Pradesh, Nagaland and Manipur are contiguous with Kachin State and Sagaing Region of Myanmar. These Indian states share a border of over 1,400 km with Myanmar. The Northeastern states of India are distant and lie in a remote region far from the rest of India. Access to the India's heartland is a detour around Bangladesh and through the narrow piece of land known as the 'chicken's neck' which lies between Nepal, Bhutan and Bangladesh.

India and the CLMV countries have already established the Mekong-Ganga Cooperation (MGC), a sub-regional forum for cooperation among the six member countries namely, India, Myanmar, Cambodia, Laos, Thailand and Vietnam. Four areas of cooperation have been identified: tourism, culture, education and transportation linkage. This cooperation provides a good foundation for future trade and investment in the sub-region.

In September 2012, the Sixth Ministerial meeting of the MGC was convened in New Delhi and it was decided to expand the areas of cooperation to include health issues and pandemic management. The cooperation between the CLMV countries and the Northeastern states of India can be carried out under this sub-regional arrangement. In the above context, this chapter focuses on the Myanmar's cooperation with India's Northeast frontier states.

Myanmar's Cooperation with the Northeast States of India

As mentioned earlier, Myanmar's geographic location is of immense strategic significance to India. India's strategic interests vis-à-vis Myanmar lie mainly in the following domains:

a) Overall security interest of India with particular emphasis on the Northeastern frontier.

b) Suppression and eradication of the insurgency problem in the remote Northeastern states.

c) Economic development of the Northeastern states turning this region into a commercial hub between Southeast Asia including the CLMV countries, China and India.

d) Access to the sea, i.e. the Bay of Bengal for the landlocked Northeastern states.

e) Source of energy for India from Myanmar's potentially rich natural gas reserves offshore and hydro-electricity.

f) Physical connectivity between India and Southeast Asia.

Myanmar and India have cooperated in these areas for several years but much more needs to be done in order to enhance this cooperation both vertically as well as horizontally. There is a need to expand the cooperation into other sectors such as trade and investment, tourism, culture, people-to-people contact, etc.

Security Cooperation

Myanmar has cooperated with India in the suppression and eradication of the insurgency in the Northeastern frontier of India. Successful joint operations have been mounted in the past against the Naga separatists on the Indian side of the border dealing a heavy blow to the insurgents.

Non-traditional security issues such as drug trade, arms smuggling and extremism/terrorism are other major areas of cooperation between the two countries. Mechanism both at the national as well as the local level have been established under which both sides meet regularly to coordinate cooperation on these matters.

Close cooperation between the two countries to eliminate the nexus between drug trade, arms smuggling and extremism/terrorism was agreed recently at the 18th National level meeting held in New Delhi on December 2012. In addition to the Border Liaison Offices (BLO) established earlier, a third BLO has been opened between Changlang, India and Pangsau, and Myanmar. A fourth BLO will be opened in Nagaland between Ukhul, Manipur, India and Somra, and Myanmar. Cooperation between the law enforcement agencies of Myanmar and India for peace and tranquillity along the border is expected to be further enhanced through the BLOs.

Economic Development

The mainstay of the economy of Northeast India is agriculture. Small scale industry such as plywood factory, sawmills, fruit preservation, etc. exist but their role in the economy does not bear much significance. Myanmar can well serve as a source of consumer goods and daily necessities for the peoples of India's Northeastern states. It will be less time consuming and less expensive to outsource these goods from Myanmar rather than by transporting them from the other parts of India.

In this respect both sides have agreed to establish three border trading posts at Manipur, Mizoram and Nagaland. Two of these are operational now: Moreh, Manipur, India and Tamu Sagaing Region, Myanmar; and at Reid, Mizoram, India and Khampai Reid, Chin State, Myanmar. Goods from other ASEAN countries as well as from China could flow through Myanmar to reach the Northeastern states of India.

As the region is abound rich in natural resources in terms of forests and minerals, India could consider setting up Special Economic Zones in its northeast and invite foreign investment including that of the ASEAN countries. Among the CLMV countries, Vietnam stands as a potential investor whose financial resources and technical expertise could be invested in the northeastern region. Myanmar could possibly be another candidate country for such investment.

Another area of cooperation with the CLMV countries would be in tourism. The northeast offers scenic landscapes where many ethnic groups such as the Bodos, Kukis, Ahoms, Nagas reside. Ecotourism combined with trekking in the villages and outlying areas could provide visitors with an opportunity to enjoy the scenic beauty of the region and also observe and learn about the culture and civilisation of the tribal people. India should promote the region as a tourist destination which undoubtedly will draw visitors from other countries including ASEAN countries. Naturally, India has to initially invest in infrastructure for both the economic zone and the tourism sector. Both these sectors are important for the socio-economic development of the northeast.

Access to the Sea

Access to the sea, i.e. the Bay of Bengal through Myanmar for the land-locked states of Northeastern India will be facilitated when the flagship project undertaken with India's financial and technical assistance is completed by the end of 2016. It is a multi-modal transport project linking Mizoram with Sittwe, the capital of Rakhine state in Myanmar using road and river transport. At Sittwe a deep seaport is being built with India's assistance. This transport network will open up Mizoram and through Mizoram to the other Northeastern states enabling them to export and import goods thus benefiting the northeast's economic development.

Energy Cooperation

Myanmar is endowed with rich deposits of natural gas in its offshore areas. The natural gas is now being extracted from three major offshore areas; two off the coast of Tanintharyi—the Yetagun and Yadanar gas fields and one off the coast of Rakhine state—the Shwe gas fields. Gas is already exported to Thailand from the first two fields while preparations are being made to export the gas from the third field to China. India could benefit from the Shwe gas field's production facility. The possibility of building a pipeline to transport the gas to the state of Mizoram could be examined by both sides.

Another important source of energy is the hydro-electric power which could be generated from the rivers in Myanmar. India has shown strong interest in the construction of a major hydro-electric power station at Tamanthi, an estuary of the Chindwin River in Sagaing region, Myanmar. This power station has a potential of generating up to 1,300 MW of electricity and the electric power could be exported to the hinterlands of Northeastern India where there is a shortage of electricity.

Physical Connectivity between the CLMV Countries and India

At present connectivity between the CLMV countries and India has not been fully developed. There is no direct air connection between the CLMV countries and the Northeastern region of India. Passengers have to transit through Kolkata to reach their destinations in the northeast of India. This is time consuming and cumbersome. Feasibility study could be undertaken whether there is enough traffic to justify direct flights from the CLMV countries to the Northeastern states. In fact, this could become a reality if the northeast states of India could attract investment and tourists from the ASEAN countries.

An important feature of land connectivity is the Trilateral Highway Project initially launched under the auspices of the Mekong-Ganga Cooperation forum and later incorporated into the transport sector of BIMSTEC. This is an ambitious project calling for the construction of 1,360 km of highway estimated to cost around US$ 700 million at the time of initiation. The highway will link Moreh, Manipur, India with Mae Sot, Karnchanaburi, Thailand via Bagan, Myanmar. The trilateral highway will also facilitate connection between India and the Asian Highway Network (AHN) boosting trade between India and ASEAN to reach US$ 100 billion during the five year period of its commission. Furthermore, this project will boost trade potential of India, Myanmar and Thailand currently using the sea route.

India stands to benefit from this highway by the transformation of its Northeastern region to a regional trading hub. A year ago, Ayeyarwady Bridge (Pakkoku) was put into service marking an important milestone towards the realisation of the trilateral highway. This bridge is the longest bridge in Myanmar with rail and road system. A major portion of this highway lies in Myanmar and most of it already built. However, as the condition of the road is not up to international standards, much work needs to be done in upgrading and expanding the existing network.

After the historic visit of the Indian Prime Minister Manmohan Singh to Myanmar in May 2012, the Indian government decided to allocate US$ 500 million for the project so that it could be completed by 2016. In December 2012, a car rally was organized which originated in Indonesia and traversed through Singapore, Malaysia, Thailand, Cambodia, Laos and Myanmar to end in Guwahati, Assam. In effect, the trip took about 16 days from start to finish and tested the conditions of the major portion of the planned trilateral highway which runs through Myanmar. This highway will connect the CLMV countries with the Northeastern states of India via the East-West corridor passing through Thailand and Cambodia to Vietnam and Laos. Recently, India and Myanmar agreed to put a regular bus service between Manipur and Mandalay. This would greatly facilitate people-to-people contact between the two regions.

On the land connectivity, Myanmar railways network enables train service from Kalay in the northwest to Thanbyuzayat in the southeast region. This route passes through Mandalay, Nay Pyi Taw and Yangon. Its length is approximately 1,300 km. The missing links are between Guwahati, Assam, India and Kalay, Myanmar in the northwest while in the southeast between Thanbyuzayat, Myanmar and Nam Tok, Thailand. The entire length of the missing links comes to around 500 km. A feasibility study for the missing link with India has been undertaken but funding remains a major constraint.

As for the missing link with Thailand, the Myanmar Railways have decided that with or without overseas assistance, it will undertake the task using its own resources. This announcement by the Myanmar Railway is encouraging. Upon completion, this spur line will connect the entire Myanmar railways network with that of ASEAN and through it to the planned Singapore-Kunming railway line.

Challenges

There are a number of challenges for implementing projects relating to land connectivity. With a proper synergy between ASEAN and India, these obstacles could be overcome. First and foremost of these is a need for clear and well defined international borders among the countries concerned. Certain portions of the India-Myanmar border remain to be demarcated while the same is true for the Myanmar-Thai border. This point is particularly important because the trilateral highway passes through the border sector where it is not clearly defined.

Next, the prevalence of stability and tranquillity of the borders is critical for some projects. On the Indian side of the border especially in some of the Northeastern states the problem of insurgency still persists. Despite mutual cooperation and firm action in the security sphere, it has not been possible to completely eradicate the problem. A political solution must be found domestically for mitigating the problem. Incentives must be given to these ethnic people in the economic and social spheres so that their living standards could be raised. Such a multi-pronged approach may provide a settlement to the issue. On Myanmar side the present government has achieved peace negotiations with the armed groups. It is now secure and safe to drive through areas which hitherto were under the control of the armed groups.

The third issue that needs to be examined and worked out among the countries concerned is the consistency and uniformity of Customs and Immigration procedures at the borders for smooth and efficient transportation of people and goods. Other related questions such as quarantine, driving license, etc. need also to be addressed.

The most important and formidable challenge is the issue of acquisition of funds for the implementation of the projects. Part of the funds could be sourced from Governments while others could be raised from the private sector if the project is to be carried out on a PPP (Public Private Partnership) basis. Financial assistance could also be sought from international financial institutions such as the ADB and the World Bank. Since the western governments have either lifted or suspended sanctions on Myanmar, it would be possible to explore ways and means of acquiring loans from these banks. Yet another possibility is to secure loans from foreign governments interested in the projects.

Conclusion

The Northeastern Indian states comprise Assam and its six sister states: Meghalaya, Arunachal Pradesh, Nagaland, Manipur, Mizoram and Tripura. The size of these states combined is said to be as big as England and Scotland combined and the population stands at around 40 million people. Therefore its importance in terms of size and population is significant for economic development.

Northeastern states are essentially landlocked and outside of India this region is rarely known and few visitors from abroad visit it since it is not promoted as a tourist destination. Although abundant in natural resources such as forests, bamboos and minerals, economic development in the Northeastern states overall lags behind the other states in India. India should open up the northeast so as to interact with the rest of the world thereby bringing socio-economic development to its inhabitants. In this respect India could consider what China has done to open up and develop its south-western hinterland of Yunnan which also is an essentially landlocked province that used to be poor and lagged behind in the development.

Chapter 13

Connecting CLMV Countries with North-East India: A Comprehensive Approach

Tan Tai Yong

Northeast India occupies a total land area of 262,230 square kilometres (about 8 per cent of India's total area), and has a population of nearly 39 million (less than 4 per cent of the country's population). The combined GDP of the eight constituent states (including Sikkim) in 2011 was US$ 38.6 billion. Linked to the Indian mainland by just a tiny corridor, the region, which shares borders with China, Bhutan, Myanmar and Bangladesh, is one of the most impoverished and least-developed regions in the country. Politically, it is one of the most complex places in the subcontinent, with over 200 ethnic groups packed into a relatively small piece of territory, which for years has been beset with a myriad of separatist insurgencies, communal and ethnic conflicts.

Although the region is endowed with rich natural resources, its economy remains largely underdeveloped because of geographical isolation, political unrest, ineffective governance and poor infrastructure. De-colonisation and the establishment of national boundaries in 1947 broke up an erstwhile trading zone that incorporated northeast India, Southeast Asia and parts of Southern China. Partition led to the loss of a major chunk of physical connection between mainland India and Northeast region and disrupted the land and sea trade connections on which the region had traditionally depended for commerce and trade; following independence the region lost most of its traditional markets in her neighbourhood, particularly to Bangladesh, and commercial activities became impossible because of political boundaries, insurgency and diplomatic tensions. Poor connectivity and the lack of access to markets have thus imposed major constraints on the region's economy.

The Impetus for Connectivity

When the Indian government launched its Look East policy in 1992, it hoped to re-establish the old trading networks by connecting its northeast region with its immediate Southeast Asian neighbourhood. The Indian government has long recognized the need for economic growth as a necessary condition for tackling the political and social problems in the region. However, difficulties in mobilising resources in the region, the cultural remoteness of the area, as well as challenging political and geographical terrains have retarded efforts at economic and other forms of development.

The Look East policy offered a way forward. As it evolved its policy toward its eastern neighbours, India hoped that closer and deeper economic links between Northeast India and Southeast Asia would not only contribute to greater connectivity between India and Southeast Asia, but would also serve as a strategy to advance the economic development of the Northeast region. Here, it is worthwhile to reproduce the strategic thrust of its Northeast Vision 2020 document, which seems to promote a 'Look East through Northeast' strategy:

> *With 96 per cent of the borders of the North Eastern Region constituting international boundaries, and in explicit recognition of the need to break the fetters of the geo-political isolation of the Region, it is necessary to factor in what the Minister of External Affairs has described as 'new inputs' in foreign, defence, internal security and international trade policy. To this end, the immediate priority is to build the required infrastructure right up to the border areas, establishing connectivity and communication links to the cross-border points through which trade and economic exchanges with the countries neighbouring the North Eastern Region are proposed to be promoted under the Look East policy. This priority is to be accorded by all Central agencies concerned and State Governments because while the Look East policy has yielded few returns to the Region thus far…. it is in North East India that South-East Asia begins and, as such, it is for the North East to be enabled to play the arrow-head role in the further evolution of this Policy. This requires a redefining of the Look East policy to resolve outstanding issues of trade, transit and investment with the countries neighbouring the region. It also involves*

promoting Indian investment in infrastructure in partner countries, especially Myanmar, particularly in respect of ports such as Sittwe and international highways to connect the North Eastern Region to ASEAN.

Such investment might also be encouraged where required for transit between the Region and the rest of India, as also for trade with the neighbourhood and beyond.

However, in such a process, we recognize that it is critical to address the challenges of border management, especially with regard to cross border migration, terrorism, drugs and arms supply and other forms of non-conventional security threats for ensuring the rights and traditions of local ethnic groups comprehensively in the context of global forces of change.[1]

The Vision 2020 document highlights three central tenets: the importance of overland trade with Southeast Asia as a fundamental economic strategy for growth in the region; the need to develop infrastructure as a critical condition for trade and investments to happen; and the importance of maintaining political stability and security for development to take place. Thus, while promising to increase the connectivity of the region, the plan envisaged the creation of employment through state investments in infrastructure, encouraging private investment especially in natural resources and agriculture, increasing border trade and promoting tourism in the 'paradise unexplored'.[2]

The infrastructural development would include the construction of huge hydropower dams in order to harness the power potential of the region.[3] Further, there were provisions for 'feel good' initiatives to build people-to-people contact between India and its eastern neighbours such as joint tourism development, trade fairs,[4] direct flights,[5] sporting events[6] and 'cultural exchanges'.[7]

With enhanced connectivity and the opening of trade routes, Northeast India's high potential for exports could be exploited. While major exports from India include textiles, chemicals, engineering goods, gems and jewellery, which together account for more than 60 per cent of export earnings, lines in which the

[1] North Eastern Region Vision 2020 Document. The Vision Statement. pp. vi-vii.
[2] North Eastern Region Vision 2020 Document. pp. 223-225.
[3] North Eastern Region Vision 2020 Document. p. 3.
[4] North Eastern Region Vision 2020 Document. pp. 39 & 80.
[5] North Eastern Region Vision 2020 Document. p. 132.
[6] North Eastern Region Vision 2020 Document. p. 200.
[7] North Eastern Region Vision 2020 Document. p. 204.

Northeast region might participate are likely to be found outside of these four categories.[8] These include the following items as research has shown[9]:

a) Food or fruit processing, bamboo and cane products, floriculture, aromatic plants, aromatic and medicinal herbs, spices, rubber, environmentally sound forest products, natural resource products, tea, etc.

b) The region has a rich heritage of artistic craftsmanship and the handicrafts are almost entirely produced from locally available raw materials. Handloom products are unique and are produced by succeeding generations of weavers. Sericulture and silk production are traditional.

c) Business Process outsourcing (BPO) and IT-related services are good opportunities in some states due to proficient English speaking skills.

d) There is enormous potential for inland and freshwater fishing industry.

e) With its snow-capped mountains, thick forests and scenic lakes, tourism is an almost untapped industry.

While the potential for trade and exports are evident, domestic uncertainties, infrastructure deficiencies and the transaction costs of border trade remains major challenges. There are also concerns among the local population that the opening of the region to market forces could have adverse effects of traditional livelihoods and possibly lead to increased settlement of mainlanders to the region. The preferred approach is therefore one of regulated opening through the involvement and cooperation of the local people.

Status of Connectivity Projects

ASEAN's own view is that India's trade with Cambodia, Laos, Myanmar and Vietnam will serve as an "opportunity to help these newer, less-developed members of the organization catch up and further intra-ASEAN trade and unity".[10] The combined GDP of Cambodia, Lao, Myanmar and

[8] Hans Peter Brunner (ed.) *North East India: Local Economic Development and Global Markets,* (New Delhi: Sage Publications, 2010).

[9] Ibid.

[10] Pavin Chachavalpongpun. 'Look East Meets Look West: India-Southeast Asia Evolving Relations', *FPRC Journal* vol. 8 (Special Issue: India's Look East Policy, 2011).

Vietnam is US$ 196.22 billion and the four countries have a total population of over 173 million. In the connection between Northeast India and CLMV, Thailand with GDP of US$ 346 billion and a population of 67 million, has a critical role. Since the 1990s, a number of initiatives have been launched to enhance the connectivity of the region. These are described in the following paragraphs.

In 1997, with Thailand taking the initiative, India became a founding member of a sub-regional grouping called Bangladesh, India, Myanmar, Sri Lanka and Thailand Economic Cooperation (BIMSTEC) which subsequently changed its name to the Bay of Bengal Initiative for Multi-Sectoral Technical and Economic Cooperation, while retaining its acronym. However, it was only in 2002 that BIMSTEC gained strategic importance "when it coincided with India's change in attitude towards regional trade agreements".[11]

In 2000, India along with Thailand, Cambodia, Laos, Myanmar and Vietnam launched the Mekong-Ganga Cooperation (MGC), with the objective of restoring old religious-cultural ties and to demonstrate a close geographical proximity between them through sub-regional co-operation in tourism, culture, infrastructure and information technology. The priority of infrastructure cooperation included the development of transport links, through road, rail and air, connecting Northeast India with the countries in Southeast Asia, and eventually Northeast Asia.

Physical connectivity between India and Southeast Asia was also pursued through the Trilateral Highway Agreement and the Trans-Asian Railway initiative under the Asian Land Transport Infrastructure Development (ALTID) Project. ALTID, in turn, has been a priority project under the New Delhi Action Plan on Infrastructure Development in Asia and the Pacific (1997-2006).[12]

At a summit, in Phnom Penh in 2002, Mr. Vajpayee brought up the idea of linking New Delhi and Hanoi with a railway line, an idea that was first mooted in 1992 by the Transport Department of United Nations Economic and Social Council for Asia Pacific (UNESCAP). At the time, it was reported that the Indian Home Ministry raised serious objections. It was feared that it could lead to an increase in the smuggling of drugs and arms to militants in India.[13] The idea behind the development of a rail link is that it will boost trade between India and ASEAN substantially and that Cambodia, Laos, Vietnam

[11] See Chak Mun, *India's Strategic Interests in Southeast Asia and Singapore*, p. 75.

[12] Development of the Asian Highway, UNESCAP. http://www.unescap.org/jecf/p06highway.htm.

[13] 'Race with China on Hanoi Train– PM Breathes Life into Plan for Transnational Track' (2012, September 5), *The Telegraph*, http://www.telegraphindia.com/1030905/asp/frontpage/story_2335157.as

and Myanmar — the four newest members of ASEAN, all of whom will be on the rail route — along with Singapore, have been portrayed as being most vocal in pushing India's case for closer ties with ASEAN.

Currently, the rail connectivity among Myanmar, Vietnam, Laos and Cambodia is poor. During Prime Minister Manmohan Singh's visit to Myanmar in May 2012, an agreement was signed to set up a joint committee to explore the possibility of developing rail infrastructure from India, through Myanmar, to Hanoi and other destinations in Southeast Asia.[14] On the Indian side, the infrastructure development needed to focus on the border region.

The work on the Kaladan multi-modal project, linking Mizoram in the Northeast through inland waterway and roads to Sittwe, Myanmar began in 2008 and is due for completion by 2015.[15] Another agreement signed in 2012, as part of the commitment to the Trilateral Highway Project, will see the development of a road link from Moreh in Manipur to Myanmar that will eventually reach Mae Sot in Thailand. The target date of completion for this is 2016.

Northeast India and Myanmar

The economic and political reforms in Myanmar over the last couple of years have given a fillip to the idea of greater connectivity between India and Southeast Asia and the process has gained momentum though not much happened on the ground.

India's imports from Myanmar (US$ 876.13 million in 2010-2011) are dominated by agricultural and forest-based products including beans, pulses, timber and wood products. On the other hand, India's exports (US$ 194.75 million) to Myanmar, though small, are diverse, ranging from primary commodities to manufactured products and is dominated by pharmaceutical products besides iron and steel, electrical machinery, mineral oil, rubber and plastics. [16]

India's investments in Myanmar are focused on a few large state-sponsored infrastructure projects. Indian companies OVL, GAIL and Essar Oil have undertaken

[14] Media Briefing by Foreign Secretary in Nay Pyi Taw on Prime Minister's Ongoing Myanmar Visit. Ministry of External Affairs, Govt. of India. http://www.mea.gov.in/mystart.php?id=190019561.

[15] Prime Minister's address to think-tanks and business community at an event organized by Myanmar Federation of Chambers of Commerce and Industry and the Myanmar Development Resource Institute in Yangon on India and Myanmar: A Partnership for Progress and Regional Development. Ministry of External Affairs, Govt. of India. http://www.mea.gov.in/mystart.php?id=190019561.

[16] India-Myanmar Economic and Commercial Relations, Embassy of India in Myanmar. http://www.indiaembassy.net.mm/index.php?option=com_content&view=article&id=165%3Aeconomic-a-commercial-relations&catid=10%3Aindia-myanmar&Itemid=62&lang=en

five major projects, estimated at US$ 189 million. Jubilant Energy won the contract for the onshore block PSC-I in 2011. In addition to the above, Indian companies like Punj Lloyd, L&T, Apollo Hospitals, Tata Motors, Essar, NHPC, VNL, Jindal Steel, Nipha Exports, etc. are active in Myanmar in various sectors.[17]

Although trade in traditional goods on head-load basis has been the customary practice for a long time, the Border Trade Agreement signed in 1994 gave it a legal framework. The Moreh-Tamu point in the Manipur sector was operationalised in April 1995 and a second border trade point at Champhai-Rhi in the Mizoram sector was opened in 2004. There are plans to open a third border trade point at Avakhung-Pansat/Somrai. India has also proposed to build a 45-hectare Integrated Customs Station at Moreh.

India and Myanmar have agreed to upgrade the status of Border Trade to Normal trade and have expanded the tradable list items from 18 to 40 since 2008. With an estimated border trade of US$ 12.8 million (2010-11), major items bought by Myanmar traders from the Indian side are cotton yarn, auto parts, soya bean meal and pharmaceuticals (there are reported smuggling of items like fertilizers and vehicles, especially two wheelers, etc.); betel nut, dried ginger, green mung beans, black matpe, turmeric roots, resin and medicinal herbs.[18]

According to the Myanmar Department of Border Trade, the border trade turnover between India and Myanmar has ranged from US$ 10 million to US$ 22 million, though it is probably higher if informal arrangements are taken into account.

In 2004, India and Myanmar signed an agreement to construct the Tamanthi Dam Hydro project in the Chindwin River in West Myanmar, east of Nagaland. India had to bear the cost of this project and 80 per cent of the electricity produced from the Dam is to be used by India and the rest will be used in Monywa Copper Mine, Sagaing Division (Myanmar). After much delay, work commenced in 2011 but is still facing difficulties. Many communities along Nagaland and Manipur have protested against the construction of the dam amidst fear of serious environmental damage, loss of biodiversity and human displacement.[19]

[17] Ibid.

[18] Laldinkima Sailo (2012), 'Northeast India-Southeast Asia Connectivity: Barrier to Bridge'. ISAS Working Paper No 162. p. 10.

[19] Ibid.

Other Areas of Connectivity[20]

Some of the other areas that have been suggested, where greater connectivity can benefit the two regions include:

a) India-ASEAN Power grid connectivity: Given the thrust on development of Hydro power dams, the development of integrated grids can benefit power producers in Southeast Asia – especially CLMV and Thailand – as well as India. The East-West transfer of power can be leveraged in a way that off peak excess power in Southeast Asia can be channelled to peak time demand in India and vice versa. (ASEAN is ahead of India in time zone, this facilitates East to West transfer of power. India's evening peak demand comes when ASEAN is asleep. Similarly morning peak demand of India is later than ASEAN. ASEAN can profitably off-peak power to India at near peak rates).

b) Virtual Learning Resources Sector: The development of Virtual Learning Resource Centres (VLRC) has also been suggested as a potential game changer in the development of human resources in the region (i.e. India and Southeast Asia) and there is a great scope for the private sector to participate. It has been deemed that the PPP mode can work very well in this sector. Further, the development of VLRCs can also be beneficial for supply chain management and in facilitating greater people to people connections.

Challenges

From the above, it is evident that there has been no shortage of initiatives and plans to bring about greater connectivity between Northeast India and the neighbouring states of Southeast Asia. However, despite the best intentions and efforts, these initiatives have not always yielded the desired outcomes. Three sets of factors might help to explain why the tasks of establishing greater connectivity can be especially daunting.

The physical challenges of developing infrastructure in difficult geographical terrain cannot be overstated. There are huge 'gaps' in the border

[20] Presentation of Mr Brijeshwar Singh, Ex-Chairman, National Highway Authority of India at the ASEAN-India Seminar on Master Plan on ASEAN Connectivity and Public-Private Partnerships. 27th November 2012 in Singapore.

areas where there are absolutely no roads or connecting networks between these localities. Without existing routes, it is virtually impossible to conduct survey and planning. Underdevelopment, militancy and land acquisition problems are also major causes of delays and breakdown of projects.

If regional integration is to succeed, it is essential to build or strengthen national, sub-regional and regional institutions involved in infrastructure development within an effective international institutional framework. According to an ADB report,[21] the existing institutional structure is neither adequate nor effective in view of the many challenges that such development projects face. These challenges include financing, coordination and integration of efforts from regional to international levels. It is generally accepted that more innovative ideas are needed so that government-to-government or public-private partnerships can be built for better effect.

Lack of political will and bureaucratic inertia are sometimes to blame for lack of progress in some of these major initiatives. In the case of India, security agencies have sometimes been suspicious of opening the region for fear of inviting more trouble in the form of arms smuggling, insurgency, drugs and influx of Chinese goods. Bilateral and multilateral efforts and agreement on managing of the border areas as well as the development of infrastructure that connects borders can also be improved. These are matters that require sustained and effective diplomacy as there is usually no shortage of sensitive border issues for countries that border each other.

Singapore and the Northeast India

If the development of the Northeast Region (NER) will deepen trade links between India and Southeast Asia, Singapore certainly has an interest to see how it can contribute to make this happen. The Institute of South Asian Studies (ISAS) at the National University of Singapore is trying to make its contribution in this regard by facilitating research and studies on the region, from the perspective of developing a better understanding of the challenges faced by the region, as well as the opportunities for trade and development.

ISAS organized a workshop on the theme, "India's Northeast Region (NER) and Southeast Asia: Exploring Potential Collaboration" at the India international Centre in New Delhi, on July 13, 2012 to coincide with Prime

[21] Biswa Nath Bhattacharyay. 'Concepts and Challenges Facing Asian connectivity' (ADB Institute working Paper Series No 220, 2010). http://www.adbi.org/working-paper/2010/06/25/3915.institutions.asian.connectivity/concept.and.challenges.facing.asian.connectivity/

Minister Lee Hsien Loong's state visit to India. Mr. Paban Singh Ghatowar, Minister for the Development of Northeastern Region, delivered the Keynote Address. The participants of the workshop that included policy makers, scholars, academics and members of civil society from the Northeast as well as those working on the Northeast highlighted some of the key issues related to the region. Further, a situation study of individual states has been prepared by ISAS researchers and will be brought out in March 2013.

The second ISAS workshop on Northeast India, "Connecting India to ASEAN: Opportunities and Challenges in India's Northeast" was scheduled for March 20, 2013. This workshop would bring together scholars and those involved in policy debates from Northeast India and Southeast Asia, including views from Myanmar, Bangladesh and stakeholders like Japan. Some of the key issues that this workshop would attempt to explore include geo-political issues, perception of people in the Northeast Region, opportunities for development of border trade as well as major governmental planning and policies with regard to the economic development of Northeast India, particularly those related to greater engagement with Southeast Asian.

Chapter 14

Illustrating Cooperation between CLMV Countries and North-East India

Sunand Sharma

The private sector has been alluded to in one format or the other in this conference and therefore, it would be pertinent to focus on building a trans-CLMV rail road. Alstom has been in India for 101 years, and it is engaged in the sectors of renewable thermal power, transmission of electricity, and the building of rail-roads and metros. So, it is easy to understand how things work in this sector. Professional People sitting in various countries of CLMV who belong to this field exchange ideas continuously on a continuous basis. For instance, a visit to Myanmar and conducting workshops in Bangkok related to investment in Myanmar and also into the Northeast India provides us good opportunities to know the subject. Currently, the largest hydro electric power plant for India is being built in Subansiri in Assam as also at others in Arunachal Pradesh. This experience may provide us some knowledge to talk about the issue being discussed here.

Alstom has grown 500 per cent in size in five years time both in terms of people employed, number of factories built and the scale at which it is working to the point that that this company headquartered in Paris has now the second largest of its investments in India. Further, the second largest in employment too is actually India and not China which now occupies number three position.

By the year 2015, India would have created the full capacity to produce everything it needs in the format of thermal power boilers, steam turbines, transmission grids, renewable power, hydroelectric power, big or small and solar power. But that means that in the year 2015 India will have the capacity to produce 30000 MW of power equipment per year, which is never, ever been planned to be that way, but was caused to become that way by the surge of demand internally and by the very fact that most of the major companies like Alstom saw the Chinese walk into India and walk away with our lunch in approximately two and half years time.

The reaction was to build 11 factories such as Alstom, GE, Toshiba, Siemens, Mitsubishi, Hitachi etc. Alstom has built in a record time of 18 months a railway coach-manufacturing factory north of Chennai and actually in Andhra Pradesh in the district of Chitoor.

In Southern Bhutan in Gelafu, Alstom is now building a service workshop to service all the hydroelectric power plants of Bhutan. Heavy engineering of the heaviest kind ever imagined can and should be taken to the Northeast. And the reason is very simple. If all of the hydroelectric power plants are going to come up in Arunachal Pradesh and Assam and then across the border in Sitwe or Thamanti, the nearest point to manufacture would actually be the Northeast and which is definitely on the agenda of the company.

The only thing which holds the company back is the actual progress of these projects, the day Thamanti is announced, the day any of the projects in the Northeast is announced, that is the day Alstom is ready to build a factory immediately on the back of that. The company has built a factory in Baroda to supply Subansiri and 20000 tonnes of manufactured equipment has been transferred from Baroda to Subansiri. Baroda to Subansiri is definitely shorter than Guwahati to Subansiri as an example, or when the road is ready and someone is able to cross the border into Myanmar from North-East it's much easier to transfer equipment between them.

As multinational companies of the large kind come to India such as Ikea, Carrefour, Wal-Mart etc. they would do a lot of sourcing form the Northeast and the connectivity that you would be important because all of these things are already developed in the areas of the CLMV, and if the transportation links can be found, it would be very easy. Then the people of the Northeast would not necessarily have to come to southern India to find jobs, they can stay there and find jobs; and there should be encouragement and methodologies created for these things to happen in forest, in timber, in agriculture and in food processing.

Part V
Expanding Networks through Connectivity: Land, Sea and Air

Mr. Brijeshwar Singh

Mr. K.L. Thapar

Professor Hidetoshi Nishimura

Dr. S. Narayan

Ambassador Pradap Pibulsonggram

Chapter 15

Indo-ASEAN Connectivity: An Assessment

Brijeshwar Singh

ASEAN has expressed its views on Intra-ASEAN connectivity in the Master Plan on ASEAN connectivity. This outlines three areas of connectivity of interest to India: (a) Physical connectivity, (b) Institutional connectivity and (c) People-to-People connectivity. India's views on India-ASEAN connectivity have been outlined in numerous policy statements on its Look East policy of which the most recent is the statement by the Hon. External Affairs Minister of India released on February 20, 2013.

In fact India and ASEAN must cooperate in all the three areas of connectivity outlined in the ASEAN Master Plan. However this chapter will concentrate on physical connectivity. Within Physical connectivity, three areas suggest themselves as being the best candidates for substantial spinoffs to both partners. These are: (a) power grid connectivity – this is a key action point relating to the regional energy security framework, (b) ASEAN Virtual learning resource centres (AVLRC) – this is key action point 13 of the master plan and (c) completion of the Asian highway network – key action point for one of the Master Plan. In addition marine connectivity must supplement surface connectivity.

India-ASEAN Power Grid Connectivity

This will in fact benefit both areas and will spill over to much of South Asia. The basic principle involved is the fact that ASEAN is ahead of India in time zone. By virtue of being to the East of India, both the morning and evening peak demands of ASEAN come earlier than India.

India's evening peak demand in fact comes when ASEAN is asleep, and its morning peak comes at midday in ASEAN. As a result ASEAN off-peak power, which coincides with the morning and evening peak demands in South Asia, can be profitably sold to South Asia at near peak rates. Inter-connections between the Indian power grid and Bhutan and Nepal are being implemented.

Between India and Sri Lanka a high voltage direct current (HVDC) inter-connection has been proposed. The Indian power grid is rapidly maturing having the following features:

a) 96,216ckt km of transmission lines at 800/765 kv, 400 kv, 220 kv and 132 kv EHVAC and 500 kv HVDC lines.

b) 158 substations.

c) Transformation capacity of about 1,51,303 MVA.

d) Availability of network greater than 99 per cent.

One of the greatest beneficiaries of such an inter-connection would be Myanmar which has a small and inadequate grid. With the expected rapid industrialisation of Myanmar, power demand and generation will increase manifold and sales from both its East and West will help it to meet its future power demands.

Virtual Learning Connectivity

For Virtual learning possibilities, India's nodal institution is C-DAC (Centre for Development of Advanced Computing) in Hyderabad which has developed an e-learning framework called e-shikshak. C-DAC also conducts a national seminar every four years called 'E-learning and E-learning technologies' or ELETECH INDIA. For course contents IGNOU (Indira Gandhi National Open University) is a good source. More importantly, India has been changing the relative roles of face-to-face interactions with a human teacher on one hand and e-learning on the other.

It is now felt that e-learning offers a quick and reliable method for imparting theoretical concepts and basic framework. The scarce resource of the human teacher is best utilised in clarifying concepts and improving skills of problem solving. The classroom is therefore evolving into a problem solving workshop with theoretical learning done through e-learning.

Another important aspect of e-learning is its application for small and medium business and rural development. Here some of the Indian systems would be of interest to ASEAN. E-SAVy is a supply chain management system for the SME sector developed by C-DAC, while India Development Gateway (INDG) is knowledge sharing about product and services for rural development. In addition there are a large number of private sector firms active in e-learning. These firms have been able to utilise the talent of some of the most eminent professors in the fields of engineering and management in particular. India also has an enormous skill development programme with the Prime Minister's Office who has a National Skill Development Advisor (Mr. S. Ramadorai) who oversees the national programme.

Virtual learning perhaps justifies the broader theme of institutional connectivity at the non-governmental level. NGO networks critiquing the Washington consensus are perhaps the earliest examples of India-ASEAN Institutional connectivity. There has also been considerable collaboration among other forms of social activists. In fact this activity preceded and perhaps facilitated connectivity at the level of institutions of higher learning in the social sciences. Governmental connectivity has been a successor to this. Connectivity at the level of chambers of commerce or industry has proceeded somewhat sporadically.

An important aspect of Institutional connectivity should be the working out of common educational and professional standards. A mutual acceptance for professional or educational qualifications will be one of the best ways to promote a wider exchange of technical and professional personnel between India and ASEAN.

Physical Connectivity

Efforts to promote India-ASEAN connectivity have really cantered on two important transport links. First, the completion of the Asian highway network and secondly the development of marine connectivity through the new Dawei port in Myanmar. Each of these will be considered in turn.

The Asian highway network was pioneered by ESCAP and has been accepted by all the member countries. However progress has remained patchy and it is indeed doubtful whether the links will meet modern standards of communication even by 2020. India and ASEAN should in fact specify the technical level they desire of the interconnecting highways. At the very least these highways should be capable of accommodating tractor-trailer type of container traffic with at least a 6 wheel trailer. This is necessary to ensure that highway links encourages rapid container based trade. The technical standards will also have to accommodate trailer traffic, so that road geometries are suitably designed for longer vehicles, particularly on curves where a wide radius of curvature should be planned and implemented, as well as on hill gradients and bridge crossings which must be designed for ever longer vehicles. It should be possible for a trailer-truck to safely carry cargo at an average speed in excess of 60 km/h in order to ensure rapid and safe movement of cargo.

Looked at from this standard, the proposed inter-connections seem to fall short of the requirements significantly. The Indian NHDP (National Highways Development Programme) relies on a East-West highway to connect to Myanmar and then ASEAN. Unfortunately the section of this highway through North Bengal (NH-31D) is still in a very preliminary state of pre-construction activity and it is unlikely that work on it will commence before 2014 or in fact be finished before 2017-18. In the next Eastern most state of Assam, the East-West highway terminates at Silchar at Southern Assam which is still over 300 km from the Myanmar border.

No plans have yet been sanctioned for the upgrading of Silchar-Imphal-Moreh/Tamu highway to a four lane status. On the Myanmar side of the border, once again the planning and implantation of four laned highways is lagging. In effect there will be a four lane highway up to Dawei in Southern Myanmar and from there to Silchar in Southern Assam, truck traffic will have to flow along two laned highways, and be carried by shorter length trucks. This will lead to considerable trans-shipment costs.

A bolder initiative is needed therefore to overcome the geographical challenges in the Dawei to Silchar stretch of the interconnections. The Patkhai ranges which run along the India-Myanmar border are marked by conical hills with steep gradients and lush jungle. There are numerous streams and rivulets. Because of the torrential monsoon rainfall, stream volumes change dramatically between the dry the wet seasons, and erosion of hill slopes is severe wherever the jungle is cleared for a highway. Soils are often unstable and require considerable improvements to bear the heavy load of highway traffic and modern slope stabilisation technology is necessary to prevent land slips and blockages in the monsoon.

The conical nature of the hills makes it difficult to accommodate the flat gradients (about 1 per cent slopes) which are necessary to permit safe and fast container traffic. In fact road engineers should not be attempting the current strategy of hair pin bends along these sections. The highway connections between India and Myanmar should ideally be based on a combination of valley crossing through bridges and tunnel boring through the hills so that a straight alignment can be maintained, distances and time reduced, and safety enhanced to ensure rapid and safe movement of goods and passengers. The current strategy of hill hugging roads should be abandoned in the interests of quicker and safer traffic movement.

A more fundamental issue is the relative underdevelopment of India's Northeast as well as Myanmar. The first major industrial zone in India is centred around Kolkata in southern-west Bengal, which is more than 2000 km from the proposed Indo-Myanmar highway interconnection. The long loop around Bangladesh which the highway traverses adds substantially to the transit distance and time. Myanmar in turn has relatively little industry and only a small degree of cross-border trade with India.

The nearest major industrial zone being projected is around Dawei port and this lies almost 4000 km by road from the Indian industrial region around Kolkata. It is rather doubtful if exchange of goods between two such widely separated industrial concentrations would ever be sufficient to justify the costs of the proposed highway interconnections. It is therefore absolutely necessary for India and ASEAN to configure a strategy to develop the greater Mekong region in a broader East-West configuration beginning from South Vietnam and ending in the Brahmaputra Valley in lower Assam.

Only sustained development of a wider international industrial zone would be able to justify a higher level of road connectivity. Both Myanmar and India's northeast are relatively low users of energy per capita, and have not developed an industrial culture. Substantial complementary investments in energy and skill development are necessary before the highway programme can fulfil its promise. The need for better governance and improved law and order situation in this zone can hardly be overstressed.

On the marine side the most important coast for India's future marine trade with ASEAN is undoubtedly the East coast of India along the Bay of

Bengal. Along this littoral port development has been particularly rapid in the middle section of Andhra Pradesh. It thins out in the northern littoral states of Orissa, which has only two ports of importance: Paradip and Dhamra; and the northern most state of West Bengal which has a single port complex Kolkata – Haldia along the river Hooghly. The northern most stretch of this coast line in Orissa and West Bengal also lacks a port capable of handling container traffic.

Vishakhapatnam in Andhra Pradesh is the northern most port which is capable of handling a significant volume of container traffic. In fact the volume of the containers it handles is almost equal to that handled by Chennai port in Tamil Nadu. There are considerable logistic difficulties of moving containers from Vishakhapatnam to West Bengal and Assam, to support any sustained industrialisation following a planned western extension of the greater Mekong corridor. Development of a major container port along the northern stretches of this coast is therefore absolutely essential. In the short run Dhamra in Orissa appears a likely candidate. However a new deep sea port is being proposed for West Bengal and this should be able to handle a large volume of container traffic.

The southern stretches of the Bay of Bengal are relatively better equipped with container ports. Vishakhapatnam and Chennai are the leading container terminals. However Krishnapatanam in southern Andhra Pradesh and Tuticorin in southern Tamil Nadu are other important container terminals. Gangavaram in Andhra Pradesh is a private port just south of Vishakhapatnam. It boasts the deepest draught of any Indian port and is able to handle CAPEMAX size cargo vessels. It may develop a major container handling facility in the future. The plans of other ports are as yet unclear.

The projections of Dawei port are in fact presuppose a single maritime corridor namely Dawei to Chennai as the major trunk route for India-ASEAN trade. The existence of other container terminals on the east coast suggests other alternative paths and foci for this trade. However the pattern of industrialisation along the east coast is extremely patchy. In the north there is an important industrial zone around Kolkata in West Bengal. Orissa lacks industries in the coastal belt. It is still a mining and commodity driven economy. Industries of Andhra Pradesh are not very substantial along its coast line and its major industrial areas lie inland. There is a major industrial area around Chennai in northern Tamil Nadu which is slowly developing into an industrial corridor along the Chennai-Bangalore axis. Not unnaturally the projections for Dawei port seek to take advantage of this industrial corridor development.

Looked at from the narrow angle of this developing industrial corridor, three ports will play a complementary role namely Krishnapatanam, Ennore and Chennai ports. If container facilities can be developed in any of the minor ports south of Chennai such as Cuddalore, Karaikal or Nagapatanam, these ports could also play some role in facilitating trade between the Bangalore-Chennai zone and ASEAN. Development of the proposed expressway between Chennai and Bangalore is therefore an extremely important step in cementing the proposed trade relationship between Dawei and the southern India industrial zone.

At present all the ports along the Bay of Bengal are first generation ports and do not take any responsibility for delivering cargo to the final destination. Indeed none of these ports have taken a proactive role in developing internal linkages from the port to the final destination. Such linkages could be by waterways, railways or highways. Waterways provide a possible avenue of inland delivery of cargoes for ports in West Bengal, as the Hooghly River is connected through waterways in Bangladesh to Assam. A certain amount of waterways also exist in Orissa which could possibly be exploited. Railway development both along the littoral and perpendicular to it leading to inland destination is neglected and almost no new line or doubling of tracks is being proposed. As a result the burden of inland communication has fallen entirely on the highway sector.

Fortunately the NHDP has provided a number of important East-West links leading away from the Bay of Bengal. The Chennai-Bangalore has already been mentioned but in addition the entire Golden Quadrilateral from Mumbai to Pune to Bangalore to Chennai and then along the east coast from Chennai to Kolkata is being taken up for 6 laning. The highway from Machilipatanam on the Andhra coast to Vijayawada and then the major industrial zone of Hyderabad and further west to Pune has also been taken up for 4 laning and modernisation, and rapid progress has been made on this stretch. The Hyderabad-Vijayawada section is already 4 laned and has reduced transit times by half. The Pune-Sholapur in Maharashtra is expected to finish by 2014. This will be a major artery to convey goods from the Andhra ports inland.

More fundamentally we should consider what would be the likely pattern of trade between ASEAN and India. Sixty per cent of India's industrial production is concentrated in the narrow corridor between Ahmadabad in Gujarat and Mumbai in Maharashtra. The major industrial centre in east India, Kolkata, is still to be connected to Mumbai by a 4 lane highway. It is hoped that this highway will be finished by 2018. At present road traffic of these two centres can take up to 14 days. Development of rapid East-West corridors across peninsular India is necessary for ASEAN to be able to utilise Bay of Bengal ports as access or entry points for trade with the Western Industrial concentration in the Mumbai-Ahmadabad belt.

New Economic Geography

ERIA has pioneered the use of new economic geography in thinking about ASEAN development. This approach has been incorporated in much of the ASEAN master plan on connectivity. New economic geography also significantly influences ASEAN's approach to India-ASEAN connectivity. Indeed areas studied and geographical models for the impact of the national highway development programme remains the leading geographical model examining the NHDP.

Unfortunately there has been no corresponding use of new economic geography by Indian planning bodies. This is an important aspect of institutional connectivity which needs to be remedied. As a result studies of ASEAN interconnectivity and India-ASEAN connectivity have not received the wide scrutiny in India which they deserve.

At the heart of the ERIA model lies a simple econometric model. And like all econometric models it delivers conclusions consistent with the values of the parameters fed into it. Broadly it correctly predicts the economic development which has taken place along the Golden Quadrilateral (GQ) of India's NHDP. However, it also predicts economic development along the North-South corridor. Contrary to this the North-South corridor appears to have had a negligible impact on economic development. Similarly the model predicts a high level of economic development along the East-West corridor, this is only partially correct. The western portion of the East-West corridor has shown improved economic growth, and in contrast the eastern portion seems to have no acceleration of its growth rate; this naturally leads to the question of where is this model going wrong and in what ways should its parameters be reset?

Economic development depends on a combination of factors including governance, energy availability, other infrastructure such as railways, educational attainments and law and order. Not all of these can be captured by the model; however energy availability and energy consumption per capita perhaps is the largest missing determinant. Once this is factored in, the low impact of transportation development on the rate of growth in eastern India becomes explicable. The conundrum of the uneven development along the East-West highway becomes more readily explained. However, along the North-South highways low level of energy consumption does not seem to explain the negligible impact of highways on economic development along its length. This needs more careful analysis.

It seems that the ERIA model also appears to be two-dimensional in its geography. It consistently predicts a higher model of economic development in upland and hill regions than can actually be observed. It is much better in predicting economic development in river valley areas. The 3rd dimension, the vertical dimension which acts as an important constraint in economic development where mountains pose barriers more difficult than oceans, somehow needs to be factored in. Once this is done, India-ASEAN connectivity really reduces to an exercise in joining together the coastal river valleys of Thailand, Cambodia and Vietnam with the river valleys of Myanmar and then the valleys of Barak-Brahmaputra systems in Northeast India in one hand and joining together the littoral concentrations of industry on the Indian coast line and the ASEAN coast line on the other hand.

A failure to recognize the difficulty in traversing mountain ranges will lead to an overemphasis on surface linkages such as highways and railways. Perhaps the most striking illustration of this can be offered by the case of the famous Stilwell road executed during WWII to carry supplies from Ledo in Upper Assam across Northern Burma and to the KMT Capital of Chungking in China. The road was built as a feat of engineering and took a heavy toll of human life. It is rather surprising to note that even after its completion, allied forces continued to ship a larger volume of supplies by the aerial route, flying across the Burma Hump, than they ever did by land based truck convoys. In a logistic sense the Stilwell road was a failure, and could not achieve its aim of reducing dependence on air transport. Unless the difficulties posed by mountainous terrain are tackled in a more modern method, it is quite possible that we will be equally disappointed by the actual volume of traffic generated by highway linkages between India and ASEAN.

In conclusion, multiple port marine connectivity, easier customs facilitation, and better modes of inland transport to carry goods from the ports to the hinterland industrial zones could provide a quicker and cheaper method of fostering India-ASEAN trade. At the same time the experience of WWII should alert us to the fact for valuable cargoes. Air transport will always play an important role and the development of air cargo hubs on both sides must be an important part of our joint planning.

Chapter 16

Expanding Networks through Connectivity

K.L. Thapar

Geography has always determined the trade patterns and the Indo-ASEAN region is no exception. India has been a sea faring and trading nation. In the middle of the 19th Century international trade accounted for 25 per cent of its GDP with distinct trade patterns. North India traded with countries to the West of India, especially the Arab world and North Africa, south India traded with the countries to the east of India in addition to the bourgeoning trade with Arabia.

The crucial factor in the pattern was the topography of South Asian land mass. The Himalayas effectively discouraged much trade with the North and the East while the trade routes with the West were open. As well as the large number of rivers which required fording and smaller mountains that required crossing made the terrain a formidable obstacle to high volumes of trade. But in the South, the jutting and tapering landmass of South Asia meant that seaborne trade was possible both with the West and the East. Besides the impediment of terrain, the colonial heritage of the countries of the region also affected the trade patterns.

The region became a set of colonies. India's share in the world GDP dropped from 25 per cent to 2 per cent. The colonial powers developed transport corridors which largely flowed from North to South to suit their commercial and political interests. This also resulted in the emergence of different technology platforms thereby increasing the disconnect between the countries. Until recently South Asia was a single geographic entity where trade flow was uninterrupted. This geographic entity was broken in 1947 and Northeast India became almost a landlocked area. It is this region which provides land connectivity with ASEAN. Hence, while developing land transport linkages the countries have to contend with geographical impediments; historical distortions and the disconnect that prevail at various levels. In a sense improved seamless connectivity by road and rail remains the last frontier. In the interim the main means of connectivity between countries remain the sea.

India has taken several welcome initiatives such as trilateral highway, second highway linking India-Myanmar-Lao, PDR-Vietnam-Cambodia and Delhi-Hanoi rail link. The Delhi-Hanoi rail link project will take years to materialize keeping in view the resources required and the extensive missing links. The trans-Asian railway network does provide an acceptable blueprint. About the trans-Asian highway, the important thing to note is that all the countries have accepted these routes for the first time in the history and they can provide the blueprint for further development of the linkages.

Distance does matter and more so in the context of looming depletion of fossil fuels. Rising freight charges will give a fillip to the trend towards making products closer to the market. Regional, rather than global production networks are likely to become more important in future. Availability and access to relevant technologies in the neighbouring countries would be cost effective in the long run and would also bring about harmonisation of technologies. While the ground infrastructure is underway, harmonisation of technology platforms needs to be addressed at different levels. For instance, it is in the interest of the smaller railway systems to develop compatible technologies.

In reality the partition of India has meant the death of the railway system in several countries, be it in Sri Lanka or Myanmar. If we go across the Southeast Asian countries the smaller railway systems do not have the minimum critical mass to sustain themselves and they have different gauges, different technologies and hence it is the imperative need that before we continue to talk of development of the ground infrastructure we also talk in terms of harmonisation of technology platforms.

India should aim at integrating with ASEAN master plan for regional connectivity. With regard to the resource mobilisation, India may consider joining ASEAN Infrastructure Fund which was set up in collaboration with

ADB to finance regional connectivity projects and lastly India may consider building the proposed cross-country highways passing through Myanmar at its own cost and this has been done in the past as well.

With regard to the maritime transport, there are no direct links at the present moment available between India and ASEAN. Exports through current maritime network suffer from multiple handling and transhipments and increases the travel time and costs. The proposed port at Dawei will reduce the sailing time and provide direct access to the Southeast Asian landmass. This is an important development which has gone unnoticed that the moment a port gets built over there at Dawei, we are able to move into the landmass of Southeast Asia much easier.

Air transport linkages are lacking at present, India and ASEAN can work towards developing a single aviation market and use bilateral air services agreements for this purpose. There is a need to provide direct air links from India to Vietnam and the neighbouring countries both on commercial and cultural considerations.

Finally, the digital connectivity is also important. The world has moved to new realms of digital connectivity which can be provided by submarine cables, optic fibres and satellites. The trans-border optic fibres can be laid alongside the railway lines and highways. Indeed these corridors can become economic corridors for multiple purposes.

Non-government organisations having a regional base also have an important role to play. UNESCAP Ministerial Conference noted with appreciation the valuable role of Asian Institute of Transport Development (AITD) in arranging training courses for railway personnel from South and Southeast Asia and this is a singularly important contribution. AITD will be running the 14th training course for which we have invited. Finally, AITD has also promoted Asian Railway Association which has been established to promote cooperative research, harmonisation of hardware, technologies and operational practices. Nurturing merit and talent through award of scholarships is one of the initiatives which we have taken. AITD proposes to extend this programme to South and Southeast Asian countries.

Chapter 17

India-ASEAN Connectivity and its Missing Links

Hidetoshi Nishimura

The chapter highlights India-ASEAN Connectivity and its missing links. To have a comprehensive understanding of this subject, first it is essential to introduce Economic Research Institute for ASEAN and East Asia (ERIA) and its origin. ERIA's establishment was agreed by 16 EAS countries' national leaders at the 3rd East Asia Summit in November 2007. The ASEAN Economic Community Blueprint was adopted on the same occasion, at the 13th ASEAN Summit. ERIA's primary mandate is to provide policy recommendations to the ASEAN/East Asia Summit.

ERIA drafted the 'Comprehensive Asia Development Plan' (CADP) to support the establishment of an integrated economic region through both soft and hard infrastructure development, engendering a competitive and globally connected East Asia which would be at the heart of the world's growth centre. The final report of CADP was submitted to the 5th East Asia Summit in October 2010.

CADP provides the following features:

a) A grand spatial design for infrastructure development in East Asia armed with a consistent conceptual framework based on the new waves of the international trade theory such as the fragmentation theory and new economic geography.

b) Simulation analyses on the impacts of logistic enhancement to the region using the Geographical Simulation Model (IDE/ERIA-GSM).

c) A long list of prospective infrastructure projects in consistence with the aforementioned conceptual framework.

ERIA is following up all the 695 CADP projects in the region. Many of them are now in the operational and construction stages in the Mekong region. However, there have been delays in the projects in Myanmar, especially for Dawei, which is a critical node for connecting ASEAN and India. Utilising the knowledge gained by CADP, ERIA has also helped the ASEAN Secretariat, together with ADB, UNESCAP and World Bank, to draft the ASEAN Connectivity Master Plan. ERIA is proud to be a part of this activity, and hopes this contribution will pave the way for improved internal connectivity in ASEAN, and its open connectivity with other regions.

ERIA has also drafted the Comprehensive Asia Development Plan Phase 2 which focuses on India-ASEAN Connectivity. The economic impacts of the 'Golden Quadrilateral (GQ)' and 'North-South and East-West Highways (NSEW)' of India should be highlighted since some regions get economic advantages from these highway projects while others are negatively impacted. With the development of GQ and NSEW, economic activities along these economic corridors are revitalized, leading to a higher GRDP. In principle, domestic connectivity enhancement benefits the Indian economy. In addition to domestic connectivity enhancement, India will have additional benefits of India-ASEAN connectivity. Our Geographical Simulation Model showed that the Mekong-India Economic Corridor (MIEC), the Trilateral Highway and other India-ASEAN Connectivity projects as well as market liberalisation will bring additional positive impacts for India and the Mekong region.

In this regard, ERIA is supporting the Myanmar Government with longer development vision through the Myanmar Comprehensive Development Vision (MCDV) project. In this project, we focus on some of the emerging and important routes of India's connectivity with ASEAN including the 'Trilateral Highway'. Bangkok is connected with the Northeastern States of India, via Myanmar. As the road infrastructure in Thailand is basically well developed, the remaining issues are the sections in Myanmar and the Northeastern part of India. More importantly, trade and transport facilitation across two national borders between Thailand and Myanmar, and Myanmar and India needs to be addressed with a promise of commitment from all the involved countries.

With growing trade and investment linkages, the Mekong India Economic Corridor (MIEC) shall provide opportunities to Myanmar, Thailand, Cambodia, Vietnam and India to build a strong economic and industrial base and a world-class infrastructure. The emphasis of the corridor is on expanding the manufacturing base and also to expand trade with the rest of the world, particularly India. The corridor will enable these economies to further integrate with each other and collectively emerge as a globally competitive economic bloc.

MIEC is expected to enhance trade with India by reducing travel distance between India and MIEC countries and removing supply side bottlenecks. In order to optimize the development of the corridor, MIEC includes all key economic centres and seaport locations along their western coasts. However, there remain significant missing links in this corridor. In addition, the connectivity between the countries of MIEC should be enhanced through upgradation of the road infrastructure (physical connectivity) and various trade and transport facilitation measures (institutional connectivity).

Now Myanmar is on its way to all-round reform. Current economic and social reforms in Myanmar and Thilawa Development will benefit Myanmar by taking economic agglomeration to Yangon and the Dawei project shall have a huge economic impact on the Mekong region and is beneficial for Northeast India. Moreover, equitable development of Myanmar is crucial for the sustainable economic growth of the country and the region. In the MCDV project, ERIA has proposed a Two-Polar (Yangon and Mandalay) development, connectivity enhancement in the domestic economic corridors and border development. This strategic combination will achieve both high economic growth and equitable development and bring additional benefits to India and the Mekong region.

In conclusion, connectivity is the key to enhancing the strengths of ASEAN and India by joining the production networks. A combination of physical and institutional connectivity is critical. And lastly, connectivity is required to achieve both the deepening of economic integration and the narrowing of development gaps.

Chapter 18

A Comprehensive Approach to India-ASEAN Connectivity

S. Narayan

The last decade has witnessed a sea change in the relationship between India and ASEAN. There have been several significant economic and political developments that have contributed to this. First, the India's Look East policy, strongly supported by Singapore, led to the comprehensive economic cooperation agreement between the two countries, the first that India has been confident enough to ink. This has led to bilateral trade growing from a mere US$ 1.5 billion on 2002 to over US$ 17 billion in 2010. There was a confidence to enter into trade agreement negotiations with the other ASEAN members, and the India-ASEAN free trade agreement is also now a reality.

The India-ASEAN Free Trade Agreement (AIFTA), which came into effect on January 1, 2010 with Malaysia, Singapore and Thailand, is central to the country's growing engagement with the ASEAN region. Bilateral trade volume between India and ASEAN exceeded US$ 70 billion in 2012. By 2015, it is expected to reach US$ 100 billion. The share of total trade of India with Mekong countries has more than doubled in a span of 15 years. India has signed partial FTA with Thailand and Comprehensive Economic Cooperation Agreement (CECA) with Singapore. India's FTA with ASEAN was signed on August 13, 2009 and FTA with Malaysia as individual country is under negotiation and close to signing.

Secondly, increased trade has brought about increased investment into the ASEAN member countries from India. Indian companies use Singapore as the hub for their financial, legal and investment activities. Indian entities are investing in natural resources in the ASEAN countries including coal mining in Indonesia, Palm oil and Rubber plantations in Malaysia and Laos, and in retail opportunities for Indian goods. Indian brand names are being found in retail malls in Singapore, Kuala Lumpur and Thailand.

Thirdly, there is increasing tourism and MICE traffic from India into ASEAN. There are over 300 flights every week from different destinations in India to Singapore every week now, as against only around 50 flights a decade ago. This is contributing to the tourism, hotel, transport and entertainment industries in the ASEAN, and there is an estimate of US$ 5 billion outflow from India in 2011 on this account. In return, there are inwards remittances from workers and professionals of Indian origin in the ASEAN countries. While disaggregated figures are not readily available, anecdotal evidence indicates that this has grown manifold in the last decade.

Next, at the international level, security cooperation and participation by India at the meetings of regional bodies and networks has increased. There is cooperation in joint defence exercises as well as opportunities of training in India for defence personnel. The architecture of security for the Straits of Malacca is now a joint concern, and India is also a participant in all the discussions on the South China Seas. For several years now, there have been joint naval exercises with Singapore, and Singapore air force pilots avail training opportunities in India.

Finally, the opening up of Myanmar is of strategic and trade importance to India. Pulses, rice and other agricultural produce find a ready market in India, and the trade routes are traditional and go back to colonial days. There is a growing influence of China in the region, where the ASEAN countries need to examine the rebalance of influence between their northern neighbour and India. There is increasing appreciation of the need to balance the influence of the two large economies in the region, and the realisation that each one of them has distinct opportunities for trade and development to offer.

Several aspects of this rapid change have happened sui generis, and only some aspects like security co-operation and trade agreements have been due to strategic policy level agreements on both the sides. Nowhere is this more evident than in the Northeast of India. The seven North Eastern Indian states have had a geographical disadvantage of poor linkage with the rest of India.

The narrow land corridor from India has offered limited access to trade with the rest of India. The opening of the land routes from Manipur and Mizoram have multiplied trade with Myanmar manifold in the last couple of years, and increasing informal trade across the border of retail consumer items from China is now flooding the markets in Manipur and Aizawl.

Interestingly, it is the Myanmar trade that is growing rapidly, but over the years, one can expect goods from China to arrive in increasing quantities along the border. It is a geographical reality that the Northeastern States of India share a much longer and integrated land border with the ASEAN countries than even with their motherland, India, and it is only natural that economic opportunities for this region arise from greater connectivity with ASEAN. Greater connectivity is essential for the realisation of the full benefits of the regional free trade and cooperation agreements, since one of the major obstacles to the expansion of trade between India and ASEAN is the high cost of moving goods across the borders.

There is an unsaid parameter in these developments. The initiatives taken by China to develop a rail network in Tibet, and a road network to connect with several points in the Kunming province, is likely to open up a number of opportunities for inter-regional trade. The road trade across the Nathu La pass, which was opened in 2008, is now flourishing, with the gradual addition of permissible goods. Substantial infrastructure has been developed on the Chinese side, and similar infrastructure is being developed on the Indian side. The presence of China in the trade investment and development patterns of all ASEAN countries would be quite significant, and India needs to pick and choose the advantages, develop co-operation, and avoid conflict prone situations. Diplomacy and international relations would have as much of a role to play as design and construction of infrastructure.

These ground level developments have led to a flurry of activity among the governments to encourage, develop and regulate the opportunities of inter-linkages between India and the ASEAN countries, and to examine the entire issue of connectivity in a comprehensive manner. At the 17th ASEAN Summit in 2010, the East Asia Summit (EAS) leaders adopted the Master Plan on ASEAN Connectivity, which identifies key strategies and actions to enhance the region's connectivity in three dimensions: physical, institutional and people-to-people. The Comprehensive Asia Development Plan (CADP), designed by Economic Research Institute for ASEAN and East Asia (ERIA) for EAS members, provides a grand spatial design for infrastructure development in East Asia. The India-ASEAN Connectivity Report by RIS

(Research and Information System for Developing Countries) advocates the enhancement of connectivity between India and ASEAN with an emphasis on two major axes: land connectivity with the Northeastern region and air, and sea connectivity with the southern region, with a thrust on the Chennai-Ennore area.

Land Transport

The most important of the proposed linkages involve land transport. In particular, the road network offers a number of challenges: poor quality of roads and incomplete road networks, including missing links. Highway lanes, lighting system and quality of roads differ across countries in Asia, and there is a lot of work to be done in standardisation of highway construction.

With a long international border and landlocked position, accompanied by a hilly terrain, access to the Northeastern region has been a challenge. Development of roads and railway networks to connect this region to ASEAN partners will provide an avenue for cross-border trade while simultaneously expediting economic development in this region.

Completion of the ASEAN Highway Network, including the Trilateral Highway connecting Thailand, Myanmar and India has been adopted as one of the priorities of the Master Plan on ASEAN Connectivity. The project is expected to be completed by 2016. At the plenary session of the India-ASEAN Commemorative Summit held in December 2012, Prime Minister Manmohan Singh proposed that a second track of the trilateral highway be launched to connect India with Myanmar, Lao, Cambodia and Vietnam.

The planned Mekong-India Economic Corridor (MIEC) will integrate Myanmar, Thailand, Cambodia and Vietnam (Mekong Countries) with India through its east coast. It is proposed to connect Ho Chi Minh City (Vietnam) with Dawei (Myanmar) via Bangkok (Thailand) and Phnom Penh (Cambodia) and further linking to Chennai in India. MIEC should be included in the designated Trade Transport Routes (TTRs), which receive special emphasis for implementation by 2015 under transport cooperation in ASEAN.

The completion of national road projects such as the Chennai-Ennore Port Road Connectivity Project, the National Highway Development Programme and Dedicated Freight Corridor Projects to improve national connectivity is essential to allow smooth flow of goods and services.

Rail is not widely used as a mode of transport in Mekong countries. The share of rail transport in total freight is low at 3 per cent (excluding Cambodia). Presently, the rail network has severe capacity constraints to deliver efficient and reliable services for heavy usage as axle load is low at less than 20 tonnes (except Thailand). The lack of inter-operability constrains the use of rail as a transport method in the region. Track gauges, voltages and signalling systems differ from one country to another.

However, multimodal transportation hubs could be created that would leverage existing rail connectivity. Investments in standardisation of tracks, signals and procedures, along with linkages to markets through a road work, would require the development of a master plan that would take into account national priorities and existing infrastructure. In India, technological upgradation and modernisation of existing infrastructure and assets needs to be undertaken in the railways sector.

There is a plan to establish a rail link from Kolkata to Ho Chi Minh City via Myanmar, Thailand, Cambodia and Vietnam, but this project is more a wish list than a reality on planning and design. The investments required are likely to be substantial, and it is not clear whether international traffic alone will provide adequate returns for this investment. Further, there is the question whether such a route would pass through Bangladesh, or use the existing Indian railways network.

Air Transport

Air transport is an important mode of transportation for high-value fragile goods, perishable commodities and passengers; the trade in these goods is expected to grow significantly. The passenger flow will also multiply as the tourism potential of corridor is enhanced and new sites are developed. There is considerable interest in the ASEAN countries for tourism in the Northeast of India, and considerable travel by citizens of the seven states to the rest of Asia. The 14th ASEAN Transport Ministers' meeting held in Makati, Metro, Manila, Philippines in 2008 upheld the proposed Open Skies Agreement and India's keen interests to join the ASEAN Member States in an Open Skies Regime, covering airfreight and passenger services.

Collaboration with Singapore and Malaysia to improve airport infrastructure may be explored by India and other ASEAN nations. Air transport network is expected to be enhanced by the ongoing initiatives to establish the ASEAN

Single Aviation Market (ASAM) and the ASEAN's air transport agreements with its Dialogue Partners including India, China and Korea. The implementation of the Single Aviation Market is likely to permit integrated trade agreements.

Sea Transport

Port network and sea transportation will be the main trade link of ASEAN region, particularly for bulk transport. But many ASEAN countries (except Singapore and Malaysia) rank poorly in the UNCTAD Liner Shipping Connectivity Index. Capacity utilisation at most gateway ports in the region is fairly high, indicating that investments in port expansion are required. Current port capacity will have to be increased after 2014, particularly in India and the Mekong region, in order to meet the expected increase in demand for port services.

A JICA study on 47 designated ports in ASEAN revealed a number of challenges in providing a more efficient shipping network services given the varying levels of port infrastructure development. There is a significant mismatch in the port facilities offered in different countries; these infrastructure gaps create difficulties for port users. Operational efficiency of Indian ports needs to be enhanced significantly to bring them at par with international ports. The construction of new ports in Dawei, Kyaukphyu and Pakbara are in the pipeline and the expansion/upgrading of existing ports, such as Yangon, Sittwe and Chennai, are expected. Inland waterways along the Kaladan River and Ganga can also enhance the connectivity between the mainland and Northeast India via Myanmar and Bangladesh, respectively.

In April 2008, India and Myanmar signed the agreement for the Kaladan Multi-Modal Transit Transport Project, financed by India's Ministry of External Affairs. The project will connect the port of Kolkata with Sittwe port in Myanmar. It will then link Sittwe to Mizoram via river and road transport. The Project is scheduled for completion in 2014. This project will reduce distance from Kolkata to Sittwee by approximately 1328 km and provide an alternative transport route to the narrow Siliguri corridor.

Conclusion

The benefits, in India, are likely to flow not only to the Northeastern states, but to other regions as well. Increasingly, it is being realized that sea trade should be directed to the southern part of India, perhaps to the ports of Chennai, Krishnapatnam and Vishakapatnam. There are historical as well as logistical reasons for this. Historically, there is a large presence of South Indian (primarily Tamil) traders in the South East Asian countries, more so in Malaysia and Singapore. Traders from the south, primarily Andhra Pradesh, have been at the helm of commodity trade with Malaysia and Myanmar. Substantial quantity of pulses, primarily Toor Dhall, and also rice and oil seeds, is being imported from the ASEAN countries in the south. The trade in pulses and rice is in the hands of Andhra traders, while oilseeds are more the forte of Gujarati and Marwari traders.

These traditional trading patterns in India have existed for centuries, and are now getting strengthened through increased volumes and enhanced opportunities. These goods, after landing on the eastern ports, use the local railway and road logistics to move the products to relevant markets. The volumes of trade in these commodities have been growing at a compounded annual growth rate close to 25 per cent in the last five years, driven by increased incomes and changing consumption. There is a strong Indian argument for improved connectivity in terms of lowering costs and increasing reliability, thereby raising the efficiency of trade.

In the eastern part of India, Kolkata has traditionally been a gateway to product and retail markets of Bihar and Bengal, and the improvement in connectivity will improve opportunities for this bilateral movement. With enhanced connectivity, less developed regions may expand their economic activities to leverage their location and resource advantages, particularly in India's Northeast region and Myanmar. Industrial agglomerations like Chennai and Bangkok will lead economic growth for the region by providing large markets of goods for neighbouring regions. Integrated connectivity plans will especially benefit smaller countries by giving them access to the international market at a lower cost. Improved infrastructure and connectivity must be accompanied by trade facilitation. Conducive trade climate through appropriate policies, regulation and private sector participation need to be created.

The key to making all this happen is not just physical connectivity. Physical connectivity should be developed in conjunction with institutional connectivity, in the form of institutional arrangements to facilitate cross-border movement of goods and services. Currently, a substantial quantum of trade takes place across informal channels, especially in Manipur and Mizoram. The formal procedures are still quite rigid and time consuming.

As an example, agricultural goods and products coming into India require a certification, for which facilities are available only in Guwahati in Assam – it is more expedient to move these through informal channels. Facilitation of trade, better customs and border clearance infrastructure, as well as more channels of transportation would increase formal trade and increase revenues.

It is possible to consider some tariff reductions in the case of locally procured agricultural goods and commodities that are used for retail consumption rather than trade, to improve the flow of these goods. Currently, the growth of these informal channels is giving rise to a parallel and underground economy that is to be viewed with concern, especially in the states where there is a history of insurgency and terrorism. It would be worthwhile for the Indian revenue authorities to study the pattern of trade across these borders, and to set up more venues for road movement, improve infrastructure at check points and also to expedite procedures. Infrastructure is still poor, and the trade is small, it should be possible for the revenue authorities to develop some rapid clearance mechanisms for these small value items. Investments in processes and in procedural facilitation are as urgent as investment in infrastructure.

The funding requirement for transport infrastructure is huge and at least a part of it must be solicited from the private sector through PPPs. In order to improve risk allocation and operational efficiency, India should collaborate with countries that have technological/operational expertise in these areas. Quick project execution in difficult areas requires a considerable degree of planning and logistics management, and collaborative efforts with the ASEAN neighbour countries are likely to lead to substantial gains in time and costs.

It is clear that better connectivity between India and ASEAN nations will help bridge the existing development gaps, lead to increased trade and investment, fuel economic growth and create employment. It is now important to convert ideas and wishes into reality through investment in planning, design and institutional improvements. It is also obvious that in terms of each of these aspects, India has considerable leeway to make up. Many of the ASEAN countries, with probably the exception of Myanmar, have the institutional capabilities as well as the financial muscle to carry out their part of the programme – in India this needs to be developed , funded, implemented and monitored.

The benefits of improved connectivity are obvious. Apart from enhancing trade and development, they provide employment and livelihood opportunities. These would arise initially in project construction, and later in logistics, warehousing, trading and retail as well as in tourism and entertainment sectors. The Nathu La trade has enhanced state GSDP of Sikkim by close to one per cent, bestowing considerable benefit on its local population in terms of increased incomes and employment. There is a need and opportunity to do the same for the Northeast to ASEAN corridors.

Chapter 19

India-ASEAN Connectivity: Realising the Potential

Pradap Pibulsonggram

Centuries of multi-faceted interactions between the countries that are now members of ASEAN and India have seen many highs and lows, reflecting the evolution of each country and the geopolitical situations in Asia and the world. The deep impact of these relationships, nonetheless, upon our social fabrics is for all to witness, and this has been succinctly stated by Prime Minister Manmohan Singh of India:

> " ... India and Southeast Asia have centuries-old links. People, ideas, trade, art, and religions have long criss-crossed this region. A timeless thread of civilization runs through all our countries. While each one of us has a unique and rich heritage, there are abiding linkages of culture and custom, of art and pluralism in our region...."

> "... The breadth and intensity of India's engagement with Southeast Asia is unmatched by any of our other regional relationship. We have institutionalized annual summits; many of our sectoral dialogues have been elevated into ministerial consultations; and nearly 25 mechanisms for dialogue and cooperation between us cover virtually every field of human endeavour."

The past 20 years have brought these countries and peoples closer again, with a firm commitment on the part of the leaders to raise India-ASEAN relationships to the level of 'Strategic Partnership'. In this age of networking, it is important that joint effort on enhancing the existing physical connectivity is concentrated upon. Despite state-of-the-art tools that are prevalent in our societies to promote networking, nothing could replace the direct contact among these peoples; the entrepreneurs, innovators, producers and the ones who desire a better life and wellbeing.

Potentials of India-ASEAN Partnership

The potentials of India-ASEAN partnership are evident and recognized as expressed by Prime Minister Singh recently:

> "... India-ASEAN trade has grown over ten times in the ten years since we launched annual summits. Following the implementation of our FTA in Goods, trade grew by 41 per cent in Indian fiscal year 2011-12. Two-way flows in investments have also grown rapidly to reach US$ 43 billion over the past decade. As ASEAN investments into India have multiplied, ASEAN countries too have emerged as major destinations for Indian companies. From energy resources to farm products, from materials to machinery, and from electronics to information technology, Indian and ASEAN companies are forging new partnerships of trade and investment."

Similarly, the Prime Minister of Thailand, Mr. Yingluck Shinawatra emphasized the need for these countries to "work diligently and innovatively" to fulfil the heightened expectations from the "Vision Statement (which) lays out a comprehensive roadmap for political, economic, socio-cultural and development cooperation."

With a community of 1.8 billion people and a combined GDP of US$ 3.8 trillions, ASEAN and India indeed possess great potentials. Optimistically, the bilateral trade volume is projected to expand to US$ 200 billion by 2020. Services and investments likewise will continuously increase and multiply on the foundation of the concluded negotiations of FTA in these two areas. In the case of Thailand, with 60 years of diplomatic relations, the people are now reaching out more to each other. In 2012, over a million Indian citizens had spent their time at various tourist attractions in Thailand, and 80 Indian couples held their wedding ceremonies. In Thailand, 500 or so movies were filmed at different locations. In 2003, the two countries signed the Free Trade Agreement, and by 2011 the bilateral trade passed the US$ 8 billion ceiling, an increase of 23.2 per cent over the previous year.

The Possibility for Closer Physical Connectivity

The long existing common interests between the ASEAN member countries and India, coupled with the vast potential for stronger partnership, naturally guide and lead them to forge a wider and deeper network. The key strategy is to enhance their physical connectivity with each other by land, sea and air. Intensified efforts are underway, with real possibility for achieving such a goal considering that India has land, sea and air borders with ASEAN primarily through Myanmar, 'the gateway'. The Eminent Persons Group, established by ASEAN/India leaders last year to review our dialogue relations, mindful of the significance of India's proximity to ASEAN, clearly advocated "the leverage of (the) recommended Strategic Partnership through enhanced connectivity to reap the benefits...."

On the ASEAN side, the 2010 Master Plan on ASEAN Connectivity (MPAC), which is designed to demonstrate to the world in 2015 that ASEAN has become a 'Community' with concrete and functional connectivity, has its aim to also link ASEAN to India. MPAC has identified 84 key actions for the enhancement of ASEAN's physical, institutional and people-to-people connectivity, within specific timelines mostly by 2015. The physical pillar deals with the ASEAN Highway Network (23 designated routes, 38,400 km), Transport Transit Routes (over 21,000 km), Rail Link from Singapore to Kunming passing through Thailand, utilisation of inland waterways (51,000 km), multimodal transport system, competitive maritime (47 designated ports) and aviation services, ICT (ASEAN Broadband Corridor) and energy (gas pipelines and electricity-grids).

MPAC: Physical Connectivity Strategies

There are seven strategies listed under Master Plan on ASEAN Connectivity. These include: (a) Complete the ASEAN Highway Network (AHN), (b) Complete the implementation of Singapore Kunming Rail Link (SKRL) project, (c) Establish an efficient and integrated inland waterways network, (d) Accomplish an integrated, efficient and competitive maritime transport system, (e) Establish integrated and seamless multimodal transport systems to make ASEAN the transport hub in the East Asia region, (f) Accelerate the development of ICT infrastructure and services in each of the ASEAN Member States and (g) Prioritise the processes to resolve institutional issues in ASEAN energy infrastructure projects.

By land, ASEAN and India are already connected via 1360 km trilateral highway, which is linking Thailand (Mae Sot) to Myanmar (Myawaddy) and Myanmar (Pakoku-Chaungma-Kalewa) to India (Tamu/Moreh). One of the 84 key actions is to promote Mekong-India Economic Corridor (MIEC) as a land bridge. The four-prong approaches are: (a) Construct the Mekong bridge in Neak Loung (National road no1 in Cambodia), (b) Develop the Dawei deep sea port (by 2020), (c) Build the highway between Kanchanaburi and Dawei (by 2020) and (d) Conduct a feasibility study and preliminary design for the railway spur line between Kanchanaburi and Dawei.

By 2016, the upgrading of the trilateral highway Thailand-Myanmar-India is expected to be completed. To showcase the latest development on the land transport connectivity, the Car Rally was arranged which started from Indonesia on November 26, 2012 and passed through Singapore, Malaysia, Thailand, Cambodia, Vietnam, Lao PDR, Myanmar and ended up in India at Guwahati (Assam) on December 20, 2012. India provided 31 XUV 500 Mahindra, while Thailand 'the Detroit of Asia' complemented the convoy with additional locally-made SUVs when passing through twice. The eleven-nation drivers covered 7,714 km in 22 nights. Under MPAC, the ASEAN Highway Network will by 2015 be extended to India via the northern part of Laos and Myanmar.

By sea, India has ten container ports along its eastern coast which links it to ASEAN. As India is looking East and ASEAN looking West, a multimodal transport system is being developed to connect Indian ports particularly Chennai with the planned deep sea port in Dawei, Myanmar. Rail and plane facilities in the project pipelines will bring goods and peoples to Thailand and other ASEAN countries as well as beyond to our plus three dialogue partners China, Japan and South Korea.

Maritime connectivity between the nations of ASEAN and India could be traced back to the 10th century or even earlier. From September 15 to March 26, 2012; India has demonstrated and refocused the region's attention to the importance of this 'route of monsoon trade winds', by sending the Navy's sail training ship 'INS Sudarshini' on a commemorative expedition to retrace the ancient ports and the modern ones in ASEAN and India. The captain, officers and crew have created much excitement and interest at every port of call.

By air, the ten leaders of ASEAN have supported a strategy to develop ASEAN Single Aviation Market (ASAM) by 2015, the timeline as defined in the Roadmap for Integration of Air Travel Sector. ASEAN member countries have signed and are in the process of implementing the following three important air agreements, in recognition of the vital role of air transportation and the 'accelerated restructuring of the global aviation market': (a) The Multilateral Agreement on the Full Liberalisation of Air Freight Services (MAFLAFS), (b) The Multilateral Agreement on Air Services (MAAS) and (c) The Multilateral Agreement on the Full Liberalisation of Passenger Air Services (MAFLPAS).

Current air traffics between cities in ASEAN and India will benefit and considerably enhance and deepen the interactions among our peoples once these three agreements are fully carried out. The soon-to-be concluded ASEAN/India Air Transport Agreement will complement and serve to accelerate the pace of our network expansion effort.

India-ASEAN: 21st Century Mindset

At the latest ASEAN/India 10th Anniversary Commemorative Summit on December 20, 2012 in New Delhi, our leaders have set a clear 'Vision' for the peoples to pursue politically, economically and socially. Enhanced connectivity will expand the networks and make us close neighbours. The success of our mission is for the peoples to adjust the mindset and fulfil the urgent need to get to know one another better and well. We are fortunate to live in the digital age, which greatly facilitates the flow of information and communications. What will confront us all in the years or the decades ahead are not only the positive and constructive opportunities, but the unimaginable challenges posed by the continual changes in technology, the dwindling essential natural resources and shortages in the productive workforce.

Special Remarks

Ms. Jyotsna Suri

Ms. Jyotsna Suri

Senior Vice President, FICCI & Chairperson & Managing Director, Bharat Hotels Ltd., India

It is my great honour and privilege to address you all at this Valedictory Session of Delhi Dialogue V, titled 'India-ASEAN: Vision for Partnership and Prosperity'. I understand that we had some very insightful sessions at Delhi Dialogue V. These deliberations should provide fresh policy thinking in line with our vision for the ASEAN region to be a zone of shared Peace, Progress and Prosperity.

We, at FICCI, feel that we have an opportunity to establish a new set of objectives for a community of 1.8 billion people with a combined GDP of US$ 3.8 trillion, which would synergize with India's Look East policy.

I would like to highlight three of them. First, we must set a new trade target. The growing trade volume between ASEAN and India at US$ 79 billion has surpassed the 2012 target. In the spirit of our Prime Minister's vision, I urge the industry to pursue trade with ASEAN to exceed US$ 100 billion by 2015 and US$ 200 billion in 10 years from now. A FTA covering trade, investment and services, will go a long way in achieving this target.

Secondly, people-to-people connectivity by expanding networks through land, sea and air. This is a perfect opportunity for the airlines, shipping and infrastructure industry in India and ASEAN. Needless to mention, this will be a huge boost to trade and tourism.

Thirdly, we need to initiate and promote extensively the India-ASEAN cooperation in food and energy security. As the fastest growing economies in the world, with the ambitions of a young population, food and energy needs are to be addressed as there are opportunities within India and ASEAN to complement each other in this aspect.

I would like to leave you all with these thoughts, which I feel are very important for taking India-ASEAN relations to the next level.

Valedictory Address

H.E. Mr. Sanjay Singh

H.E. Mr. Sanjay Singh

Secretary (East), Ministry of External Affairs, Government of India

It is indeed a privilege and honour for me to deliver the Valedictory Address as the proceedings of Delhi Dialogue V came to an end. Ever since the inception of Delhi Dialogue in 2009, this annual forum has come a long way and has emerged as one of the premier ASEAN-centric platforms for active discussions on regional and international issues of mutual importance to India and ASEAN. It has facilitated debate, dialogue and discussion among policy makers, opinion makers and eminent personalities from academia, reputed think tanks and civil society at large.

As in previous years, this year too, Delhi Dialogue V has been successful in drawing wide participation from across the region, and in promoting thought-provoking discussions on a range of topical issues of particular relevance to the region. The course of the day has seen interactive discussions on themes such as India-ASEAN security cooperation, tackling non-traditional security challenges, assessing the role of new and renewable energy in sustainable development, analysing the opportunities and challenges in promoting greater cooperation between CLMV countries and Northeast India and enhancing land, sea and air connectivity between ASEAN and India, issues that are central to our collective objectives of growth and development.

Delhi Dialogue V is being held at an opportune time, as it takes place two months after the convening of the special ASEAN-India Commemorative Summit on the theme 'ASEAN-India: Partnership for Peace and Shared Prosperity' at New Delhi in December 2012. The Commemorative Summit was notable in more ways than one, as it not only commemorated the 20th anniversary of ASEAN-India dialogue relations and the 10th anniversary of ASEAN-India Summit-level relations, but also because it elevated the ASEAN-India partnership to a strategic level, thereby envisioning further intensification and deepening of our cooperation into the future. The ASEAN-India Commemorative Summit, attended by nine Heads of States/Heads of Government of ASEAN countries, marked an important milestone and led to the adoption of the Vision Statement, which outlines the way forward during the coming decade.

It was in the early 1990s that India embarked upon its Look East policy. However, ASEAN countries and India share a historical relationship of several millennia. The free flow of people, merchandise, cultures and ideas across our land and maritime borders has manifested itself in the richness of our cuisines, languages, religions and architecture. This two-way link has made India and ASEAN natural partners in more recent times to meet contemporary challenges in a globalized world. Over the last two decades, and especially in recent years, our relationship has transformed, reflecting the emergence of our shared region as a new engine of growth and our increasing interdependence. As emphasised by the Prime Minister of India, India's relationship with ASEAN remains one of the cornerstones of its foreign policy and the very foundation of our Look East policy. India and ASEAN, having successfully implemented the first Plan of Action for the period 2005-2010, are currently intensifying efforts towards the full implementation of the new Plan of Action for the period 2010-2015 titled 'ASEAN-India: Partnership for Peace, Progress and Shared Prosperity'.

In the run up to the Commemorative Summit, the year 2012 witnessed an intensification of activities across the political, economic and socio-cultural pillars of ASEAN-India cooperation. A number of high level G-2-G meetings, in the sectors of agriculture and trade & commerce, and first ever ministerial level meetings in the sectors of environment and new & renewable energy have been held. The Ministers for Tourism of ASEAN countries and India signed an MoU on Strengthening Tourism Cooperation between ASEAN and India, thereby making India the first Dialogue Partner to sign such an MoU. We have a newsletter on agriculture, an aseanindia website and social media sites, and, more recently, also a website on tourism. We held the first ever meeting of the Heads of Space Agencies of India and ASEAN countries last summer. An ASEAN-India Artists Camp, an ASEAN-India Civilizational Dialogue Conference and the fusion gala cultural performance by 10 ASEAN and 18 Indian cultural troupes were other highlights. People-to-people interactions have witnessed specific intensification last year, with visits arranged for students, media personnel, diplomats, parliamentarians, farmers and research scholars.

Two activities, in particular, the ASEAN-India Car Rally 2012 and the Expedition by INS Sudarshini to ASEAN countries were major undertakings in our respective capitals. The ASEAN-India Car Rally 2012, which was flagged off from Yogjakarta, Indonesia, traversed nearly 8,000 kms in 22 days across eight ASEAN countries and was flagged-down at Guwahati, in addition to a ceremonial flag down of the rally by the Leaders of ASEAN and India in New Delhi on the sidelines of the Commemorative Summit. The Sailing Ship INS Sudarshini Expedition was flagged off from Kochi in September 2012 and is currently continuing its voyage, tracing the ancient trade routes along the monsoon winds, highlighting India's maritime linkages with Southeast Asia. A number of Marker Events – both commercial and cultural – such as business seminars, tourism road-shows and cultural performances, along their routes, were successful in drawing enthusiastic participation from the ASEAN countries and India. Both these events reinforced the importance of strengthening connectivity in all its dimensions between India and ASEAN, and in creating a web of linkages to unleash the vast economic synergy in the region.

Our strength is that ASEAN and India together account for a combined population of 1.8 billion and a combined GDP of US$ 3.8 trillion with significant synergies of capacity and expertise. Indian Industry could well benefit from the ASEAN experience in key sectors of economy such as infrastructure, agro-processing, retail and value-added manufacturing. Equally, Indian companies can be invaluable partners for ASEAN economies in augmenting their productivity. Bilateral trade between ASEAN and India has been robust, having surpassed the US$ 70 billion mark targeted for 2012. Negotiations on the ASEAN-India Services and Investment Agreements have come to a conclusion. This development would help in realising the full potential of the ASEAN-India Free Trade Agreement and in achieving the trade target of US$ 100 billion by 2015, as outlined in the Vision Statement. It can also have a defining influence on the regional economic architecture.

As we pursue the full implementation of the ASEAN-India Dialogue Relations across the whole spectrum of political and security, economic, socio-cultural and development cooperation, we look forward to new ideas and concepts emanating from the Delhi Dialogue.

We need to find ways to empower our growing populations, especially the youth. We need to better integrate technology into resource utilisation. We need to capitalize on comfort levels with each other that stand out for the absence of irritants. This is the calendar for the future and Delhi Dialogue allows us to widen the involvement and participation in the ASEAN India Strategic Partnership to the constituency that matters most – the people of ASEAN and India. I recall that one idea that came up at Delhi Dialogue IV last year was the proposal to establish an ASEAN-India Centre. This proposal is now on our sights, as it has figured not only as a recommendation in the Report of the ASEAN-India Eminent Persons Group, but also in the Vision Statement adopted at the Commemorative Summit, where the Leaders of ASEAN and India agreed to establish an ASEAN-India Centre.

I thank you for inviting me to share with you the past, present and future of the ASEAN-India relationship. I wish Delhi Dialogue much more success in the coming years.

Vote of Thanks

Dr. A. Didar Singh

Dr. A. Didar Singh

Secretary General, FICCI, New Delhi

It gives me immense pleasure to have you all at the Valedictory Session of Delhi Dialogue V. This is the fifth series of this annual dialogue to promote greater engagement between the ASEAN countries and India. As all of you know, India and ASEAN have already made considerable progress in terms of their economic and political relations over the years. With the Delhi Dialogue V, this commemorative year of our relations, holds much more value.

It may be pertinent to mention that during the Commemorative Year 2012, FICCI organized many business events with support from both the Ministry of External Affairs and Ministry Commerce & Industry. This includes Business Marker events coinciding with India ASEAN Sailing Ship Expedition and 2nd India ASEAN Business Fair & Business Conclave.

The Delhi Dialogue has emerged as one of the premier ASEAN-centric platforms for discussions on regional and international issues of mutual importance. In addition, the recommendations of the ASEAN-India Eminent Persons Group (AIEPG), for forging an even closer partnership for peace, progress and shared prosperity makes Delhi Dialogue of this greater significance. Specially the evolution of the concept that India-ASEAN future will be driven by the bonds of connectivity, these physical bonds will be strengthened by digital links, together, this web of linkages will help unleash the vast economic potential of our region, accelerate development and deepen our Strategic Partnership.

India's connectivity with ASEAN in all its dimensions, physical, institutional and people-to-people, is a strategic priority for India. India-ASEAN connectivity is central to India's growing engagement with its eastern neighbours and the benefits of better connectivity would be plenty for both India and ASEAN. Some of these aspects were discussed earlier during the day.

Hence, I would like to express my gratitude to Mr Sanjay Singh, Secretary East for his leadership to this position of Delhi Dialogue. Mr. Singh your Valedictory address has highlighted the potential areas for enhanced cooperation between India and ASEAN.

The various topics that were discussed at the Delhi Dialogue V, given the diversity of eminent speakers and participants, will help to emanate fresh policy thinking, suggest innovative solutions to challenges facing the region and give an impetus to our growing partnership, for investment and trade.

The deliberations that have taken place since yesterday at the Delhi Dialogue V will take India-ASEAN relations to the next level. We are very delighted to have partnered with the Ministry of External Affairs and Indian Council of World Affairs (ICWA) for this platform. This Partnership between industry, think tanks and government is very unique.

Hence, our appreciation and thanks to Secretary General, ASEAN H.E. Le Luong Minh, whose support to the India-ASEAN relationship is very important. Thanks to all the dignitaries, eminent persons and speakers who are present here to share with us the benefit of their vision. I would also like to thank the ASEAN Heads of Missions in India and our own Ambassador to Indonesia and ASEAN, Mr. Gurjit Singh.

Finally, I would like to convey our sincere thanks to each of the delegates and guests present here, whose contribution and presence are central to whatever success we achieve in our endeavours and it encourages us to do more. I look forward to having you all with us for Delhi Dialogue VI.

Notes on Contributors

Notes on Contributors

H.E. Mr. Salman Khurshid,
Hon'ble External Affairs Minister, Government of India

H.E. Mr. Salman Khurshid is the External Affairs Minister of India. Mr. Khurshid took office as the External Affairs Minister on 28 October 2012. He is a renowned lawyer-educationist-writer-politician.

During his earlier term in the Lok Sabha from 1991 to 1996, he served as the Deputy Minister of Commerce and later as the Minister of State for External Affairs. He has also held various important portfolios such as the Minister of State with independent charge of Minority Affairs and Corporate Affairs. Later, he was elevated to Union Minister of Water Resources and Minority Affairs. In July 2011, he took over as the Union Minister of Law and Justice with additional charge of Minority Affairs.

Mr. Khurshid has a passion for writing. His acclaimed books include *Sons of Babur* (which has been made into a popular play), *At Home in India* and *If Winter Comes*.

H.E. Mr. Sanjay Singh, Secretary (East), Ministry of External Affairs, Government of India

H.E. Mr. Sanjay Singh joined the Indian Foreign Service in 1976. He has served in Indian Missions in Mexico, Germany, Ghana and France and in the Ministry of External Affairs, New Delhi as Director in the Office of the External Affairs Minister and Joint Secretary and Head of Division dealing with Latin American Countries. From October 1997 to June 2001, he was India's Consul General in Ho Chi Minh City and from July 2001 to August 2004, Deputy Chief of Mission in Paris. He served as Joint Secretary and Additional Secretary for Gulf and Haj from March 2005 to March 2009. He served as Ambassador of India to Iran from March 2009 to March 2011. He took over as Secretary (East) in the Ministry of External Affairs on 18th March, 2011.

Mr. Sanjay Singh has a Masters in Physics from Delhi University. He is married to Mrs. Sujatha Singh.

H.E. Mr. Le Luong Minh, Hon'ble Secretary-General, ASEAN

H.E. Mr. Le Luong Minh is the Secretary-General of ASEAN. Before assuming his post as ASEAN Secretary-General, he was Vietnam's Deputy Minister for Foreign Affairs.

From 2004 to 2011, Mr. Minh was Vietnam's Ambassador Extraordinary and Plenipotentiary, Permanent Representative to the United Nations. From August 2007 to December 2008, he was concurrently Assistant Minister for Foreign Affairs and from December 2008 till the end of his tenure in June 2011 concurrently Deputy Minister for Foreign Affairs.

Mr. Minh has had a long career in Vietnam's Ministry of Foreign Affairs. He was appointed Deputy Director-General for International Organizations in 1993. In 1995, he was appointed as Ambassador – Permanent Representative to the United Nations Office and Other International Organizations in Geneva. Two years later, he was appointed as Ambassador – Deputy Permanent Representative to the United Nations at the Headquarters.

Mr. Minh studied Diplomacy at the University of Foreign Affairs, Hanoi, Vietnam. He then studied linguistics and English literature at Jawaharlal Nehru University, New Delhi, India.

H.E. Dr. Soeung Rathchavy, Secretary of State, Ministry of Foreign Affairs, Cambodia

H.E. Dr. Soeung Rathchavy is presently the Secretary of State, Ministry of Foreign Affairs, Cambodia. Dr. Rathchavy has served in the Ministry of Foreign Affairs of Cambodia in various capacities.

Prior to the current appointment, Dr. Soeung Rathchavy has held the position of Under Secretary of State, Advisor to Deputy Prime Minister and Minister of Foreign Affairs. Dr. Rathchavy was also Deputy Secretary General of ASEAN for Socio-Cultural Community, ASEAN Secretariat, Jakarta, Indonesia.

Dr. Soeung Rathchavy has also been Professor at Royal Academy of Cambodia, Council of Ministers, Cambodia. She is also the recipient of the Gold Medal of Labour and Silver Medal of Labour.

H.E. Mr. I. Gusti Agung Wesaka Puja, Director General of ASEAN Cooperation, Ministry of Foreign Affairs, Indonesia

H.E. Mr. I. Gusti Agung Wesaka Puja is currently the Director General of ASEAN Cooperation, Ministry of Foreign Affairs, Indonesia. Prior to this he was the Ambassador Extraordinary and Plenipotentiary of the Republic of Indonesia to the Republic of Austria, Republic of Slovenia and Permanent Representative to the United Nations and other International Organizations in Vienna.

He joined the Ministry of Foreign Affairs in 1986 and has since served at various missions of Indonesia. He has also served as the Coordinator of the ASEAN Vienna Committee in 2010, and has served on a special assignment as a Member of Government Negotiators for Peace Agreement between the Government of the Republic of Indonesia and the Free Aceh Movement.

He is a recipient of various awards including the Bintang Jasa Utama Award in 2010.

H.E. Y.B. Senator A. Kohillan Pillay, Deputy Minister of Foreign Affairs, Malaysia

H.E. Y.B. Senator A. Kohillan Pillay was appointed as Deputy Minister of Foreign Affairs, Malaysia in the Cabinet reshuffle in April 2009. After primary education in Malaysia, he obtained his Bachelor of Economics (Hons) degree at Connaught University, Ireland (1991) and Master of Science in Commercial and Industrial Economy from Pacific Western University, USA (1992).

Y.B. Senator A. Kohillan Pillay served at various positions in the Gerakan Party before being appointed as Municipal Councilor of Selayang Municipal Council, State of Selangor in 1998, which he continued till 2008. In 2008, he was appointed as Senator of the Upper House, and was later appointed as Deputy Minister of Plantation Industries and Commodities.

During 2008, he also taught Economics and Business Studies as Senior Lecturer and Lecturer in Stamford College, Ampang, Regent School of Economics and Olympia College.

H.E. Mr. U. Zin Yaw, Deputy Foreign Minister of Myanmar

H.E. Mr. U. Zin Yaw is the Deputy Foreign Minister of Myanmar since September 2012. He was Ambassador of Myanmar to India from 2010 to 2012.

Earlier, H.E. Mr. U. Zin Yaw served the Defence Services in various capacities during the period 1974 to 2010. He holds a B.Sc. (DSA) and a M.A. in Defence Studies.

H.E. Ms. Erlinda F. Basilio, Under Secretary for Policy and SOM Leader, Philippines

H.E. Ms. Erlinda F. Basilio is currently the Under Secretary for Policy and SOM Leader, Philippines. She began her career at the Department of Foreign Affairs (DFA) as Chief of the Division of American Affairs, Office of Economic Affairs.

Ms. Erlinda F. Basilio has served in the Philippine embassies in Japan and Cuba; envoy to Sweden, Denmark, Norway, Finland, Estonia, Latvia and Lithuania; and Permanent Representative to the United Nations in Geneva. She has also served as the Executive Director of the Office of Asian and Pacific Affairs under the DFA. Subsequently, Ms. Basilio was Assistant Secretary of the Office of Association of Southeast Asian Nations (ASEAN) Affairs. She has been appointed as Under Secretary for Policy since 2006.

She is the recipient of various awards, including the Lakandula Award from the President of the Republic of the Philippines in 2007 and the Distinguished Service Award from the Secretary of Foreign Affairs in 2012.

H.E. Mr. Simon Wong Wie Kuen, Deputy Secretary of Foreign Affairs, Singapore

H.E. Mr. Simon Wong Wie Kuen is currently Deputy Secretary (International) of the Ministry of Foreign Affairs. Prior to taking up his current appointment, H.E. Mr. Simon Wong Wie Kuen was Ambassador (2009 to 2012) in the Singapore Embassy in Hanoi.

H.E. Mr. Simon Wong Wie Kuen joined the Singapore Foreign Service in 1990 where he held the post of Country Officer/Western Europe (1990 to 1992) in the Policy, Planning and Analysis Directorate II. He then served as First Secretary in the Singapore Embassy in Seoul (1992 to 1995).

Mr. Wong served as Counsellor and Deputy Chief of Mission (2000 to 2004) and subsequently as Acting Minister-Counsellor and Deputy Chief of Mission (2004 to 2005) in the Singapore Embassy in Beijing.

H.E. Mr. Simon Wong Wie Kuen was appointed Director/Americas (2005 to 2007). He was also concurrently Director/Europe (2005 to 2006) and subsequently Director/Northeast Asia from April 2006.

H.E. Mr. Nopadol Gunavibool, Deputy Permanent Secretary, Ministry of Foreign Affairs, Thailand

H.E. Mr. Nopadol Gunavibool is presently the Deputy Permanent Secretary, Ministry of Foreign Affairs, Thailand. As a career diplomat, Mr. Gunavibool joined the Ministry of Foreign Affairs in 1982, and since then has served in various capacities.

From 1989 to 1992, he began his involvement in ASEAN affairs as Desk Officer for ASEAN Senior Officials Meeting (SOM). He went on to serve as Director of Division 1, Department of East Asia Affairs, handling ASEAN political and security and Thailand's bilateral relations with Vietnam and Cambodia. He has also served as Director-General of Department of East Asian Affairs, in charge of Thailand's bilateral relations with nine ASEAN member countries as well as China, Japan, South Korea, Mongolia, North Korea and Timor-Leste.

From March 2006 to September 2007, he became Director-General of the Department of ASEAN Affairs and was later appointed Ambassador Extraordinary and Plenipotentiary of Thailand to the Republic of Singapore from 2007 to 2011.

H.E. Mr. Pham Quang Vinh, Deputy Minister of Foreign Affairs, Vietnam

H.E. Mr. Pham Quang Vinh is presently the Deputy Minister of Foreign Affairs, Vietnam. Prior to this he held the position of Assistant Minister of Foreign Affairs and Vietnam's ASEAN SOM Leader.

From 2007 to 2008 he also served as Director General, Vietnam's ASEAN SOM Leader. He has held the position of both Deputy Director General and Director General of the Ministry of Foreign Affairs, Vietnam. Apart from serving in various missions of Vietnam, he has also served as Minister-Counsellor, Deputy Permanent Representative of Vietnam to the United Nations, New York.

He is a graduate from the University of Foreign Affairs in Hanoi, Vietnam and completed his post-graduate programme from Canberra College of Advanced Education, Australia.

Chief Organisers

Ambassador Rajiv Kumar Bhatia, Director General, Indian Council of World Affairs, New Delhi

Ambassador Rajiv Kumar Bhatia is the Director General, Indian Council of World Affairs (ICWA), New Delhi since June 2012.

Earlier, as a career diplomat, he served India with distinction for over 37 years. He was India's Ambassador/High Commissioner in four countries – Kenya, Myanmar, Mexico and South Africa.

Presently, he is member of the Academic Council of Jawaharlal Nehru University, member of the Governing Council of the National Institute of Design and Member-Secretary of the Governing Council of ICWA.

Known for his intellectual inclinations, Mr. Bhatia enjoys writing and speaking on a wide range of foreign policy-related issues. Since his retirement from the Indian Foreign Service in end of 2009, he has published over 95 articles on international affairs and diplomacy in India's national dailies, journals and periodicals.

He has delivered lectures at the National Defence College, Foreign Service Institute, universities and other institutions in India. He has been interviewed by BBC, Bloomberg News, AP, NDTV, Doordarshan, Lok Sabha and Rajya Sabha TV.

Ms. Naina Lal Kidwai, President, FICCI, Country Head - India & Director - Asia Pacific, HSBC Ltd., New Delhi, India

Ms. Naina Lal Kidwai, Country Head, India, and Executive Director on the board of HSBC Asia-Pacific, heads the Indian operations of the HSBC group.

She is actively engaged in trade and industry issues and is President of the Federation of Indian Chambers of Commerce and Industry (FICCI); member of the Government of India's Industry Task Force, and the Working Group on Banking, Financial Sector Legislative Reforms Commission. She is also a Global Advisor for Harvard Business School and the Chair of its India Advisory Board and Chairman of the City of London's Advisory Council for India.

Her interest in environmental issues and livelihood creation for women are evident through her representation on the Shakti Sustainable Energy Foundation Board, the TERI Advisory Board, the World Economic Forum's Global Agenda Council on Climate Change, and the US State Department International Council on Women's Business Leadership.

An MBA from Harvard Business School, she is the recipient of many awards and honours. She received the *Padma Shri*, for her contribution to Trade and Industry from the Government of India in 2007.

Mr. R. Ravindran, Chairman, SAEA Group Research, Singapore

Mr. Ravindran is currently the Chairman of SAEA Group Research, Singapore. He is a Legal Consultant with INCA Law LLC. He also sits as a director on the board of SGX listed companies and some private companies.

He was a Singapore Member of Parliament for the Marine Parade Group Representation Constituency and the Bukit Timah Group Representation Constituency.

Other prior appointments include Chairman of the Government Parliamentary Committee for Defence and Foreign Affairs, Board Member of the People's Association and Deputy Chairman in the Government Parliamentary Committee for Home Affairs and Law. He was also a member of the Jurong Town Council and Marine Parade Town Council, the South East Community Development Council, the Singapore Institute of Directors and the Singapore Academy of Law.

Dr. A. Didar Singh, Secretary General, FICCI, New Delhi

Dr. A. Didar Singh is Secretary General FICCI, a former civil servant of the Indian Administrative Service (IAS). Until recently, he was Secretary to Government of India in the Ministry of Overseas Indian Affairs. Prior to this, he was Member (Finance), National Highways Authority of India, Department of Road Transport and Highways at New Delhi. He was earlier Joint Secretary in the Ministry of Heavy Industries, and before that in the Ministry of Commerce (Foreign Trade).

Dr. Singh obtained a Bachelors and Masters from St. Stephens College, Delhi University. He has a Masters in Development Administration from Birmingham University, UK, and has the distinction of having done the first Ph.D. in India on the Policy and Administration of e-Commerce.

Dr. Didar Singh is an internationally known expert in e-commerce and ICT development and has done several studies in this area for international agencies like International Trade Centre, World Health Organization etc.

Plenary Session 1: India-ASEAN Security Cooperation: Towards Peace and Stability

Professor Kanti Prasad Bajpai, Professor and Vice Dean Research, Lee Kuan Yew School of Public Policy, National University of Singapore

Professor Kanti Prasad Bajpai is the Vice Dean Research at the Lee Kuan Yew School of Public Policy, National University of Singapore. Earlier, he was Professor in the Politics and International Relations of South Asia, Oxford University; Professor of International Politics in the Centre for International Politics, Organization and Disarmament of the School of International Studies, Jawaharlal Nehru University, New Delhi.

Professor Bajpai has held various fellowships: Resident Fellow of the Rajiv Gandhi Institute for Contemporary Studies, Rajiv Gandhi Foundation, New Delhi; Visiting Fellow at the Joan B. Kroc Institute for Peace, Notre Dame University; the Brookings Institution, Washington, D.C.; Visiting Fellow at the Australian Defence Force Academy (ADFA), Canberra; Wesleyan University, Middletown, Connecticut and the University of Illinois, Urbana-Champaign.

Profesor Bajpai's most recent book is *Roots of Terrorism.* He is presently finishing books on Indian strategic thought and India-China relations.

Professor Rommel C. Banlaoi, Chairman and Executive Director, Philippine Institute for Peace, Violence and Terrorism Research (PIPVTR), Manila

Professor Rommel C. Banlaoi is the Chairman of the Board and Executive Director of the Philippine Institute for Peace, Violence and Terrorism Research (PIPVTR) and Head of its Center for Intelligence and National Security Studies (CINSS). He is also the Editor of *Homeland Voice: The Journal of World Security.* He currently serves as the Vice President of the Philippine Association of Chinese Studies (PACS), a Senior Fellow at the Yuchengco Center of De La Salle University (DLSU), Manila and a Faculty Member at the Department of International Studies, Miriam College, the Philippines. He received the prestigious Albani Philippine Peace Prize Award in 2011 for his contribution to peace research and national security education.

Professor Rommel served as a Professor of Political Science and International Relations at the National Defense College of the Philippines (NDCP) from 1998 to 2008 and has single-authored eight books, co-authored four books and contributed at least 50 book chapters and international journal articles.

Dr. K.S. Balakrishnan, Head, Department of International and Strategic Studies, Faculty of Arts and Social Sciences, University of Malaya, Kuala Lumpur, Malaysia

Dr. K. S. Balakrishnan is currently the Head of Department and Senior Lecturer at the Department of International and Strategic Studies, Faculty of Arts and Social Sciences, University of Malaya. His previous appointments include Senior Researcher at Institute of International and Strategic Studies (ISIS, Malaysia) (1993-97) and Lecturer at Monash University, KL Campus (1999-May 2000).

His research areas include Malaysia's Foreign and Defence Policy, ASEAN Security and Regionalism and Asia Pacific Security. He is also invited by ministries, military colleges, think tanks, media, political parties, NGOs and government agencies for various evaluation services, guest lectures and other expertise. He has visited over 20 countries and is renowned in the strategic studies and international relations.

His works have been published as books, chapters and articles in national and international journals.

Dr. Evi Fitriani, Head, International Relations Department, University of Indonesia, Jakarta

Dr. Evi Fitriani joined the University of Indonesia in January 1996, where she teaches undergraduate as well as master programmes of the International Relations and European Studies. Dr. Evi has extensively published research reports, journal articles and newspaper articles on topics related to Indonesia's foreign policy, ASEAN, Asia-Pacific regionalism and European Union. Since 2008, her research has focussed on China.

Dr. Evi completed her doctorate in Political Science and International Relations at Australian National University (ANU) under the Australian Development Scholarship. She graduated with two master programmes from Leeds University, UK, 1994, funded by the British Chevening award, and from Ohio University, USA, supported by the Fulbright Scholarship.

At the University of Indonesia, Evi has also worked in administrative positions including Director of the Office and Member of Senate. Dr. Evi has travelled extensively and lived in the UK, the USA, the Netherlands, Japan and Australia.

Concurrent Session 2A: Non-Traditional Security Challenges: Food Security, Water Management and Pandemics

Professor Nayan Sharma, Head of Department, Department of Water Resource Development and Management, Indian Institute of Technology (IIT), Roorkee

Professor Nayan Sharma teaches in Water Resources Development & Management Department at IIT Roorkee. His areas of specialisation are water resources, river engineering and hydraulic structures. During 30 years with IIT-Roorkee, he guided 151 M.Tech. dissertations and 18 Ph.D. theses. He has 115 research publications. He is also a member of 54 national and international level technical committees. He has undertaken over 60 consulting and 9 national and international research projects.

Professor Sharma authored two books published by Springer Publishers and INCID. Professor Sharma received the prestigious Indo-Swiss Bilateral Research Award as Visiting Professor in Swiss Federal Institute of Technology, Lausanne, Switzerland. Professor Sharma lectured at The Imperial College London, Southampton University, Edinburgh University, EPFL Lausanne, Iowa University, IST Lisbon and Gottingen University, Germany. In 2010, he delivered the Dr. K. L. Rao Memorial Lecture at the 26th National Convention of Civil Engineers of Institution of Engineers (India).

Dr. Termsak Chalermpalanupap, ASEAN Studies Centre, Institute of Southeast Asian Studies, Singapore

Dr. Termsak Chalermpalanupap is a Visiting Research Fellow at ISEAS and Lead Researcher for Political and Security Affairs. He retired from the ASEAN Secretariat in Jakarta in July 2012 after nearly 20 years of service in the political and security field of ASEAN cooperation.

Throughout his ASEAN career, Dr. Termsak has contributed opinion pieces, articles and book chapters and presentations on various aspects of ASEAN political and security cooperation, including human rights, nuclear non-proliferation, ASEAN regionalism and the ASEAN Charter among others.

Dr. Termsak is also a Global Associate of the Centre for International Law (CIL) at the National University of Singapore. He has a B.A. in Political Science from Chulalongkorn University, Bangkok, Thailand and a M.A. and Ph.D. in Political Science from the University of New Orleans, USA.

Dr. Dinna Wisnu, Director, Paramadina Graduate School of Diplomacy, Paramadina University, Jakarta, Indonesia

Dr. Dinna is the Co-founder and Dean/Director of 'Paramadina Graduate School of Diplomacy', the first post-graduate school of diplomacy in Indonesia at Paramadina University. Her area of specialization is international political economy, especially on social welfare policies, the political economy of development, labour and industrial relations and diplomacy.

She has published articles in journals, books, reports and newspapers extensively in Indonesia, and also writes for audience in the US, South Korea and other countries. She is often quoted and asked for opinion in various media, including from other countries. She advises various government projects and programmes in several Ministries.

Dr. Wisnu's most recent book is titled *Politik Sistem Jaminan Sosial* ('Politics of Social Security System'), (Jakarta: PT Gramedia Pustaka Utama, 2012). She earned Ph.D. and M.A. in Political Science from The Ohio State University, USA, and B.A. in International Relations from the University of Indonesia.

Concurrent Session 2B: Future of Global Energy Market: Role of New and Renewable Energy in Sustainable Development

Mr. Harish Hande, Managing Director, SELCO Solar Light Private Limited, India

Mr. Harish Hande is an engineer and a renewable energy entrepreneur with extensive grassroots experience in meeting the energy requirements of rural households. He is the co-founder of SELCO-India of which he is the Managing Director.

SELCO-India is a rural energy service in Bangalore, India. Since 1995, SELCO-India has installed over 160,000 solar lighting systems in rural households. His experience includes a large number of health, education and water related projects; over 500 small rural and urban health clinics; over 1000 rural and semi-urban schools and dormitories and over 1500 irrigation and drinking water systems.

Mr. Harish Hande also is on the board of many national and international organisations. He was recently awarded the 2011 Ramon Magsaysay Award recognising his efforts to build a social enterprise that brings customised, affordable and sustainable electricity to India's vast rural population.

Mr. Gautam Vivek, World Energy Council, New Delhi, India

Mr. Gautam Vivek is Additional General Manager (Corporate Planning) in NTPC Ltd. and is currently in-charge of World Energy Council India, Secretariat. World Energy Council works in the area of sustainable use and supply of energy and it covers entire spectrum of energy.

A post-graduate in Geology, Mr. Gautam Vivek joined NTPC as a finance trainee and was extensively involved in financial appraisal of NTPC projects by World Bank and other international financial institution. He has been an integral part of NTPC's major strategic planning process and has exposure to key facets of the Indian power sector industry.

Mr. Gautam Vivek is presently involved in organisational transformation of WEC India into 'foremost energy think-tank in the country and voice of the sector'. His current assignment gives him a wide exposure to complex and intricate issues relating to global energy sector.

Mr. Vivek is a keen student of 'transformation' and passionately involved, among others, in the work of Energy Poverty issues.

Plenary Session 3: Cooperation between CLMV Countries and North-East India: Opportunities and Challenges

Professor Gautam Barua, Director, Indian Institute of Technology (IIT), Guwahati

Professor Gautam Barua is the Director of Indian Institute of Technology (IIT), Guwahati, India since March 2003 and Professor, Department of Computer Science and Engineering since 1995. He graduated from IIT Bombay with B.Tech. (1976) and M.Tech. (1978) degrees in Electrical Engineering. He obtained a Ph.D. degree in Computer Engineering from the University of California, Santa Barbara, USA in 1981. He was at IIT Kanpur from 1982 till 1995. His areas of interest are Operating Systems and Networks.

Professor Gautam Barua is on the Governing Boards of the following organisations: IIM Shillong, NIT Meghalaya, Assam Institute of Management, Assam Health University, Cotton College University, Oil India Ltd., Brahmaputra Cracker and Polymer Ltd., the AICTE and is in the High Level Committee of the National Knowledge Network. He is an IT consultant to the Government of Assam and a number of public enterprises. He is a member of ACM and the Computer Society of India.

Ambassador U. Nyunt Maung Shein, Head, Myanmar Institute of Strategic and International Studies, Yangon, Myanmar

Ambassador U. Nyunt Maung Shein is the Chairman of the Myanmar Institute of Strategic and International Studies (MISIS) since January 2013. He has served the Government of Myanmar for 40 years before retiring as Ambassador/Permanent Representative to the United Nations Office in Geneva in 2008. He held various diplomatic positions at Myanmar Missions in Bern, Hanoi, Bangkok, Dhaka and Tokyo.

He was Ambassador Extraordinary and Plenipotentiary to the Republic of Korea (2001-02) and the Federal Republic of Germany (2002-05) with concurrent accreditation to Austria, Poland, Finland and the Czech Republic as well as the Ambassador/Permanent Representative to the UNIDO, UNODC and IAEA, Vienna. He has served in the Political Department in different capacities and has represented his country at the Senior Official's Meeting (SOM) and other related meetings of ASEAN including Summits.

He holds a B.Sc. Degree and Master of International Public Policy from SAIS, the Johns Hopkins University, USA.

Professor Tan Tai Yong, Director, Institute of South Asian Studies (ISAS), National University of Singapore (NUS), Singapore

Professor Tan Tai Yong has been an integral part of Institute of South Asian Studies (ISAS), Singapore since its inception. He was the Acting Director of the Institute from July 2004 to July 2006, and April 2007 to May 2008. He was appointed as Director of ISAS on 1 June 2008.

Professor Tan, a historian, is concurrently Vice Provost (Student Life) at the National University of Singapore. Prior to this, he was Dean of the Faculty of Arts and Social Sciences at the National University of Singapore from 2004 to 2009.

Professor Tan has written extensively on South Asian history as well as on Southeast Asia and Singapore. His recent books include Singapore – *A 700 Year History* (2009); *Creating 'Greater Malaysia': Decolonisation and the Politics of Merger* (2008); *Partition and Post-Colonial South Asia: A Reader* (co-edited, 2007); *The Garrison State* (2005); *The Aftermath of Partition in South Asia* (co-authored, 2000) and *The Transformation of Southeast Asia: International Perspectives on De-colonisation* (co-edited, 2003).

Mr. Sunand Sharma, Country President, Alstom India and South Asia, India

Mr. Sunand Sharma is the Country President, Alstom India & South Asia and Chairman of Alstom India Ltd. (a public listed company). During his present tenure, which commenced in 2006, he has contributed to the expansion of the presence of Alstom in India and South Asia. In this period, the company has made major investments, whilst strengthening its position in Thermal Power, Renewable Power and Transport, and integrated the business of Grid in India and South Asia.

Prior to joining Alstom, he led the Business Development effort of GE in India in the 1980s and 1990s that established GE's leadership in India in Aircraft Engines, Gas Turbines and Medical Systems. From the mid 1990s till 2006 he provided strategic advice to various leading global companies including Nokia Telecommunications of Finland, Owens Corning Fiberglas Inc. of USA, Energy Developments Limited of Australia, Vialle Alternative Fuel Systems and the Royal Cebeco Group of the Netherlands, GE Wind Energy of USA and Acciona Energia of Spain.

Plenary Session 4: Expanding Networks through Connectivity: Land, Sea and Air

Mr. Brijeshwar Singh, Former Chairman, National Highways Authority of India, India

Mr. Brijeshwar Singh joined the Indian Administrative Service in 1975 and served in the Government of India as well as the government of Tamil Nadu. He has more than three decades of experience in infrastructure, beginning with his role of officer On Special Duty for the 9th Asian Games held in New Delhi in 1982. He has worked in the Tamil Nadu Electricity Board and has served on the Boards of companies dealing with electronics, transportation, industrial development and agro-industries. He retired in 2010 as Chairman of National Highways Authority of India (NHAI).

He holds a Master's Degree from Delhi School of Economics and Master's in Economics from Oxford University. He has worked in agriculture including tenure with FAO. He served as a member on the Task Force for reviewing

National Security systems from 2010-2011. He now works as a private consultant in New Delhi.

Mr. K.L. Thapar, Chairman, Asian Institute of Transport Development, New Delhi

Mr. Thapar is former Principal Adviser and Secretary, Planning Commission, Government of India. He has been Adviser and Consultant to several international bodies including United Nations, World Bank, ADB and has served in a number of countries.

Mr. Thapar is the Founder Chairman of the Asian Institute of Transport Development. It has been granted special consultative status with United Nations. Its extensive country-level membership facilitates its role of fostering regional cooperation for overall welfare of the communities.

Mr. Hidetoshi Nishimura, Executive Director, Economic Research Institute of ASEAN and East Asia (ERIA), Jakarta, Indonesia

Mr. Hidetoshi Nishimura is the founding Executive Director of Economic Research Institute for ASEAN and East Asia (ERIA) since June 2008. Prior to taking up this position, he worked for the establishment of ERIA as Special Assistant to the Chairman on ERIA matters in JETRO.

During his long career, he has held important positions in the Policy Division pertaining to environment protection, territorial trade policy pertaining to Europe, Africa and Middle East. He has also held the position of the Representative of the Asia-Pacific Region of the Japan Overseas Development Corporation, Director of the Southeast Asia and Pacific Division of the Trade Policy Bureau, Vice Governor for International Affairs of Ehime Prefecture, Director-General of the Business Support Department of the Small and Medium Enterprise Agency and other prestigious appointments.

He is a strong advocate of ASEAN-India Connectivity and has steered two major ERIA research on this theme named Comprehensive Asia Development Plan-Phase I and II.

Dr. S. Narayan, Head of Research, Institute of South Asian Studies (ISAS), National University of Singapore (NUS), Singapore

Dr. S. Narayan is the Head of Research and Visiting Senior Research Fellow at the Institute of South Asian Studies, National University of Singapore since 2005.

He has nearly four decades of engagement in public service in the State and Central Governments, in Development Administration and was the Economic Adviser to the Prime Minister during 2003-04. Prior to this assignment, Dr. S. Narayan served the Government of India as Finance and Economic Affairs Secretary, Secretary in the Departments of Revenue, Petroleum and Industrial Development.

Dr. S. Narayan obtained his Ph.D. from the Indian Institute of Technology in New Delhi, MPhil (Development Economics) from Cambridge University, Master of Business Management (Finance) from the University of Adelaide and an M.Sc. (Physics) from the University of Madras (Madras Christian College).

Dr. Narayan has authored a book, edited two books and written numerous policy papers, reports and book chapters. He writes regularly in newspapers, both locally and internationally.

Ambassador Pradap Pibulsonggram, Member, ASEAN Connectivity Coordination Committee, Thailand

Ambassador Pradap Pibulsonggram is an Adviser to Thailand's National Coordinator on the Master Plan on ASEAN Connectivity. In addition, he represents Thailand on the ASEAN Connectivity Coordinating Committee, currently under the Chairmanship of Brunei Darussalam. He is also an independent Board Director of the Siam City Cement Public Co. Ltd., and a Corporate Advisor of TEAM GROUP Consulting Engineering and Management.

During his 36 years of diplomatic service, Ambassador Pibulsonggram was responsible for numerous assignments relating to ASEAN affairs and was actively involved in the ASEAN integration process. He represented Thailand as Head of Mission in 11 countries including Hungary, Switzerland and Italy.

After his retirement in 2009, he was appointed as Thailand Representative on High Level Task Force on Master Plan of ASEAN Connectivity. At present, he has been assigned to join his ASEAN colleagues in tracking the implementation of the Master Plan and the concrete feature of ASEAN Community 2015.